Charlotte Mary Yonge

The chaplet of pearls

The white and black Ribaumont

Charlotte Mary Yonge

The chaplet of pearls
The white and black Ribaumont

ISBN/EAN: 9783744646819

Printed in Europe, USA, Canada, Australia, Japan

Cover: Foto ©Andreas Hilbeck / pixelio.de

THE

CHAPLET OF PEARLS;

OR,

THE WHITE AND BLACK RIBAUMONT.

BY THE

AUTHOR OF "THE HEIR OF REDCLYFFE."

IN TWO VOLUMES.

VOL. II.

London:

MACMILLAN AND CO.

1868.

CONTENTS OF VOL. II.

CHAPTER XL.

CHAPTER XLI.

CHAPTER XLII.

CHAPTER XLIII.

CHAPTER XLIV.

THE CHAPLET OF PEARLS;

OR,

THE WHITE AND BLACK RIBAUMONT.

CHAPTER XXV.

THE VELVET COACH.

"No, my good Lord, Diana—"
All's Well that Ends Well.

A LATE autumn journey from the west coast to Paris was a more serious undertaking in the sixteenth century than the good seaman Master Hobbs was aware of, or he would have used stronger dissuasive measures against such an undertaking by the two youths, when the elder was in so frail a state of health; but there had been a certain deceptive strength and vigour about young Ribaumont while under strong excitement and determination, and the whole party fancied him far fitter to meet the hardships than was really the case. Philip Thistlewood always recollected that journey as the most distressing period of his life.

They were out of the ordinary highways, and therefore found the hiring of horses often extremely difficult. They had intended to purchase, but found no animals that, as Philip said, they would have accepted as a gift, though at every wretched inn where they had to wait while the country was scoured for the miserable jades, their proposed requirements fell lower and lower. Dens of smoke, dirt, and boorishness were the great proportion of those inns, where they were compelled to take refuge by the breaking down of one or other of the beasts, or by stress of weather. Snow, rain, thaw and frost alternated, each variety rendering the roads impassable; and at the best, the beasts could seldom be urged beyond a walk, fetlock-deep in mire or water. Worse than all, Berenger, far from recovered, and under the heavy oppression of a heartrending grief, could hardly fail to lose the ground that he had gained under the influence of hope. The cold seemed to fix itself on the wound in his cheek, terrible pain and swelling set in, depriving him entirely of sleep, permitting him to take no nourishment but fragments of soft crumbs soaked in wine or broth—when the inns afforded any such fare—and rendering speech excessively painful, and at last unintelligible.

Happily this was not until Philip and Humfrey both had picked up all the most indispensable words to serve their needs, and storming could be done in any language. Besides, they had fallen in at La Motte-Achard with a sharp fellow named Guibert, who had been at sea, and knew a little English, was a Norman by birth, knew who the Baron de Ribaumont was, and was able to make himself generally useful, though ill supplying the place of poor Osbert, who would have been invaluable in the present predicament. Nothing was so much dreaded by any of the party as that their chief should become utterly unable to proceed. Once let him be laid up at one of these little *auberges*, and Philip felt as if all would be over with him; and he himself was always the most restlessly eager to push on, and seemed to suffer less even in the biting wind and sleet than on the dirty pallets or in the smoky, noisy kitchens of the inns. That there was no wavering of consciousness was the only comfort, and Philip trusted to prevent this by bleeding him whenever his head seemed aching or heated; and under this well-meant surgery it was no wonder that he grew weaker every day, in spite of the most affectionate and assiduous watching on his brother's part.

Nearly six weeks had been spent in struggling along the cross-roads, or rather in endless delays; and when at last they came on more frequented ways, with better inns, well-paved *chaussées*, and horses more fit for use, Berenger was almost beyond feeling the improvement. At their last halt, even Philip was for waiting and sending on to Paris to inform Sir Francis Walsingham of their situation; but Berenger only shook his head, dressed himself, and imperatively signed to go on. It was a bright morning, with a clear frost, and the towers and steeples of Paris presently began to appear above the poplars that bordered the way; but by this time Berenger was reeling in his saddle, and he presently became so faint and dizzy, that Philip and Humfrey were obliged to lift him from his horse, and lay him under an elm-tree that stood a little back from the road.

"Look up, sir, it is but a league further," quoth Humfrey; "I can see the roof of the big Church they call Notre-Dame."

"He does not open his eyes, he is swooning," said Philip. "He must have some cordial, ere he can sit his horse. Can you think of no place where we could get a drop of wine or strong waters?"

"Not I, Master Philip. We passed a convent wall but now, but 'twas a nunnery, as good as a grave against poor travellers. I would ride on, and get some of Sir Francis's folk to bring a litter or coach, but I doubt me if I could get past the barrier without my young Lord's safe-conduct."

Berenger, hearing all, here made an effort to raise himself, but sank back against Philip's shoulder. Just then, a trampling and lumbering became audible, and on the road behind appeared first three horsemen riding abreast, streaming with black and white ribbons; then eight pair of black horses, a man walking at the crested heads of each couple, and behind these a coach, shaped like an urn reversed, and with a coronet on the top, silvered, while the vehicle itself was, melon-like, fluted, alternately black, with silver figures, and white with black landscapes; and with white draperies, embroidered with black and silver, floating from the windows. Four lacqueys, in the same magpie-colouring, stood behind, and outriders followed; but as the cavalcade approached the group by the road-side, one of the horsemen paused, saying lightly, "Over near the walls for an affair of honour? Has he caught it badly? Who was the other?"

Ere Guibert could answer, the curtains were thrust aside, the coach stopped, a lady's head and hand appeared, and a female voice exclaimed, in much alarm, "Halt! Ho, you there, in our colours, come here. What is it? My brother here? Is he wounded?"

"It is no wound, madame," said Guibert, shoved forward by his English comrades, "it is M. le Baron de Ribaumont who is taken ill, and—ah! here is Monsieur Philippe."

For Philip, seeing a thick black veil put back from the face of the most beautiful lady who had ever appeared to him, stepped forward, hat in hand, as she exclaimed, "Le Baron de Ribaumont! Can it be true? What means this? What ails him?"

"It is his wound, madame," said Philip, in his best French;

"it has broken out again, and he has almost dropped from his horse from *défaillance.*"

"Ah, bring him here—lay him on the cushions, we will have the honour of transporting him," cried the lady; and, regardless of the wet road, she sprang out of the coach, with her essences in her hand, followed by at least three women, two pages, and two little white dogs which ran barking towards the prostrate figure, but were caught up by their pages. "Ah, cousin, how dreadful," she cried, as she knelt down beside him, and held her essences towards him. Voice and scent revived him, and with a bewildered look and gesture half of thanks, half of refusal, he gazed round him, then rose to his feet without assistance, bent his head, and making a sign that he was unable to speak, turned towards his horse.

"Cousin, cousin," exclaimed the lady, in whose fine black eyes tears were standing, "you will let me take you into the city—you cannot refuse."

"Berry, indeed you cannot ride," entreated Philip; "you must take her offer. Are you getting crazed at last?"

Berenger hesitated for a moment, but he felt himself again dizzy; the exertion of springing into his saddle was quite beyond him, and bending his head he submitted passively to be helped into the black and white coach. Humfrey, however, clutched Philip's arm, and said impressively, "Have a care, sir; this is no other than the fine lady, sister to the murderous villain that set upon him. If you would save his life, don't quit him, nor let her take him elsewhere than to our Ambassador's. I'll not leave the coach-door, and as soon as we are past the barriers, I'll send Jack Smithers to make known we are coming."

Philip, without further ceremony, followed the lady into the coach, where he found her insisting that Berenger, who had sunk back in a corner, should lay his length of limb, muddy boots and all, upon the white velvet cushions, richly worked in black and silver, with devices and mottoes, in which the crescent moon, and eclipsed or setting suns, made a great figure. The original inmates seemed to have disposed of themselves in various nooks of the ample conveyance, and Philip, rather at a loss to explain his intrusion, perched himself awkwardly on the edge of the cushions in front of his brother, thinking that Humfrey was an officious, suspicious fellow, to distrust this lovely lady, who seemed so exceedingly shocked and grieved at Berenger's condition. "Ah! I never guessed it had been so frightful as this. I should not have known him. Ah! had I imagined——" She leant back, covered her face, and wept, as one overpowered; then, after a few seconds, she bent forward, and would have taken the hand that hung listlessly down, but it was at once withdrawn, and folded with the other on his breast.

"Can you be more at ease? Do you suffer much?" she asked, with sympathy and tenderness that went to Philip's heart, and he explained. "He cannot speak, madame; the shot in his cheek" (the lady shuddered, and put her handkerchief to her eyes) "from time to time causes this horrible swelling and torture. After that he will be better."

"Frightful, frightful," she sighed, "but we will do our best to make up. You, sir, must be his *trucheman.*"

Philip, not catching the last word, and wondering what kind of man that might be, made answer, "I am his brother, madame."

"*Eh! Monsieur son frère.* Has *Madame sa mère* a son so old?"

"I am Philip Thistlewood, her husband's son, at your service, madame," said Philip, colouring up to the ears; "I came with him, for he is too weak to be alone."

"Great confidence must be reposed in you, sir," she said, with a not unflattering surprise. "But whence are you come? I little looked to see Monsieur here."

"We came from Anjou, madame. We went to La Sablerie," and he broke off.

"I understand. Ah! let us say no more! It rends the heart;" and again she wiped away a tear. "And now——"

"We are coming to the Ambassador's to obtain"—he stopped, for Berenger gave him a touch of peremptory warning, but the lady saved his embarrassment by exclaiming that she could not let her dear cousin go to the Ambassador's when he was among his own kindred. Perhaps Monsieur did not know her; she must present herself as Madame de Selinville, *née* de Ribaumont, a poor cousin of *ce cher Baron*, "and even a little to you, *M. le frère*, if you will own me," and she held out a hand, which he ought to have kissed, but not knowing how, he only shook it. She further explained that her brother was at Cracow with Monsieur, now King of Poland, but that her father lived with her at her hotel, and would be enchanted to see his dear cousin, only that he, like herself, would be desolated at the effects of that most miserable of errors. She had been returning from her Advent retreat at a convent, where she had been praying for the soul of the late M. de Selinville, when a true Providence had made her remark the colours of her family. And now, nothing would serve her, but that this dear Baron should be carried at once to their hotel, which was much nearer than that of the Ambassador, and where every comfort should await him. She clasped her hands in earnest entreaty, and Philip, greatly touched by her kindness and perceiving that every jolt of the splendid but springless vehicle caused Berenger's head a shoot of anguish, was almost acceding to her offer, when he was checked by one of the most imperative of those silent negatives. Hitherto, Master Thistlewood had been rather proud of his bad French, and as long as he could be understood, considered trampling on genders, tenses, and moods, as a manful assertion of Englishry, but he would just now have given a great deal for the command of any language but a horseboy's, to use to this beautiful gracious personage. "*Merci, madame, nous ne fallons pas, nous avons passé notre parole d'aller droit à l'Ambassadeur's et pas où else,*" did not sound very right to his ears; he coloured up to the roots of his hair, and knew that if Berry had had a smile left in him, poor fellow, he would have smiled now. But this most charming and polite of ladies never betrayed it, if it were ever such bad French; she only bowed her head, and said something very pretty—if only he could make it out—of being the slave of one's word, and went on persuading. Nor did it make the conversation easier, that she inquired after Berenger, and mourned over his injuries as if he were unconscious, while Philip knew, nay, was reminded every instant, that he was aware of all that was passing, most anxious that as little as possible should be said, and determined against being taken to her hotel. So unreasonable a prejudice did this seem to Philip, that had it not been for Humfrey's words, he would have doubted whether, in spite of all his bleeding, his brother's brain were not wandering.

However, what with Humfrey without, and Berenger within, the turn to the Ambassador's hotel was duly taken, and in process of time a hearty greeting passed between Humfrey and the porter; and by the time the carriage drew up, half the household were assembled on the steps, including Sir Francis himself, who had already heard more than a fortnight back from Lord Walwyn, and had become uneasy at the non-arrival of his two young guests. On Smithers's appearance, all had been made ready; and as Berenger, with feeble, tardy movements, made courteous gestures of thanks to the lady, and alighted from the coach, he was absolutely received into the dignified arms of the Ambassador. "Welcome, my poor lad, I am glad to see you here again, though in such different guise. Your chamber is ready for you, and I have sent my secretary to see if Maître Paré be at home, so we will, with God's help, have you better at ease anon."

Even Philip's fascination by Madame de Selinville could not hold out against the comfort of hearing English voices all round him, and of seeing his brother's anxious brow expand, and his hand and eyes return no constrained thanks. Civilities were exchanged on both sides; the Ambassador thanked the lady for the assistance she had rendered to his young friend and guest; she answered with a shade of stiffness, that she left her kinsman in good hands, and said she should send to inquire that evening, and her father would call on the morrow; then, as Lady Walsingham did not ask her in, the black and white coach drove away.

The lady threw herself back in one corner, covered her face, and spoke no word. Her coach pursued its way through the streets, and turned at length into another great courtyard, surrounded with buildings, where she alighted, and stepped across a wide but dirty hall, where ranks of servants stood up and bowed as she passed; then she ascended a wide carved staircase, opened a small private door, and entered a tiny wainscotted room, hardly large enough for her farthingale to turn round in. "You, Véronique, come in—only you," she said, at the door; and a waiting woman, who had been in the carriage, obeyed, no longer clad in the Angevin costume, but in the richer and less characteristic dress of the ordinary Parisian *femme de chambre.*

"Undo my mantle in haste!" gasped Madame de Selinville. "O Véronique—you saw—what destruction!"

"Ah! if my sweet young lady had only known how frightful he had become, she had never sacrificed herself," sighed Véronique.

"Frightful! What with the grave blue eyes that seem like the steady avenging judgment of St. Michael in his triumph in the picture at the Louvre," murmured Madame de Selinville; then she added quickly, "Yes, yes, it is well. She and you, Véronique, may see him frightful and welcome. There are other eyes—make haste, girl. There—another handkerchief. Follow me not."

And Madame de Selinville moved out of the room, past the great state bedroom and the *salle* beyond, to another chamber where more servants waited and rose at her entrance.

"Is any one with my father?"

"No, madame;" and a page knocking, opened the door and announced, "Madame la Comtesse."

The Chevalier, in easy *deshabille*, with a flask of good wine, iced water, and delicate cakes and *confitures* before him, a witty and licentious epigrammatic poem close under his hand, sat lazily enjoying the luxuries that it had been his daughter's satisfaction to procure for him ever since her marriage. He sprang up to meet her with a grace and deference that showed how different a person was the Comtesse de Selinville from Diane de Ribaumont.

"Ah! *ma belle*, my sweet," as there was a mutual kissing of hands, "thou art returned. Had I known thine hour, I had gone down for thy first embrace. But thou lookest fair, my child; the convent has made thee lovelier than ever."

"Father, who think you is here? It is he—the Baron."

"The Baron; who, what Baron?"

"What Baron? Eh, father!" she cried impetuously. "Who could it be but one?"

"My child, you are mistaken! That young hot-head can never be thrusting himself here again."

"But he is, father; I brought him into Paris in my coach! I left him at the Ambassador's."

"Thou shouldest have brought him here. There will be ten thousand fresh imbroglios."

"I could not; he is as immoveable as ever, though unable to speak! Oh, father, he is very ill, he suffers terribly. Oh, Narcisse! Ah! may I never see him again!"

"But what brings him blundering here again?" exclaimed the Chevalier. "Speak intelligibly, child! I thought we had guarded against that! He knows nothing of the survivance."

"I cannot tell much. He could not open his mouth, and his half-brother, a big dull English boy, stammered out a few words of shocking French against his will. But I believe they had heard of *la pauvre petite* at La Sablerie, came over for her, and finding the ruin my brother makes wherever he goes, are returning seeking intelligence and succour for *him*."

"That may be," said the Chevalier, thoughtfully. "It is well thy brother is in Poland. I would not see him suffer any more; and we may get him back to England ere my son learns that he is here."

"Father, there is a better way! Give him my hand."

"*Eh quoi*, child; if thou art tired of devotion, there are a thousand better marriages."

"No, father, none so good for this family. See, I bring him all—all that I was sold for. As the price of that, he resigns for ever all his claims to the ancestral castle—to La Leurre, and above all, that claim to Nid-de-Merle as Eustacie's widower, which, should he ever discover the original contract, will lead to endless warfare."

"His marriage with Eustacie was annulled. Yet—yet

there might be doubts. There was the protest; and who knows whether they formally renewed their vows when so much went wrong at Montpipeau. Child, it is a horrible perplexity. I often could wish we had had no warning, and the poor things had made off together. We could have cried shame till we forced out a provision for thy brother; and my poor little Eustacie——" He had tears in his eyes as he broke off.

Diane made an impatient gesture. "She would have died of tedium in England, or broken forth so as to have a true scandal. That is all over, father, now; weigh my proposal! Nothing else will save my brother from all that his cruel hand merits! You will win infinite credit at Court. The King loved him more than you thought safe."

"The King has not a year to live, child, and he has personally offended the King of Poland. Besides, this youth is heretic."

"Only by education. Have I not heard you say that he had so little of the Huguenot that you feared his throwing you over by an abjuration. And as to Monsieur's enmity, if it be not forgotten, the glory of bringing about a conversion would end that at once."

"Then, daughter, thou shouldst not have let him bury himself among the English."

"It was unavoidable, father, and perhaps if he were here he would live in an untameable state of distrust, whereas we may now win him gradually. You will go and see him tomorrow, my dear father."

"I must have time to think of this thy sudden device."

"Nay, he is in no condition to hear of it at present. I did but speak now, that you might not regard it as sudden when the fit moment comes. It is the fixed purpose of my mind. I am no girl now, and I could act for myself if I would;

but as it is for your interest and that of my brother thus to dispose of me, it is better that you should act for me."

"Child, headstrong child, thou wilt make no scandal," said the Chevalier, looking up at his daughter's handsome head drawn up proudly with determination.

"Certainly not, sir, if you will act for me." And Diane sailed away in her sweeping folds of black brocade.

In a few moments more she was kneeling with hands locked together before a much-gilded little waxen figure of St. Eustache with his cross-bearing stag by his side, which stood in a curtained recess in the alcove where her stately bed was placed.

"Monseigneur St. Eustache, ten wax candles every day to your shrine at Bellaise, so he recovers; ten more if he listens favourably and loves me. Nay, all—all the Selinville jewels to make you a shrine. All—all, so he will only let me love him;" and then, while taking up the beads, and pronouncing the repeated devotions attached to each, her mind darted back to the day when, as young children, she had played unfairly, defrauded Landry Osbert, and denied it; how Berenger, though himself uninjured, had refused to speak to her all that day—how she had hated him then—how she had thought she had hated him throughout their brief intercourse in the previous year; how she had played into her brother's hands; and when she thought to triumph over the man who had scorned her, found her soul all blank desolation, and light gone out from the earth! Reckless and weary, she had let herself be united to M. de Selinville, and in her bridal honours and amusements had tried to crowd out the sense of dreariness and lose herself in excitement. Then came the illness and death of her husband, and almost at the same time the knowledge of Berenger's existence. She sought excitement again in that feverish form of devotion then in vogue at Paris, and which resulted in the League. She had hitherto stunned herself as it were with penances, processions, and sermons, for which the host of religious orders then at Paris had given ample scope; and she was constantly devising new extravagances. Even at this moment she wore sackcloth beneath her brocade, and her rosary was of death's heads. She was living on the outward husk of the Roman Church, not penetrating into its living power, and the phase of religion which fostered Henry III. and the League offered her no more.

All, all had melted away beneath the sad but stedfast glance of those two eyes, the only feature still unchanged in the marred, wrecked countenance. That honest, quiet refusal, that look which came from a higher atmosphere, had filled her heart with passionate beatings and aspirations once more, and more consciously than ever. Womanly feeling for suffering, and a deep longing to compensate to him, and earn his love, nay wrest it from him by the benefits she would heap upon him, were all at work; but the primary sense was the longing to rest on the only perfect truth she had ever known in man, and thus with passionate ardour she poured forth her entreaties to St. Eustache, a married saint, who had known love, and could feel for her, and could surely not object to the affection to which she completely gave way for one whose hand was now as free as her own.

But St. Eustache was not Diane's only hope. That evening she sent Véronique to René of Milan, the court-perfumer, but also called by the malicious, *l'empoisonneur de la Reine,* to obtain from him the most infallible charm and love potion in his whole repertory.

CHAPTER XXVI.

THE CHEVALIER'S EXPIATION.

> "Next, Sirs, did he marry?
> And whom, Sirs, did he marry? One like himself,
> Though doubtless graced with many virtues, young,
> And erring, and in nothing more astray
> Than in this marriage."
>
> TAYLOR, *Edwin the Fair.*

NOTHING could be kinder than the Ambassador's family, and Philip found himself at once at home there, at least in his brother's room, which was all the world to him. Fortunately, Ambroise Paré, the most skilful surgeon of his day, had stolen a day from his attendance on King Charles, at St. Germain, to visit his Paris patients, and, though unwilling to add to the list of cases, when he heard from Walsingham's secretary who the sufferer was, and when injured, he came at once to afford his aid.

He found, however, that there was little scope for present treatment, he could only set his chief assistant to watch the patient and to inform him when the crisis should be nearer; but remarking the uneasy, anxious expression in Berenger's eyes, he desired to know whether any care on his mind might be interfering with his recovery. A Huguenot, and perfectly trustworthy, he was one who Walsingham knew might safely hear the whole, and after hearing all, he at once returned to his patient, and leaning over him, said, "Vex not yourself, sir; your illness is probably serving you better than health could do."

Sir Francis thought this quite probable, since Charles was so unwell and so beset with his mother's creatures that no open audience could be obtained from him, and Paré, who always had access to him, might act when no one else could reach him. Meantime the Ambassador rejoiced to hear of the instinctive caution that had made Berenger silence Philip on the object of the journey to Paris, since if the hostile family guessed at the residence of the poor infant, they would have full opportunity for obliterating all the scanty traces of her. Poor persecuted little thing! the uncertain hope of her existence seemed really the only thread that still bound Berenger to life. He had spent eighteen months in hope deferred, and constant bodily pain; and when the frightful disappointment met him at La Sablerie, it was no wonder that his heart and hope seemed buried in the black scorched ruins where all he cared for had perished. He was scarcely nineteen, but the life before him seemed full of nothing but one ghastly recollection, and, as he said in the short sad little letter which he wrote to his grandfather from his bed, he only desired to live long enough to save Eustacie's child from being a nameless orphan maintained for charity in a convent, and to see her safe in Aunt Cecily's care; and then he should be content to have done with this world for ever.

The thought that no one except himself could save the child, seemed to give him the resolution to battle for life that often bears the patient through illness, though now he was suffering more severely and consciously than ever he had done before; and Lady Walsingham often gave up hopes of him. He was tenderly cared for by her and her women; but Philip was the most constant nurse, and his unfailing assiduity and readiness amazed the household, who had begun by thinking him ungainly, loutish, and fit for nothing but country sports.

The Chevalier de Ribaumont came daily to inquire; and the first time he was admitted actually burst into tears at the sight of the swollen disfigured face, and the long mark on the arm which lay half-uncovered. Presents of delicacies, ointments, and cooling drinks were frequently sent from him and from the Countess de Selinville; but Lady Walsingham distrusted these, and kept her guest strictly to the regimen appointed by Paré. Now and then, billets would likewise come. The first brought a vivid crimson into Berenger's face, and both it and all its successors he instantly tore into the smallest fragments, without letting any one see it.

On the last day of the Carnival, the young men of the household had asked Master Thistlewood to come out with them and see the procession of the *Bœuf Gras;* but before it could take place, reports were flying about that put the city in commotion, caused the Ambassador to forbid all going out, and made Philip expect another Huguenot massacre. The Duke of Alençon and the King of Navarre had been detected, it was said, in a conspiracy for overthrowing the power of the Queen-mother, bringing in the Huguenots, and securing the crown to Alençon on the King's death. Downstairs, the Ambassador and his secretaries sat anxiously striving to sift the various contradictory reports; upstairs, Philip and Lady Walsingham were anxiously watching Berenger in what seemed the long-expected crisis, and Philip was feeling as if all the French Court were welcome to murder one another so that they would only let Ambroise Paré come to his brother's relief. And it was impossible even to send!

At last, however, when Ash-Wednesday was half over, there was a quiet movement, and a small pale man in black was at the bedside, without Philip's having ever seen his entrance. He looked at his exhausted patient, and said, "It is well; I could not have done you any good before."

And when he had set Berenger more at ease, he told how great had been the confusion at St. Germain when the plot had become known to the Queen-mother. The poor King had been wakened at two o'clock in the morning, and carried to his litter, where Paré and his old nurse had tended him. He only said, "Can they not let me die in peace?" and his weakness had been so great on arriving, that the surgeon could hardly have left him for M. de Ribaumont, save by his own desire. "Yes, sir," added Paré, seeing Berenger attending to him, "we must have you well quickly; his Majesty knows all about you, and is anxious to see you."

In spite of these good wishes, the recovery was very slow; for, as the surgeon had suspected, the want of skill in those who had had the charge of Berenger at the first had been the cause of much of his protracted suffering. Paré, the inventor of trephining, was, perhaps, the only man in Europe who could have dealt with the fracture in the back of the head, and he likewise extracted the remaining splinters of the jaw, though at the cost of much severe handling and almost intolerable pain: but by Easter, Berenger found the good surgeon's encouragement verified, and himself on the way to a far more effectual cure than he had hitherto thought possible. Sleep had come back to him, he experienced the luxury of being free from all pain, he could eat without difficulty; and Paré, always an enemy to wine, assured him that half the severe headaches for which he had been almost bled to death, were the consequence of his living on bread soaked in sack instead of solid food; and he was forbidden henceforth to inflame his brain with anything stronger than sherbet. His speech, too, was much improved; he still could not utter all the consonants perfectly, and could not speak distinctly without articulating very slowly, but all the discomfort and pain were gone; and though still very weak, he told Philip that now all his course seemed clear towards his child, instead of being like a dull, distraught dream. His plan was to write to have a vessel sent from Weymouth, to lie off the coast till his signal should be seen from La Motte-Achard, and then to take in the whole party and the little yearling daughter, whom he declared he should trust to no one but himself. Lady Walsingham remonstrated a little at the wonderful plans hatched by the two lads together, and yet she was too glad to see a beginning of brightening on his face to make many objections. It was only too sad to think how likely he was again to be disappointed.

He was dressed, but had not left his room, and was lying on cushions in the ample window overlooking the garden, while Frances and Elizabeth Walsingham in charge of their governess tried to amuse him by playing and singing to the lute, when a message was brought that M. le Chevalier de Ribaumont prayed to be admitted to see him privily.

"What bodes that?" he languidly said.

"Mischief, no doubt," said Frances Walsingham. "Send him word that you are seriously employed."

"Nay, that could scarce be, when he must have heard the twanging of the lute," said her sister. "Come away, sister."

"But M. le Baron has not yet heard Mr. Sidney's last madrigal, and I was to send him his opinion of it," pouted Frances; "and I know that would do him good, while the old grasshopper knight always wearies and chafes him."

"Nevertheless, kind Mistress Frances," said Berenger, "methinks I had better face the enemy and have the matter over."

The ladies took the hint and vanished, but Philip remained

till the Chevalier had entered, more resplendent than ever, in a brown velvet suit slashed with green satin, and sparkling with gold lace—a contrast to the deep mourning habit in which Berenger was dressed. After inquiries for his health, the Chevalier looked at Philip, and expressed his desire of speaking with his cousin alone.

"If it be of business," said Berenger, much on his guard, "my head is still weak, and I would wish to have the presence of the Ambassador or one of his secretaries."

"This is not so much a matter of business as of family," said the Chevalier, still looking so uneasily at Philip that Berenger felt constrained to advise him to join the young ladies in the garden; but instead of doing this, the boy paced the corridors like a restless dog waiting for his master, and no sooner heard the old gentleman bow himself out than he hurried back again, to find Berenger heated, panting, agitated as by a sharp encounter.

"Brother, what is it—what has the old rogue done to you?"

"Nothing," said Berenger, tardily and wearily; and for some minutes he did not attempt to speak, while Philip devoured his curiosity as best he might. At last he said, "He was always beyond me. What think you? Now he wants me to turn French courtier and marry his daughter."

"His daughter!" exclaimed Philip, "that beautiful lady I saw in the coach?"

A nod of assent.

"I only wish it were I."

"Philip," half angrily, "how can you be such a fool?"

"Of course, I know it can't be," said Philip sheepishly, but a little offended. "But she's the fairest woman my eyes ever beheld."

"And the falsest."

"My father says all women are false; only they can't help it, and don't mean it."

"Only some do mean it," said Berenger, drily.

"Brother!" cried Philip, fiercely, as if ready to break a lance, "what right have you to accuse that kindly, lovely dame of falsehood?"

"It skills not going through all," said Berenger, wearily. "I know her of old. She began by passing herself off on me as my wife."

"And you were not transported?"

"I am not such a gull as you."

"How very beautiful your wife must have been!" said Philip, with gruff amazement overpowering his consideration.

"Much you know about it," returned Berenger, turning his face away.

There was a long silence, first broken by Philip, asking more cautiously, "And what did you say to him?"

"I said whatever could show it was most impossible. Even I said the brother's handwriting was too plain on my face for me to offer myself to the sister. But it seems all that is to be passed over as an unlucky mistake. I wish I could guess what the old fellow is aiming at."

"I am sure the lady looked at you as if she loved you."

"Simpleton! She looked to see how she could beguile me. Love! They do nothing for love here, you foolish boy, save *par amour*. If she loved me, her father was the last person she would have sent me. No, no; 'tis a new stratagem, if I could only see my way into it. Perhaps Sir Francis will when he can spend an hour on me."

Though full of occupation, Sir Francis never failed daily to look in upon his convalescent guest, and when he heard of the Chevalier's interview, he took care that Berenger should have full time to consult him; and, of course, he inquired a good deal more into the particulars of the proposal than Philip had done. When he learnt that the Chevalier had offered all the very considerable riches and lands that Diane enjoyed in right of her late husband as an equivalent for Berenger's resignation of all claims upon the Nid-de-Merle property, he noted it on his tables, and desired to know what these claims might be. "I cannot tell," said Berenger. "You may remember, sir, the parchments with our contract of marriage had been taken away from Château Leurre, and I have never seen them."

"Then," said the Ambassador, "you may hold it as certain that those parchments give you some advantage which he hears, since he is willing to purchase it at so heavy a price. Otherwise he himself would be the natural heir of those lands."

"After my child," said Berenger, hastily.

"Were you on your guard against mentioning your trust in your child's life?" said Sir Francis.

The long scar turned deeper purple than ever. "Only so far as that I said there still be rights I had no power to resign," said Berenger. "And then he began to prove to me—what I had no mind to hear" (and his voice trembled) "—all that I know but too well."

"Hum! you must not be left alone again to cope with him," said Walsingham. "Did he make any question of the validity of your marriage?"

"No, sir, it was never touched on. I would not let him take her name into his lips."

Walsingham considered for some minutes, and then said, "It is clear, then, that he believes that the marriage can be sufficiently established to enable you to disturb him in his possession of some part, at least, of the Angevin inheritance, or he would not endeavour to purchase your renunciation of it by the hand of a daughter so richly endowed."

"I would willingly renounce it if that were all! I never sought it; only I cannot give up her child's rights."

"And that you almost declared," proceeded Walsingham; "so that the Chevalier has by his negotiation gathered from you that you have not given up hope that the infant lives. Do your men know where you believe she is?"

"My Englishmen know it, of course," said Berenger; "but there is no fear of them. The Chevalier speaks no English, and they scarcely any French; and, besides, I believe they deem him equally my butcher with his son. The other fellow I only picked up after I was on my way to Paris, and I doubt his knowing my purpose."

"The Chevalier must have had speech with him, though," said Philip; "for it was he who brought word that the old rogue wished to speak with you."

"It would be well to be quit yourself of the fellow ere leaving Paris," said Walsingham.

"Then, sir," said Berenger, with an anxious voice, "do you indeed think I have betrayed aught that can peril the poor little one?"

Sir Francis smiled. "We do not set lads of your age to cope with old foxes," he answered; "and it seems to me that you used fair discretion in the encounter. The mere belief that the child lives does not show him where she may be. In effect, it would seem likely to most that the babe would be nursed in some cottage, and thus not be in the city of La Sablerie at all. He might, mayhap, thus be put on a false scent."

"Oh no," exclaimed Berenger, startled; "that might bring the death of some other person's child on my soul."

"That shall be guarded against," said Sir Francis. "In the meantime, my fair youth, keep your matters as silent as may be—do not admit the Chevalier again in my absence;

and, as to this man Guibert, I will confer with my steward whether he knows too much, and whether it be safer to keep or dismiss him!"

"If only I could see the King, and leave Paris," sighed Berenger.

And Walsingham, though unwilling to grieve the poor youth further, bethought himself that this was the most difficult and hopeless matter of all. As young Ribaumont grew better, the King grew worse; he himself only saw Charles on rare occasions, surrounded by a host of watchful eyes and ears, and every time he marked the progress of disease; and though such a hint could not be given by an Ambassador, he thought that by far the best chance of recovery of the child lay in the confusion that might probably follow the death of Charles IX. in the absence of his next heir.

Berenger reckoned on the influence of Elisabeth of Austria, who had been the real worker in his union with Eustacie; but he was told that it was vain to expect assistance from her. In the first year of her marriage, she had fondly hoped to enjoy her husband's confidence, and take her natural place in his Court; but she was of no mould to struggle with Catherine de Médicis, and after a time had totally desisted. Even at the time of the St. Bartholomew, she had endeavoured to uplift her voice on the side of mercy, and had actually saved the lives of the King of Navarre and Prince of Condé; and her father, the good Maximilian II., had written in the strongest terms to Charles IX. expressing his horror of the massacre. Six weeks later, the first hour after the birth of her first and only child, she had interceded with her husband for the lives of two Huguenots who had been taken alive, and failing then either through his want of will or want of power, she had collapsed and yielded up the endeavour. She ceased to listen to petitions from those who had hoped for her assistance, as if to save both them and herself useless pain, and seemed to lapse into a sort of apathy to all public interests. She hardly spoke, mechanically fulfilled her few offices in the Court, and seemed to have turned her entire hope and trust into prayer for her husband. Her German confessor had been sent home, and a Jesuit given her in his stead, but she had made no resistance; she seemed to the outer world a dull, weary stranger, obstinate in leading a conventual life; but those who knew her best—and of these few was the Huguenot surgeon Paré—knew that her heart had been broken when, as a new-made mother, she had failed to win those two guilty lives, or to make her husband free himself from his bondage to bloody counsels. To pray for him was all that remained to her—and unwearied had been those prayers. Since his health had declined, she had been equally indefatigable in attending on him, and did not seem to have a single interest beyond his sick chamber.

As to the King of Navarre, for whose help Berenger had hoped, he had been all these months in the dishonourable thraldom of Catherine de Médicis, and was more powerless than ever at this juncture, having been implicated in Alençon's plot, and imprisoned at Vincennes.

And thus, the more Berenger heard of the state of things, the less hopeful did his cause appear, till he could almost have believed his best chance lay in Philip's plan of persuading the Huguenots to storm the convent.

CHAPTER XXVII.

THE DYING KING.

> "Die in terror of thy guiltiness,
> Dream on, dream on of bloody deeds and death,
> Fainting, despair, despairing yield thy breath."
>
> *King Richard III.*

A FEW days later, when Berenger had sent out Philip, under the keeping of the secretaries, to see the Queen-mother represent Royalty in one of the grand processions of Rogation-tide, the gentle knock came to his door that always announced the arrival of his good surgeon.

"You look stronger, M. le Baron; have you yet left your room?"

"I have walked round the gallery above the hall," said Berenger. "I have not gone downstairs; that is for to-morrow."

"What would M. le Baron say if his chirurgeon took him not merely downstairs, but up one flight at the Louvre."

"Ha!" cried Berenger; "to the King?"

"It is well-nigh the last chance, Monsieur; the Queen-mother and all her suite are occupied with services and sermons this week; and next week private access to the King will be far more difficult. I have waited as long as I could that you might gain strength to support the fatigue."

"Hope cancels fatigue," said Berenger, already at the other

end of the room searching for his long-disused cloak, sword, gloves, hat, and mask.

"Not the sword," said Paré, "so please you. M. le Baron must condescend to obtain entrance as my assistant—the plain black doublet—yes, that is admirable; but I did not know that Monsieur was so tall," he added, in some consternation, as, for the first time, he saw his patient standing up at his full height—unusual even in England, and more so in France. Indeed, Berenger had grown during his year of illness, and being, of course, extremely thin, looked all the taller, so as to be a very inconvenient subject to smuggle into the palace unobserved.

However, Ambroise had made up his mind to the risk, and merely assisted Berenger in assuming his few equipments, then gave him his arm to go down the stairs. Meeting Guibert on the way, Berenger left word with him that he was going out to take the air with Maître Paré; and on the man's offering to attend him, refused the proposal.

Paré's carriage waited in the court, and Berenger, seated in its depths, rolled unseen through the streets, till he found himself at the little postern of the Louvre, the very door whence he was to have led off his poor Eustacie. Here Ambroise made him take off his small black mask, in spite of all danger of his scars being remarked, since masks were not etiquette in the palace, and, putting into his arms a small brass-bound case of instruments, asked his pardon for preceding him, and alighted from the carriage.

This was Ambroise's usual entrance, and it was merely guarded by a Scottish archer, who probably observed nothing. They then mounted the stone stair, the same where Osbert had dragged down his insensible master; and as, at the summit, the window appeared where Berenger had waited those weary hours, and heard the first notes of the bell of

St.-Germain-l'Auxerrois, his breath came in such hurried sobs, that Paré would fain have given him time to recover himself, but he gasped, "Not here—not here;" and Paré, seeing that he could still move on, turned, not to the corridor leading to the King's old apartments, now too full of dreadful associations for poor Charles, but towards those of the young Queen. Avoiding the ante-room, where no doubt waited pages, ushers, and attendants, Paré presently knocked at a small door, so hidden in the wainscotting of the passage, that only a *habitué* could have found it without strict search. It was at once opened, and the withered, motherly face of an old woman with keen black eyes under a formal tight white cap, looked out.

"Eh! Maître Paré," she said, "you have brought the poor young gentleman? On my faith, he looks scarcely able to walk! Come in, sir, and rest a while in my chamber while Maître Ambroise goes on to announce you to the King. He is more at ease to-day, the poor child, and will relish some fresh talk."

Berenger knew this to be Philippine, the old Huguenot nurse, whom Charles IX. loved most fondly, and in whom he found his greatest comfort. He was very glad to sink into the seat she placed for him, the only one in her small, bare room, and recover breath there while Paré passed on to the King, and she talked as one delighted to have a hearer.

"Ah, yes, rest yourself—stay; I will give you a few spoonfuls of the cordial potage I have here for the King; it will comfort your heart. Ah! you have been cruelly mauled —but he would have saved you if he could."

"Yes, good mother, I know that; the King has been my very good lord."

"Ah! blessings on you if you say so from your heart, Monsieur; you know me for one of our poor Reformed.

And I tell you—I who saw him born, who nursed him from his birth—that, suffer as you may, you can never suffer as he does. Maître Ambroise may talk of his illness coming from blowing too much on his horn; I know better. But, ah! to be here at night would make a stone shed tears of blood. The Queen and I know it; but we say nothing, we only pray."

The sight of a Huguenot was so great a treat to the old woman in her isolated life, that her tongue ran thus freely while Berenger sat, scarce daring to speak or breathe in the strange boding atmosphere of the palace, where the nurse and surgeon moved as tolerated, privileged persons, in virtue of the necessity of the one to the King—of the other to all the world. After a brief interval Paré returned and beckoned to Berenger, who followed him across a large state-bedroom to a much smaller one, which he entered from under a heavy blue velvet curtain, and found himself in an atmosphere heavy with warmth and perfume, and strangely oppressed besides. On one side of the large fire sat the young Queen, faded, wan, and with all animation or energy departed, only gazing with a silent, wistful intentness at her husband. He was opposite to her in a pillowed chair, his feet on a stool, with a deadly white, padded, puffy cheek, and his great black eyes, always prominent, now with a glassy look, and strained wide, as though always gazing after some horrible sight. "Madame la Comtesse" stood in her old, wooden automaton fashion behind the Queen; otherwise, no one was present save Paré, who, as he held up the curtain, stood back to let M. de Ribaumont advance. He stood still, however, merely bowing low, awaiting an invitation to come forward, and trying to repress the startled tear called up by the very shock of pity at the mournful aspect of the young King and Queen.

Elisabeth, absorbed in her husband, and indifferent to all besides, did not even turn her head as he entered; but

Charles signed to him to approach, holding out a yellow, dropsical-looking hand; and as he dropped on one knee and kissed it fervently, the King said, "Here he is, Madame, the Baron de Ribaumont, the same whose little pleasure-boat was sucked down in our whirlpool."

All Elisabeth's memories seemed to have been blotted out in that whirlpool, for she only bowed her head formally, and gave no look of recognition, though she, too, allowed Berenger to salute her listless, dejected hand. "One would hardly have known him again," continued the King, in a low husky voice; "but I hope, sir, I see you recovering."

"Thanks, Sire, to Heaven's goodness, and to your goodness in sparing to me the services of Maître Paré."

"Ah! there is none like Paré for curing a wound *outside*," said Charles, then leant back silent; and Berenger, still kneeling, was considering whether he ought to proffer his petition, when the King continued, "How fares your friend Sidney, M. le Baron?"

"Right well, Sire. The Queen is about to confer on him the honour of knighthood."

"Not after this order," said Charles, as with his finger he traced the long scar on Berenger's face. "Our sister of England has different badges of merit from ours for her good subjects. Ha! what say they of us in England, Baron?"

"I have lain sick at home, Sire, and have neither seen nor heard," said Berenger.

"Ah! one day more at Montpipeau had served your turn," said the King; "but you are one who has floated up again. One—one at least whose blood is not on my head."

The Queen looked up uneasy and imploring, as Charles continued: "Would that more of you would come in this way! They have scored you deep, but know you what is gashed deeper still? Your King's heart! Ah! you will not come, as Coligny does, from his gibbet, with his two bleeding hands. My father was haunted to his dying day by the face of one Huguenot tailor. Why, I see a score, night by night! You are solid; let me feel you, man."

"M. Paré," exclaimed the poor Queen, "take him away."

"No, Madame," said the King, holding tight in his hot grasp Berenger's hand, which was as pale as his own, long, thin, and wasted, but cold from strong emotion; "take not away the only welcome sight I have seen for well-nigh two years." He coughed, and the handkerchief he put to his lips had blood on it; but he did not quit his hold of his visitor, and presently said in a feeble whisper, "Tell me, how did you escape?"

Paré, over the King's head, signed to him to make his narrative take time; and indeed his speech was of necessity so slow, that by the time he had related how Osbert had brought him safely to England, the King had recovered himself so as to say, "See what it is to have a faithful servant. Which of those they have left me would do as much for me? And now, being once away with your life, what brings you back to this realm of ours, after your last welcome?"

"I left my wife here, Sire."

"Ha! and the cousin would have married her—obtained permission to call himself Nid-de-Merle—but she slipped through his clumsy fingers; did she not? Did you know anything of her, Madame?"

"No," said the Queen, looking up. "She wrote to me once from her convent; but I knew I could do nothing for her but bring her enemies' notice on her; so I made no answer."

Berenger could hardly conceal his start of indignation—less at the absolute omission, than at the weary indifference of the Queen's confession. Perhaps the King saw it, for he added, "So it is, Ribaumont; the kindest service we can do our friends is to let them alone; and, after all, it was not the worse for her. She did evade her enemies?"

"Yes, Sire," said Berenger, commanding and steadying his voice with great difficulty, "she escaped in time to give birth to our child in the ruined loft of an old grange of the Templars, under the care of a Huguenot farmer, and a pastor who had known my father. Then she took refuge in La Sablerie, and wrote to my mother, deeming me dead. I was just well enough to go in quest of her. I came—ah! Sire, I found only charred ruins. Your Majesty knows how Huguenot bourgs are dealt with."

"And she——?"

Berenger answered but by a look.

"Why did you come to tell me this?" said the King, passionately. "Do you not know that they have killed me already? I thought you came because there was still some one I could aid."

"There is, there is, Sire," said Berenger, for once interrupting royalty. "None save you can give me my child. It is almost certain that a good priest saved it; but it is in a convent, and only with a royal order can one of my religion either obtain it, or even have my questions answered."

"Nor with one in Paris," said the King drily; "but in the country the good mothers may still honour their King's hand. Here, Ambroise, take pen and ink, and write the order. To whom?"

"To the Mother Prioress of the Ursulines at Luçon, so please your Majesty," said Berenger, "to let me have possession of my daughter."

"Eh! is it only a little girl?"

"Yes, Sire; but my heart yearns for her all the more," said Berenger, with glistening eyes.

"You are right," said the poor King. "Mine, too, is a little girl; and I bless God daily that she is no son—to be the most wretched thing in France. Let her come in, Madame. She is little older than my friend's daughter. I would show her to him."

The Queen signed to Madame la Comtesse to fetch the child, and Berenger added, "Sire, you could do a further benefit to my poor little one. One more signature of yours would attest that ratification of my marriage which took place in your Majesty's presence."

"Ah! I remember," said Charles. "You may have any name of mine that can help you to oust that villain Narcisse; only wait to use it—spare me any more storms. It will serve your turn as well when I am beyond them, and you will make your claim good. What," seeing Berenger's interrogative look, "do you not know that by the marriage-contract the lands of each were settled on the survivor?"

"No, Sire; I have never seen the marriage-contract."

"Your kinsman knew it well," said Charles.

Just then, Madame la Comtesse returned, leading the little Princess by the long ribbons at her waist; Charles bent forward, calling, "Here, *ma petite*, come here. Here is one who loves thy father. Look well at him, that thou mayest know him."

The little Madame Elisabeth so far understood, that, with a certain lofty condescension, she extended her hand for the stranger to kiss, and thus drew from the King the first smile that Berenger had seen. She was more than half a year older than the Bérangère on whom his hopes were set, and whom he trusted to find not such a pale, feeble, tottering little creature as this poor young daughter of France, whose round black eyes gazed wonderingly at his scar; but she was very precocious, and even already too much of a royal lady to indulge in any awkward personal observation.

By the time she had been rewarded for her good behaviour by one of the dried plums in her father's comfit-box, the order had been written by Paré, and Berenger had prepared the certificate for the King's signature, according to the form given him by his grandfather.

"Your writing shakes nearly as much as mine," said the poor King, as he wrote his name to this latter. "Now, Madame, you had better sign it also; and tell this gentleman where to find Father Meinhard in Austria. He was a little too true for us, do you see—would not give thanks for shedding innocent blood. Ah!"—and with a gasp of mournful longing, the King sank back, while Elisabeth, at his bidding, added her name to the certificate, and murmured the name of a convent in Vienna, where her late confessor could be found.

"I cannot thank your Majesty enough," said Berenger. "My child's rights are now secure in England at least, and this"—as he held the other paper for the King—"will give her to me."

"Ah! take it for what it is worth," said the King, as he scrawled his "*Charles*" upon it. "This order must be used promptly, or it will avail you nothing. Write to Ambroise how you speed; that is, if it will bring me one breath of good news." And as Berenger kissed his hand with tearful, inarticulate thanks, he proceeded, "Save for that cause, I would ask you to come to me again. It does me good. It is like a breath from Montpipeau—the last days of hope—before the frenzy—the misery."

"Whenever your Majesty does me the honour——" began Berenger, forgetting all except the dying man.

"I am not so senseless," interrupted the King sharply;

"it would be losing the only chance of undoing one wrong. Only, Ribaumont," he added fervently, "for once let me hear that one man has pardoned me."

"Sire, Sire," sobbed Berenger, totally overcome, "how can I speak the word? How feel aught but love, loyalty, gratitude?"

Charles half smiled again as he said in sad meditation—"Ah! it was in me to have been a good king if they had let me. Think of me, bid your friend Sidney think of me, as I would have been—not as I have been—and pray, pray for me." Then hiding his face in his handkerchief, in a paroxysm of grief and horror, he murmured in a stifled tone, "Blood, blood, deliver me, good Lord!"

In effect, there was so sudden a gush of blood from mouth and nose that Berenger sprang to his feet in dismay, and was *bonâ fide* performing the part of assistant to the surgeon, when, at the Queen's cry, not only the nurse Philippine hurried in, but with her a very dark, keen-looking man, who at once began applying strong essences to the King's face, as Berenger supported his head. In a few moments Paré looked up at Berenger, and setting him free, intimated to him, between sign and whisper, to go into Philippine's room and wait there; and it was high time, for though the youth had felt nothing in the stress of the moment, he was almost swooning when he reached the little chamber, and lay back in the nurse's chair, with closed eyes, scarcely conscious how time went, or even where he was, till he was partly aroused by hearing steps returning.

"The poor young man," said Philippine's kind voice, "he is fainting. Ah! no wonder it overcame any kind heart."

"How is the King?" Berenger tried to say, but his own voice still sounded unnatural and far away.

"He is better for the time, and will sleep," said Paré,

administering to his other patient some cordial drops as he spoke. "There, sir; you will soon be able to return to the carriage. This has been a sore trial to your strength."

"But I have gained all—all I could hope," said Berenger, looking at his precious papers. "But, alas! the poor King!"

"You will never, never let a word of blame pass against him," cried Philippine earnestly. "It is well that one of our people should have seen how it really is with him. All I regret is that Maître René thrust himself in and saw you."

"Who?" said Berenger, who had been too much engrossed to perceive any one.

"Maître René of Milan, the Queen-mother's perfumer. He came with some plea of bringing a pouncet-box from her, but I wager it was as a spy. I was doing my best to walk him gently off, when the Queen's cry called me, and he must needs come in after me."

"I saw him not," said Berenger; "perhaps he marked not me in the confusion."

"I fear," said Paré gravely, "he was more likely to have his senses about him than you, M. le Baron; these bleedings of the King's are not so new to us familiars of the palace. The best thing now to be done is to have you to the carriage, if you can move."

Berenger, now quite recovered, stood up, and gave his warm thanks to the old nurse for her kindness to him.

"Ah! sir," she said, "you are one of us. Pray, pray that God will have mercy on my poor child! He has the truth in his heart. Pray that it may save him at the last."

Ambroise, knowing that she would never cease speaking while there was any one to hear her, almost dragged Berenger out at the little secret door, conveyed him safely down the stairs, and placed him again in the carriage. Neither spoke till the surgeon said, "You have seen a sad sight, Monsieur le Baron: I need not bid you be discreet."

"There are some things that go too deep for speech," sighed the almost English Berenger; then, after a pause, "Is there no hope for him? Is he indeed dying?"

"Without a miracle, he cannot live a month. He is as truly slain by the St. Bartholomew as ever its martyrs were," said Paré, moved out of his usual cautious reserve towards one who had seen so much and felt so truly. "I tell you, sir, that his mother hath as truly slain her sons, as if she had sent René there to them with his drugs. According as they have consciences and hearts, so they pine and perish under her rule."

Berenger shuddered, and almost sobbed, "And hath he no better hope, no comforter?" he asked.

"None save good old Flipote. As you heard, the Queen-mother will not suffer his own Church to speak to him in her true voice. No confessor but one chosen by the Cardinal of Lorraine may come near him; and with him all is mere ceremony. But if at the last he opens his ear and heart to take in the true hope of salvation, it will be from the voice of poor old Philippine."

And so it was! It was Philippine, who heard him in the night sobbing over the piteous words, "My God, what horrors, what blood!" and, as she took from him his tear-drenched handkerchief, spoke to him of the Blood that speaketh better things than the blood of Abel; and it was she who, in the final agony, heard and treasured these last words, "If the Lord Jesus will indeed receive me into the company of the blest!" Surely, never was repentance deeper than that of Charles IX.—and these, his parting words, were such as to inspire the trust that it was not remorse.

All-important as Berenger's expedition had been, he still could think of little but the poor King; and, wearied out as he was, he made very little reply to the astonished friends who gathered round him on his return. He merely told Philip that he had succeeded, and then lay almost without speaking on his bed till the Ambassador made his evening visit, when he showed him the two papers. Sir Francis could hardly believe his good fortune in having obtained this full attestation of the marriage, and promised to send to the English Ambassador in Germany, to obtain the like from Father Meinhard. The document itself he advised Berenger not to expose to the dangers of the French journey, but to leave it with him to be forwarded direct to Lord Walwyn. It was most important, both as obviating any dispute on the legitimacy of the child, if she lived; or, if not, it would establish those rights of Berenger to the Nid-de-Merle estates, of which he had heard from the King. This information explained what were the claims that the Chevalier was so anxious to hush up by a marriage with Madame de Selinville. Berenger, as his wife's heir, was by this contract the true owner of the estates seized by the Chevalier and his son, and could only be ousted, either by his enemies proving his contract to Eustacie invalid and to be unfulfilled, or by his own voluntary resignation. The whole scheme was clear to Walsingham, and he wasted advice upon unheeding ears, as to how Berenger should act to obtain restitution so soon as he should be of age, and how he should try to find out the notary who had drawn up the contract. If Berenger cared at all, it was rather for the sake of punishing and balking Narcisse, than with any desire of the inheritance; and even for righteous indignation he was just now too weary and too sad. He could not discuss his rights to Nid-de-Merle, if they passed over the rights of Eustacie's child, round whom his affections were winding themselves as his sole hope.

The next evening Paré came in quest of Berenger, and after a calm, refreshing, hopeful Ascension-day, which had been a real balm to the weary spirit, found him enjoying the sweet May sunshine under a tree in the garden. "I am glad to find you out of doors," he said; "I fear I must hasten your departure."

"I burn to lose no time," cried Berenger. "Prithee tell them I may safely go! They all call it madness to think of setting out."

"Ordinarily it would be," said Paré; "but René of Milan has sent his underlings to see who is my new, tall assistant. He will report all to the Queen-mother; and though in this house you could scarcely suffer personal harm, yet the purpose of your journey might be frustrated, and the King might have to undergo another of those *bourrasques* which he may well dread."

"I will go this very night," said Berenger, starting up; "where is Philip?—where is Sir Francis?"

Even that very night Paré thought not too soon, and the Ascension-tide illuminations brought so many persons abroad that it would be easy to go unnoticed; and in the general festivity, when every one was coming and going from the country to gaze or worship at the shrines and the images decked in every church, it would be easy for the barriers to be passed without observation. Then the brothers would sleep at a large hostel, the first on the road to England, where Walsingham's couriers and guests always baited, and the next morning he would send out to them their attendants, with horses for their further journey back into Anjou. If any enemies were on the watch, this would probably put them off the scent, and it only remained further to be debated, whether the Norman Guibert had better be dismissed at once or taken with them. There was always a soft place in Berenger's heart for a Norman, and the man was really useful; moreover, he would certainly be safer employed and in their company, than turned loose to tell the Chevalier all he might have picked up in the Hôtel d'Angleterre. It was, therefore, decided that he should be the attendant of the two young men, and he received immediate orders that night to pack up their garments, and hold himself ready.

Nevertheless, before the hour of departure, Guibert had stolen out, had an interview with the Chevalier de Ribaumont at the Hôtel de Selinville, and came back with more than one good French crown in his pocket, and hopes of more.

CHAPTER XXVIII.

THE ORPHANS OF LA SABLERIE.

"The cream tarts with pepper in them."—*Arabian Nights.*

Hope, spring, and recovery carried the young Baron de Ribaumont on his journey infinitely better than his companions had dared to expect. He dreaded nothing so much as being overtaken by those tidings which would make King Charles's order mere waste paper; and therefore pressed on with little regard to his own fatigue, although happily with increasing strength, which carried him a further stage every day.

Luçon was a closely-guarded, thoroughly Catholic city, and his safe-conduct was jealously demanded; but the name of Ribaumont silenced all doubt. "A relation, apparently, of M. de Nid-de-Merle," said the officer on guard, and politely invited him to dinner and bed at the castle; but these he thought it prudent to decline, explaining that he brought a letter from the King to the Mother Prioress.

The convent walls were pointed out to him, and he only delayed at the inn long enough to arrange his dress as might appear to the Abbess most respectful, and, poor boy, be least likely to startle the babe on whom his heart was set. At almost every inn, the little children had shrieked and run from his white and gashed face, and his tall, lank figure in deep black; and it was very sadly that he said to Philip, "You must come with me. If she turns from me as an ogre, your bright ruddy face will win her."

The men were left at the inn with charge to let Guibert speak for them, and to avoid showing their nationality. The three months of Paris, and the tailors there, had rendered Philip much less conspicuous than formerly; but still people looked at him narrowly as he followed his brother along the street. The two lads had made up their minds to encumber themselves with no nurses, or womanfolk. The child should be carried, fondled, and fed by her boy-father alone. He believed that, when he once held her in his arms, he should scarcely even wish to give her up to any one else; and, in his concentration of mind, had hardly thought of all the inconveniences and absurdities that would arise; but, really, was chiefly occupied by the fear that she would not at first let him take her in his arms, and hold her to his heart.

Philip, a little more alive to the probabilities, nevertheless was disposed to regard them as "fun and pastime." He had had many a frolic with his baby-sisters, and this would be only a prolonged one; besides, it was "Berry's" one hope, and to rescue any creature from a convent was a good work, in his Protestant eyes, which had not become a whit less prejudiced at Paris. So he was quite prepared to take his full share of his niece, or more, if she should object to her father's looks, and he only suggested halting at an old woman's stall to buy some sweetmeats by way of propitiation—a proceeding which much amazed the gazing population of Luçon. Two reports were going about, one that the King had vowed a silver image of himself to St. Ursula, if her Prioress would obtain his recovery by their prayers; the other that he was going to translate her to the royal Abbey of Fontévrault to take charge of his daughter, Madame

Elisabeth. Anyway, high honour by a royal messenger must be intended to the Prioress, Mère Monique, and the Luçonnais were proud of her sanctity.

The portress had already heard the report, and opened her wicket even before the bell could be rung, then eagerly ushered him into the parlour, the barest and most ascetic-looking of rooms, with a boarded partition across, unenlivened except by a grated hollow, and the outer portion empty, save of a table, three chairs, and a rugged woodcut of a very tall St. Ursula, with a crowd of pigmy virgins, not reaching higher than the ample hem of her petticoat.

"Did Aunt Cecily live in such a place as this?" exclaimed Philip, gazing round; "or do they live on the fat among down cushions inside there?"

"Hush—sh," said Berenger, frowning with anxiety; for a a rustling was heard behind the screen, and presently a black veil and white scapulary appeared, and a sweet calm voice said, "Peace be with you, sir; what are your commands?"

Berenger bowed low, and replied, "Thanks, reverend Lady, I bring a letter from the King, to request your aid in a matter that touches me nearly."

"His Majesty shall be obeyed. Come you from him?"

He was forced to reply to her inquiries after the poor King's health before she opened the letter, taking it under her veil to read it; so that as he stood, trembling, almost sickening with anxiety, and scarcely able to breathe, he could see nothing but the black folds; and at her low murmured exclamation he started as if at a cannon-shot.

"De Ribaumont!" she said; "can it be—the child—of—of—our poor dear little *pensionnaire* at Bellaise?"

"It is—it is!" cried Berenger. "O Madame, you knew her at Bellaise?"

"Even so," replied the Prioress, who was in fact the Sœur

Monique so loved and regretted by Eustacie. "I loved and prayed for her with all my heart when she was claimed by the world. Heaven's will be done; but the poor little thing loved me, and I have often thought that had I been still at Bellaise when she returned she would not have fled. But of this child I have no knowledge."

"You took charge of the babes of La Sablerie, Madame," said Berenger, almost under his breath.

"Her infant among those poor orphans!" exclaimed the Prioress, more and more startled and amazed.

"If it be anywhere in this life, it is in your good keeping, Madame," said Berenger, with tears in his eyes. "Oh! I entreat, withhold her no longer."

"But," exclaimed the bewildered nun, "who would you then be, sir?"

"I—her husband—widower of Eustacie—father of her orphan!" cried Berenger. "She cannot be detained from me, either by right or law."

"Her husband," still hesitated Monique. "But he is dead. The poor little one—Heaven have mercy on her soul—wrote me a piteous entreaty, and gave large alms for prayers and masses for his soul."

The sob in his throat almost strangled his speech. "She mourned me to the last as dead. I was borne away senseless and desperately wounded; and when I recovered power to seek her it was too late! O Madame! have pity—let me see all she has left to me."

"Is it possible?" said the nun. "We would not learn the parentage of our nurslings since all alike become children of Mother Church." Then, suddenly bethinking herself, "But, surely, Monsieur cannot be a Huguenot."

It was no doubt the first time she had been brought in contact with a schismatic, and she could not believe that such respectful courtesy could come from one. He saw he must curb himself, and explain. "I am neither Calvinist nor Sacrémentaire, Madame. I was bred in England, where we love our own Church. My aunt is a Benedictine Sister, who keeps her rule strictly, though her convent is destroyed; and it is to her that I shall carry my daughter. Ah, Lady, did you but know my heart's hunger for her!"

The Prioress, better read in the lives of the saints than in the sects of heretics, did not know whether this meant that he was of her own faith or not; and her woman's heart being much moved by his pleadings, she said, "I will heartily give your daughter to you, sir, as indeed I must, if she be here; but you have never seen her."

"No; only her empty cradle in the burnt house. But I *must* know her. She is a year old."

"We have two babes of that age; but I fear me you will scarce see much likeness in either of them to any one you knew," said the Prioress thoughtfully. "However, there are two girls old enough to remember the parentage of their companions, though we forbade them to mention it. Would you see them, sir?"

"And the infants, so please you, reverend Mother," exclaimed Berenger.

She desired him to wait, and after an interval of suspense there was a pattering of little *sabots* behind the partition, and through the grating he beheld six little girls in blue serge frocks and tight white caps. Of the two infants, one with a puny, wizen, pinched face was in the arms of the Prioress; the other, a big, stout, coarse child, with hard brown cheeks and staring black eyes, was on its own feet, but with a great basket-work frame round its head to save it from falls. There were two much more prepossessing children of three or four, and two intelligent-looking girls of perhaps eight and ten, to the elder of whom the Prioress turned, saying, "Agathe, I release you from my command not to speak of your former life, and desire you to tell this gentleman if you know who were the parents of these two little ones."

"Yes, reverend Mother," said Agathe, readily; "the old name of Claire" (touching the larger baby) "was Salomé Potier: her mother was the washerwoman; and Annonciade, I don't know what her name was, but her father worked for Maître Brassier who made the kettles."

Philip felt relieved to be free from all doubt about these very uninviting little ones, but Berenger, though sighing heavily, asked quickly, "Permit me, Madame, a few questions.—Little maid, did you ever hear of Isaac Gardon?"

"Maître Isaac! Oh yes, sir. We used to hear him preach at the church, and sometimes he catechised us," she said, and her lip quivered.

"He was a heretic, and I abjure him," added the other girl, perking up her head.

"Was he in the town? What became of him?" exclaimed Berenger.

"He would not be in the town," said the elder girl. "My poor father had sent him word to go away."

"*Eh quoi?*"

"Our father was Bailli la Grasse," interposed the younger girl consequentially. "Our names were Marthe and Lucie la Grasse, but Agathe and Eulalie are much prettier."

"But Maître Gardon?" still asked Berenger.

"He ought to be taken and burnt," said the new Eulalie; "he brought it all on us."

"How was it? Was my wife with him—Madame de Ribaumont? Speak, my child."

"That was the name," said one girl.

"But Maître Gardon had no great lady with him," said

the other, "only his son's widow and her baby, and they lodged with Noémi Laurent, who made the *pâtisserie*."

"Ah!" cried Berenger, lighting up with the new ray of hope. "Tell me, my dear, that they fled with him, and where?"

"I do not know of their going," said Agathe, confused and overborne by his eagerness.

"Curb yourself, sir," said the Prioress, "they will recollect themselves and tell you what they can."

"It was the little cakes with lemoned sugar," suggested the younger girl. "Maître Tressan always said there would be a judgment on us for our daintiness. Ah! he was very cross about them, and after all it was the Maire of Luçon who ate fifteen of them all at once; but then he is not a heretic."

Happily for Berenger, Agathe unravelled this speech.

"Mademoiselle Gardon made the sugar-lemoned cakes, and the Mayor of Luçon, one day when he supped with us, was so delighted with them that he carried one away to show his wife, and afterwards he sent over to order some more. Then, after a time, he sent secretly to my father to ask him if Maître Gardon was there: for there was a great outcry about the lemon cakes, and the Duke of Alençon's army were coming to demand his daughter-in-law; because it seems she was a great Lady, and the only person who could make the cakes."

"Agathe!" exclaimed the Prioress.

"I understand," said Berenger. "The Curé of Nissard told me that she was traced through cakes, the secret of which was only known at Bellaise."

"That might be," said Mère Monique. "I remember there was something of pride in the cakes of Bellaise, though I always tried to know nothing of them."

"Well, little one, continue," entreated Berenger. "You are giving me life and hope."

"I heard my father and mother talk about it," said Agathe, gaining courage. "He said he knew nothing of great people, and would give nobody up to the Catholics, but as to Maître Isaac he should let him know that the Catholic army were coming, and that it would be the better for us if we had no pastor within our walls; and that there was a cry that his daughter's lemon cakes were made by the Lady that was lost."

"And they escaped! Ah! would that I could thank the good man!"

"Surely yes, sir, I never saw them again. Maître Tressan the elder prayed with us. And when the cruel soldiers came and demanded the Lady and Maître Isaac, and all obstinate Calvinists, our mayor and my father and the rest made answer that they had no knowledge of the Lady, and did not know where Maître Gardon was; and as to Huguenots we were all one as obstinate as the other, but that we would pay any fine within our means so they would spare our lives. Then the man in the fine coat said, it was the Lady they wanted, not the fine; and a great deal he said besides, I know not what, but my father said, 'It is our life's blood that they want,' and he put on his breastplate and kissed us all, and went away. Then came horrible noises and firing of cannon, and the neighbours ran in and said that the enemy were battering down the old crumbly bit of wall where the monastery was burnt; and just then our man Joseph ran back all pale, and staring, to tell us my father was lying badly hurt in the street. My mother hurried out, and locked the door to keep us from following."

The poor child broke down in tears, and her sister went on. "Oh, we were so frightened—such frightful sounds came close, and people ran by all blood and shrieking—and there was a glare in the sky—and nobody came home—till at last it grew so dreadful that we hid in the cellar to hear and see nothing. Only it grew hotter and hotter, and the light through the little grating was red. And at last there was a noise louder than thunder, and, oh, such a shaking—for it was the house falling down. But we did not know that; we tried to open the door, and could not; then we cried and called for father and mother—and no one heard—and we sat still for fear, till we slept—and then it was all dark, and we were very hungry. I don't know how time went, but at last, when it was daylight again, there was a talking above, a little baby crying, and a kind voice too; and then we called out, 'Oh take us out and give us bread.' Then a face looked down the grating. Oh! it was like the face of an angel to us, with all the white hair flying round. It was the holy priest of Nissard; and when one of the cruel men said we were only little heretics who ought to die like rats in a hole, he said we were but innocents who did not know the difference."

"Ah! we did," said the elder girl. "You are younger, sister, you forget more;" and then, holding out her hands to Berenger, she exclaimed, "Ah! sir, take us away with you."

"My child!" exclaimed the Prioress, "you told me you were happy to be in the good course."

"Oh yes!" cried the poor child; "but I don't want to be happy! I am forgetting all my poor father and mother used to say. I can't help it, and they would be so grieved. Oh, take me away, sir!"

"Take care, Agathe, you will be a relapsed heretic," said her sister solemnly. "For me, I am a true Catholic. I love the beautiful images and the processions."

"Ah! but what would our mother have said!" cried poor Agathe, weeping more bitterly.

"Poor child, her old recollections have been renewed," said the Prioress, with unchanged sweetness; "but it will pass. My dear, the gentleman will tell you that it is as impossible for him to take you as it is for me to let you go."

"It is so, truly, little one," said Berenger. "The only little girl I could have taken with me would have been my own;" and as her eyes looked at him wistfully, he added, "No doubt, if your poor mother could, she would thank this good Mother-prioress for teaching you to serve God and be a good child."

"Monsieur speaks well and kindly," said the Prioress; "and now, Agathe, make your curtsey, and take away the little ones."

"Let me ask one question more, reverend Mother," said Berenger. "Ah! children, did you ever see her whom you call Isaac Gardon's daughter-in-law?"

"No, sir," said the children; "but mother did, and she promised one day to take us to see the baby, for it was so pretty—so white, that she had never seen the like."

"So white!" repeated Berenger to himself; and the Prioress, struck, perhaps, by the almost flaxen locks that sparsely waved on his temples, and the hue of the ungloved hand that rested on the edge of the *grille*, said, smiling, "You come of a fair family, Monsieur."

"The White Ribaumonts," said Berenger, "and, moreover, my mother was called the Swan of England; my little sisters have skins like snow. Ah! Madame, though I have failed, I go away far happier than if I had succeeded."

"And I," she said, "shall cease to pray for that dear one as for one in the grave."

"Ah! you have prayed for me. Pray still that Heaven will have pity on us, and unite us once more."

"And reveal the true faith," began the nun; but Philip in the meantime was nudging his brother, and whispering in English, "No Popish prayers, I say! Stay, give these poor little prisoners one feast of the sweetmeats we brought."

Of this last hint Berenger was glad, and the Prioress readily consented to a distribution of the dainties among the orphans. He wished to leave a more lasting token of his gratitude to the little maiden whose father had perhaps saved Eustacie's life, and recollecting that he had about him a great gold coin, bearing the heads of Philip and Mary, he begged leave to offer it to Agathe, and found that it was received by good Mère Monique almost in the light of a relic, as bearing the head of so pious a queen.

Then, to complete Philip's disgust, he said, "I took with me my aunt's blessing when I set out; let me take yours with me also, reverend Mother."

When they were in the street again, Philip railed at him as though he had subjected himself to a spell.

"She is almost a saint," answered Berenger.

"And have we not saints enough of our own, without running after Popish ones behind grates? Brother, if ever the good old days come back of invading France, I'll march straight hither, and deliver the poor little wretches so scandalously mewed up here, and true Protestants all the time!"

"Hush! People are noticing the sound of your English."

"Let them! I never thanked Heaven properly before that I have not a drop of French——" Here Berenger almost shook him by the shoulder, as men turned at his broad tones and foreign words, and he walked on in silence, while Berenger at his side felt as one treading on air, so infinite was the burden taken off his mind. Though for the present absolutely at sea as to where to seek Eustacie, the relief from acquiescence in the horrible fate that had seemed to be hers was such, that a flood of unspeakable happiness seemed to rush in on him, and bear him up with a new infusion of life, buoyancy, and thankfulness.

CHAPTER XXIX.

IN THE KING'S NAME.

"Under which king, Bezonian? speak or die."
"Under King Harry."—*King Henry IV.*

"ONE bird in the hand is not always worth two in the bush, assuredly," said Philip, when Berenger was calm enough to hold council on what he called this most blessed discovery; "but where to seek them?"

"I have no fears now," returned Berenger. "We have not been borne through so much not to be brought together at last. Soon, soon shall we have her! A minister so distinguished as Isaac Gardon is sure to be heard of either at La Rochelle, Montauban, or Nîmes, their great gathering places."

"For Rochelle, then?" said Philip.

"Even so. We will be off early to-morrow, and from thence, if we do not find her there, as I expect, we shall be able to write the thrice happy news to those at home."

Accordingly, the little cavalcade started in good time, in the cool of the morning of the bright long day of early June, while apple petals floated down on them in the lanes like snow, and nightingales in every hedge seemed to give voice and tune to Berenger's eager, yearning hopes.

Suddenly there was a sound of horses' feet in the road before them, and as they drew aside to make way, a little troop of gendarmes filled the narrow lane. The officer, a rough, harsh-looking man, laid his hand on Berenger's bridle, with the words, "In the name of the King!"

Philip began to draw his sword with one hand, and with the other to urge his horse between the officer and his brother, but Berenger called out, "Back! This gentleman mistakes my person. I am the Baron de Ribaumont, and have a safe-conduct from the King."

"What king?" demanded the officer.

"From King Charles."

"I arrest you," said the officer, "in the name of King Henry III. and of the Queen Regent Catherine."

"The King dead?" exclaimed Berenger.

"On the 30th of May. Now, sir."

"Your warrant—your cause?" still demanded Berenger.

"There will be time enough for that when you are safely lodged," said the captain, roughly pulling at the rein, which he had held all the time.

"What, no warrant?" shouted Philip, "he is a mere robber!" and with drawn sword he was precipitating himself on the captain, when another gendarme, who had been on the watch, grappled with him, and dragged him off his horse before he could strike a blow. The other two English, Humfrey Holt and John Smithers, strong, full-grown men, rode in fiercely to the rescue, and Berenger himself struggled furiously to loose himself from the captain, and deliver his brother. Suddenly there was the report of a pistol: poor Smithers fell, there was a moment of standing aghast, and in that moment the one man and the two youths were each pounced on by three or four gendarmes, thrown down and pinioned.

"Is this usage for gentlemen?" exclaimed Berenger, as he was roughly raised to his feet.

"The King's power has been resisted," was all the answer; and when he would have bent to see how it was with poor Smithers, one of the men-at-arms kicked over the body with sickening brutality, saying, "Dead enough, heretic and English carrion!"

Philip uttered a cry of loathing horror, and turned white; Berenger, above all else, felt a sort of frenzied despair as he thought of the peril of the boy who had been trusted to him.

"Have you had enough, sir?" said the captain. "Mount and come."

They could only let themselves be lifted to their horses, and their hands were then set free to use their bridles, each being guarded by a soldier on each side of him. Philip attempted but once to speak, and that in English, "Next time I shall take my pistol."

He was rudely silenced, and rode on with wide-open stolid eyes and dogged face, stedfastly resolved that no Frenchman should see him flinch, and vexed that Berenger had his riding mask on so that his face could not be studied; while he, on his side, was revolving all causes possible for his arrest, and all means of enforcing the liberation, if not of himself, at least of Philip and Humfrey. He looked round for Guibert, but could not see him.

They rode on through the intricate lanes till the sun was high and scorching, and Berenger felt how far he was from perfect recovery. At last, however, some little time past noon, the gendarmes halted at a stone fountain, outside a village, and disposing a sufficient guard around his captives, the officer permitted them to dismount and rest, while he, with the rest of the troop and the horses, went to the village *cabaret.* Philip would have asked his brother what it meant, and what was to be done, but Berenger shook his head, and intimated that silence was safest at present, since they might be listened to; and Philip, who so much imagined treachery and iniquity to be the order of the day in France that he was scarcely surprised at the present disaster, resigned himself to the same sullen endurance. Provisions and liquor were presently sent up from the inn, but Berenger could taste nothing but the cold water of the fountain, which trickled out cool and fresh beneath an arch surmounted by a figure of our Lady. He bathed his face and head in the refreshing spring, and lay down on a cloak in the shade, Philip keeping a constant change of drenched kerchiefs on his brow, and hoping that he slept, till at the end of two or three hours the captain returned, gave the word to horse, and the party rode on through intricate lanes, blossoming with hawthorn, and ringing with songs of birds that spoke a very different language now to Berenger's heart from what they had said in the hopeful morning.

A convent bell was ringing to evensong, when passing its gateway; the escort turned up a low hill, on the summit of which stood a chateau, covering a considerable extent of ground, with a circuit of wall, whitewashed so as perfectly to glare in the evening sun; at every angle a round, slim turret, crowned by a brilliant red-tiled extinguisher-like cap; and the whole surmounted by a tall, old keep in the centre. There was a square projection containing an arched gateway, with heavy doorways, which were thrown open as the party approached. Philip looked up as he rode in, and over the doorway beheld the familiar fretted shield, with the leopard in the corner, and "*A moi Ribaumont*" round it. Could it then be Berenger's own castle, and was it thus that he was approaching it? He himself had not looked up; he was utterly spent with fatigue, dejection, and the severe headache brought on by the heat of the sun, and was only intent on rallying his powers for the crisis of fate that was probably approaching; and thus scarcely took note of the court into which he rode, lying between the gateway and the *corps de logis*, a building erected when comfort demanded more space than was afforded by the old keep, against which one end leant; but still, though inclosed in a court, the lower windows were small and iron-barred, and all air of luxury was reserved for the mullioned casements of the upper storey. The court was flagged, but grass shot up between the stones, and the trim air of ease and inhabited comfort to which the brothers were used at home was utterly wanting. Berenger was hustled off his horse, and roughly pushed through a deep porch, where the first thing he heard was the Chevalier de Ribaumont's voice in displeasure.

"How now, sir; hands off! Is this the way you conduct my nephew?"

"He resisted, sir."

"Sir," said Berenger, advancing into the hall, "I know not the meaning of this. I am peacefully travelling with a passport from the King, when I am set upon, no warrant shown me, my faithful servant slain, myself and my brother, an English subject, shamefully handled."

"The violence shall be visited on whatever rascal durst insult a gentleman and my nephew," said the Chevalier. "For release, it shall be looked to; but unfortunately it is too true that there are orders from the Queen in Council for your apprehension, and it was only on my special entreaty for the honour of the family, and the affection I bear you, that I was allowed to receive you here instead of your being sent to an ordinary prison."

"On what pretext?" demanded Berenger.

"It is known that you have letters in your possession from escaped traitors now in England, to La Noue, Duplessis Mornay, and other heretics."

"That is easily explained," said Berenger. "You know well, sir, that they were to facilitate my search at La Sablerie. You shall see them yourself, sir."

"That I must assuredly do," replied the Chevalier, "for it is the order of her Majesty, I regret to say, that your person and baggage be searched;" then, as indignant colour rushed into Berenger's face, and an angry exclamation was beginning, he added, "Nay, I understand, my dear cousin, it is very painful, but we would spare you as much as possible. It will be quite enough if the search is made by myself in the presence of this gentleman, who will only stand by for form's sake. I have no doubt it will enable us quickly to clear up matters, and set you free again. Do me the honour to follow me to the chamber destined for you."

"Let me see the order for my arrest," said Berenger, holding his head high.

"The English scruple must be gratified," said the Chevalier. And accordingly the gendarme captain unfolded before him a paper, which was evidently a distinct order to arrest and examine the person of Henri Bérenger Eustache, Baron de Ribaumont and Sieur de Leurre, suspected of treasonable practices—and it bore the signature of Catherine.

"There is nothing here said of my stepfather's son, Philip Thistlewood, nor of my servant, Humfrey Holt," said Berenger, gathering the sense with his dizzy eyes as best he could. "They cannot be detained, being born subjects of the Queen of England."

"They intercepted the justice of the King," said the captain, laying his hand on Philip's shoulder. "I shall have them off with me to the garrison of Luçon, and deal with them there."

"Wait!" said the Chevalier, interposing before Berenger's fierce, horror-struck expostulation could break forth; "this is an honourable young gentleman, son of a chevalier of good reputation in England, and he need not be so harshly dealt with. You will not separate either him or the poor groom from my nephew, so the Queen's authority be now rightly acknowledged."

The captain shrugged his shoulders, as if displeased; and the Chevalier, turning to Berenger, said, "You understand, nephew, the lot of you all depends on your not giving umbrage to these officers of her Majesty. I will do my poor best for you; but submission is first needed."

Berenger knew enough of his native country to be aware that *la justice du Roi* was a terrible thing, and that Philip's resistance had really put him in so much danger that it was needful to be most careful not further to offend the functionary of Government; and abhorrent as the proposed search was to him, he made no further objection, but taking Philip's arm, lest they should be separated, he prepared to follow wherever he was to be conducted. The Chevalier led the way along a narrow stone passage, with loophole-windows here and there; and Philip, for all his proud, indifferent bearing, felt his flesh creep as he looked for a stair descending into the bowels of the earth. A stair there was, but it went up instead of down, and after mounting this, and going through a sort of ante-room, a door was opened into a tolerably spacious apartment, evidently in the old keep; for the two windows on opposite sides were in an immensely massive wall, and the floor above and vaulting below were of stone; but otherwise there was nothing repulsive in the appearance of the room. There was a wood fire on the hearth; the sun, setting far to the north, peeped in aslant at one window; a mat was on the floor, tapestry on the lower part of the walls; a table and chairs, and a walnut chest, with a chess-board and a few books on it, were as much furniture as was to be seen in almost any living-room of the day. Humfrey and Guibert, too, were already there, with the small riding valises they and poor Smithers had had in charge. These were at once opened, but contained merely clothes and linen, nothing else that was noticed, except three books, at which the captain looked with a stupid air; and the Chevalier did not seem capable of discovering more than that all three were Latin—one, he believed, the Bible.

"Yes, sir, the Vulgate—a copy older than the Reformation, so not liable to be called an heretical version," said Berenger, to whom a copy had been given by Lady Walwyn, as more likely to be saved if his baggage were searched. "The other is the Office and Psalter after our English rite; and this last is not mine, but Mr. Sidney's—a copy of Virgilius Maro, which he had left behind at Paris."

The Chevalier, not willing to confess that he had taken the English Prayer-book for Latin, hastily said, "Nothing wrong there—no, no, nothing that will hurt the State; may it only be so with what you carry on your person, fair cousin. Stand back, gentlemen, this is gear for myself alone. Now, fair nephew," he added, "not a hand shall be laid on you, if you will give me your honourable word, as a nobleman, that you are laying before me all that you carry about you."

An instant's thought convinced Berenger that resistance would save nothing, and merely lead to indignity to himself and danger to Philip; and therefore he gave the promise to show everything about him, without compulsion. Accordingly, he produced his purse for current expenses, poor King Charles's safe-conduct, and other articles of no consequence, from his pockets; then reluctantly opened his doublet, and took off the belt containing his store of gold, which had been replenished at Walsingham's. This was greedily eyed by the captain, but the Chevalier at once made it over to Philip's keeping, graciously saying, "We do no more than duty requires;" but at the same time he made a gesture towards another small purse that hung round Berenger's neck by a black ribbon.

"On my sacred word and honour," said Berenger, "it contains nothing important to any save myself."

"Alas! my bounden duty," urged the Chevalier.

An angry reply died on Berenger's lip. At the thought of Philip, he opened the purse, and held out the contents on his palm: a tiny gold ring, a tress of black hair, a fragment of carnation-ribbon pricked with pin-holes, a string of small worthless yellow shells, and, threaded with them, a large pear-shaped pearl of countless price. Even the Chevalier was touched at the sight of this treasury, resting on the blanched palm of the thin, trembling hand, and jealously watched by eyes glistening with sudden moisture, though the lips were firm set. "Alas! my poor young cousin," he said, "you loved her well."

"Not loved, but love," muttered Berenger to himself, as if having recourse to the only cordial that could support him through the present suffering; and he was closing his fingers again over his precious hoard, when the Chevalier added, "Stay! nephew—that pearl?"

"Is one of the chaplet; the token she sent to England," he answered.

"*Pauvre petite!* Then, at least a fragment remains of the reward of our ancestor's courage," said the Chevalier.

And Berenger did not feel it needful to yield up that still better possession, stored within his heart, that *la petite* and her pearls were safe together. It was less unendurable to produce the leather case from a secret pocket within his doublet, since, unwilling as he was that any eye should scan the letters it contained, there was nothing in them that could give any clue towards tracing her. Nothing had been written or received since his interview with the children at Luçon. There was, indeed, Eustacie's letter to his mother, a few received at Paris from Lord Walwyn, reluctantly consenting to his journey in quest of his child, his English passport, the unfortunate letters to La Noue; and what evidently startled the Chevalier more than all the rest, the copy of the certificate of the ratification of the marriage; but his consternation was so arranged as to appear to be all on behalf of his young kinsman. "This is serious!" he said, striking his forehead, "you will be accused of forging the late King's name."

"This is but a copy," said Berenger, pointing to the heading; "the original has been sent with our Ambassador's dispatches to England."

"It is a pity," said the Chevalier, looking thoroughly vexed, "that you should have brought fresh difficulties on yourself for a mere piece of waste paper, since, as things unhappily stand, there is no living person to be affected by the validity of your marriage. Dear cousin,"—he glanced at the officer and lowered his voice,—"let me tear this paper; it would only do you harm, and the Papal decree annuls it."

"I have given my word," said Berenger, "that all that could do me harm should be delivered up! Besides," he added, "even had I the feeling for my own honour and that of my wife and child, living or dead, the harm, it seems to me, would be to those who withhold her lands from me."

"Ah, fair nephew! you have fallen among designing persons who have filled your head with absurd claims; but I will not argue the point now, since it becomes a family, not a State matter. These papers"—and he took them into his hand—"must be examined, and to-morrow Captain Delarue will take them to Paris, with any explanation you may desire to offer. Meantime you and your companions remain my guests, at full liberty, provided you will give me your parole to attempt no escape."

"No, sir," said Berenger, hotly, "we will not become our own jailers, nor acquiesce in this unjust detention. I warn you that I am a naturalized Englishman, acknowledged by the Queen as my grandfather's heir, and the English Ambassador will inform the Court what Queen Elizabeth thinks of such dealings with her subjects."

"Well said," exclaimed Philip, and drawing himself up, he added, "I refuse my parole, and warn you that it is at your peril that you imprison an Englishman."

"Very well, gentlemen," said the Chevalier; "the difference will be that I shall unwillingly be forced to let Captain Delarue post guards at the outlets of this tower. A room beneath is prepared for your grooms, and the court is likewise free to you. I will endeavour to make your detention as little irksome as you will permit, and meantime allow me to show you your sleeping chamber." He then politely, as if he had been ushering a prince to his apartment, led the way, pointing to the door through which they had entered the keep, and saying, "This is the only present communication with the dwelling-house. Two gendarmes will always be on the outside." He conducted the young men up a stone spiral stair to another room, over that which they had already seen, and furnished as fairly as ordinary sleeping chambers were wont to be.

Here, said their compulsory host, he would leave them to prepare for supper, when they would do him the honour to join him in the eating-hall on their summons by the steward.

His departing bow was duly returned by Berenger, but no sooner did his steps die away on the stairs than the young man threw himself down on his bed, in a paroxysm of suffering, both mental and bodily.

"Berry, Berry, what is this? Speak to me. What does it all mean?" cried Philip.

"How can I tell?" said Berenger, showing his face for a moment, covered with tears; "only that my only friend is dead, and some villanous trick has seized me, just—just as I might have found her. And I've been the death of my poor groom, and got you into the power of these vile dastards! Oh, would that I had come alone! Would that they had had the sense to aim direct!"

"Brother, brother, anything but this!" cried Philip. "The rogues are not worth it. Sir Francis will have us out in no time, or know the reason why. I'd scorn to let them wring a tear from me."

"I hope they never may, dear Phil, nor anything worse."

"Now," continued Philip, "the way will be to go down to supper, since they will have it so, and sit and eat at one's ease as if one cared for them no more than cat and dog. Hark! there's the steward speaking to Guibert. Come, Berry, wash your face and come."

"I—my head aches far too much, were there nothing else."

"What! it is nothing but the sun," said Philip. "Put a bold face on it, man, and show them how little you heed."

"How *little* I heed!" bitterly repeated Berenger, turning his face away, utterly unnerved between disappointment, fatigue, and pain; and Philip at that moment had little mercy. Dismayed and vaguely terrified, yet too resolute in national pride to betray his own feelings, he gave vent to his vexation by impatience with a temperament more visibly sensitive than his own: "I never thought you so mere a Frenchman," he said contemptuously. "If you weep and wail so like a sick wench, they will soon have their will of you! I'd have let them kill me before they searched me."

"'Tis bad enough without this from you, Phil," said Berenger faintly, for he was far too much spent for resentment or self-defence, and had only kept up before the Chevalier by dint of strong effort. Philip was somewhat aghast, both at the involuntary gesture of pain, and at finding there was not even spirit to be angry with him: but his very dismay served at the moment only to feed his displeasure; and he tramped off in his heavy boots, which he chose to wear as a proof of disdain for his companions. He explained that M. de Ribaumont was too much fatigued to come to supper, and he was accordingly marched along the corridor, with the steward before him bearing a lighted torch, and two gendarmes with halberds behind him. And in his walk he had ample time for, first, the resolution that illness, and not dejection, should have all the credit of Berenger's absence; then for recollecting of how short standing had been his brother's convalescence; and lastly, for a fury of self-execration for his own unkindness, rude taunts, and neglect of the recurring illness. He would have turned about and gone back at once, but the two gendarmes were close behind, and he knew Humfrey would attend to his brother; so he walked on to the hall—a handsome chamber, hung with armour and spoils of hunting, with a few pictures on the panels, and a great carved music-gallery at one end. The table was laid out somewhat luxuriously for four, according to the innovation which was beginning to separate the meals of the grandees from those of their household.

Great concern was expressed by the Chevalier, as Philip, in French, much improved since the time of his conversation with Madame de Selinville, spoke of his brother's indisposition, saying with emphasis, as he glared at Captain Delarue, that Maître Paré had forbidden all exposure to mid-day heat, and that all their journeys had been made in morning or evening coolness. "My young friend," as his host called him, "should, he was assured, have mentioned this, since Captain Delarue had no desire but to make his situation as little painful as possible." And the Chevalier sent his steward at once to offer everything the house contained that his prisoner could relish for supper; and then anxiously questioned Philip on his health and diet, obtaining very short and glum answers. The Chevalier and the captain glanced at each other with little shrugs; and Philip, becoming conscious of his shock hair, splashed doublet, and dirty boots, had vague doubts whether his English dignity were not being regarded as English lubberliness; but, of course, he hated the two Frenchmen all the more, and received their civility with greater gruffness. They asked him the present object of his journey—though, probably, the Chevalier knew it before, and he told of the hope that they had of finding the child at Luçon.

"Vain, of course?" said the Chevalier. "Poor infant! It is well for itself, as for the rest of us, that its troubles were ended long ago."

Philip started indignantly.

"Does your brother still nurture any vain hope?" said the Chevalier.

"Not vain, I trust," said Philip.

"Indeed! Who can foolishly have so inspired him with

a hope that merely wears out his youth, and leads him into danger?"

Philip held his tongue, resolved to be impenetrable ; and he was so far successful, that the Chevalier merely became convinced that the brothers were not simply riding to La Rochelle to embark for England, but had some hope and purpose in view; though as to what that might be, Philip's bluff replies and stubborn silence were baffling.

After the meal, the Chevalier insisted on coming to see how his guest fared; and Philip could not prevent him. They found Berenger sitting on the side of his bed, having evidently just started up on hearing their approach. Otherwise he did not seem to have moved since Philip left him; he had not attempted to undress; and Humfrey told Philip that not a word had been extracted from him, but commands to let him alone.

However, he had rallied his forces to meet the Chevalier, and answered manfully to his excuses for the broiling ride to which he had been exposed, that it mattered not, the effect would pass, it was a mere chance; and refused all offers of medicaments, potions, and *tisanes*, till his host at length left the room with a most correct exchange of good nights.

"Berry, Berry, what a brute I have been!" cried Philip.

"Foolish lad!" and Berenger half smiled. "Now help me to bed, for the room turns round!"

CHAPTER XXX.

CAGED IN THE BLACKBIRD'S NEST.

> "Let him shun castles;
> Safer shall he be on the sandy plain
> Than where castles mounted stand."
>
> *King Henry VI.*

WHILE Berenger slept a heavy morning's sleep after a restless night, Philip explored the narrow domain above and below. The keep and its little court had evidently been the original castle, built when the oddly-nicknamed Fulkes and Geoffreys of Anjou had been at daggers drawn with the Dukes of Normandy and Brittany; but it had since, like most other such ancient feudal fortresses, become the nucleus of walls and buildings for use, defence, or ornament, that lay beneath him like a spider's web, when he had gained the roof of the keep, garnished with pepper-box turrets at each of the four angles. Beyond lay the green copses and orchards of the Bocage, for it was true, as he had at first suspected, that this was the Château de Nid-de-Merle, and that Berenger was a captive in his wife's own castle.

Chances of escape were the lad's chief thought, but the building on which he stood went sheer down for a considerable way. Then on the north side there came out the sharp, high-pitched, tiled roof of the *corps du logis;* on the south, another roof, surmounted by a cross at the gable, and evidently belonging to the chapel; on the other two sides lay courts—that to the east, a stable-yard; that to the west, a small narrow, chilly-looking, paved inclosure, with enormously-massive walls, the doorway walled up, and looking like a true prison-yard. Beyond this wall—indeed, on every side—extended offices, servants' houses, stables, untidy, desolate-looking gardens, and the whole was inclosed by the white wall with flanking red-tiled turrets, whose gaudy appearance had last night made Philip regard the whole as a flimsy, Frenchified erection, but he now saw it to be of extremely solid stone and lime, and with no entrance but the great barbican gateway they had entered by; moreover, with a yawning, dry moat all round. Wherever he looked he saw these tall, pointed red caps, resembling, he thought, those worn by the victims of an *auto-da-fé*, as one of Walsingham's secretaries had described them to him; and he ground his teeth at them, as though they grinned at him like emissaries of the Inquisition.

Descending, he found Berenger dressing in haste to avoid receiving an invalid visit from the Chevalier, looking indeed greatly shaken, but hardly so as would have been detected by eyes that had not seen him during his weeks of hope and recovery. He was as resolved as Philip could wish against any sign of weakness before his enemy, and altogether disclaimed illness, refusing the stock of cooling drinks, cordials, and febrifuges, which the Chevalier said had been sent by his sister the Abbess of Bellaise. He put the subject of his health aside, only asking if this were the day that the gendarme-captain would return to Paris, and then begging to see that officer, so as to have a distinct understanding of the grounds of his imprisonment. The captain had, however, been a mere instrument; and when Philip clamoured to be taken before the next justice of the peace, even Berenger smiled at him for thinking that such a being existed in France. The only cause alleged was the vague but dangerous suspicion of conveying correspondence between England and the heretics, and this might become extremely perilous to one undeniably half English, regarded as whole Huguenot, caught on the way to La Rochelle with a letter to La Noue in his pocket; and, moreover, to one who had had a personal affray with a king famous for storing up petty offences, whom the last poor king had favoured, and who, in fine, had claims to estates that could not be spared to the Huguenot interest.

He was really not sure that there was not some truth in the professions of the Chevalier being anxious to protect him from the Queen-mother and the Guises; he had never been able to divest himself of a certain trust in his old kinsman's friendliness, and he was obliged to be beholden to him for the forms in which to couch his defence. At the same time he wrote to Sir Francis Walsingham, and to his grandfather, but with great caution, lest his letters should be inspected by his enemies, and with the less hope of their availing him because it was probable that the Ambassador would return home on the king's death. No answer could be expected for at least a fortnight, and even then it was possible that the Queen-mother might choose to refer the cause to King Henry, who was then in Poland.

Berenger wrote these letters with much thought and care, but when they were once sealed, he collapsed again into despair and impatience, and frantically paced the little court as if he would dash himself against the walls that detained him from Eustacie; then threw himself moodily into a chair, hid his face in his crossed arms, and fell a prey to all the wretched visions called up by an excited brain.

However, he was equally alive with Philip to the high-spirited resolution that his enemies should not perceive or triumph in his dejection. He showed himself at the noon-day dinner, before Captain Delarue departed, grave and silent, but betraying no agitation; and he roused himself from his sad musings at the supper-hour, to arrange his hair, and assume the ordinary dress of gentlemen in the evening; though Philip laughed at the roses adorning his shoes, and his fresh ruff, as needless attentions to an old ruffian like the Chevalier. However, Philip started when he entered the hall, and beheld, not the Chevalier alone, but with him the beautiful lady of the velvet coach, and another stately, extremely handsome dame, no longer in her first youth, and in costly black and white garments. When the Chevalier called her his sister, Madame de Bellaise, Philip had no notion that she was anything but a widow, living a secular life; and though a couple of nuns attended her, their dress was so much less conventual than Cecily's that he did not at first find them out. It was explained that Madame de Selinville was residing with her aunt, and that, having come to visit her father, he had detained the ladies to supper, hoping to enliven the sojourn of his *beaux cousins.*

Madame de Selinville, looking anxiously at Berenger, hoped she saw him in better health. He replied, stiffly, that he was perfectly well; and then, by way of safety, repaired to the society of the Abbess, who immediately began plying him with questions about England, its Court, and especially the secret marriage of Queen Elizabeth and "*ce* Comte de Dudley," on which she was so minutely informed as to put him to the blush. Then she was very curious about the dispersed convents, and how many of the nuns had married; and she seemed altogether delighted to have secured the attention of a youth from the outer world. His soul at first recoiled from her as one of Eustacie's oppressors, and from her unconvent-like talk; and yet he could not but think her a good-natured person, and wonder if she could really have been hard upon his poor little wife. And she, who had told Eustacie she would strangle with her own hands the scion of the rival house!—she, like most women, was much more bitter against an unseen being out of reach, than towards a courteously-mannered, pale, suffering-looking youth close beside her. She had enough affection for Eustacie to have grieved much at her wanderings and at her fate; and now the sorrow-stricken look that by no effort could be concealed, really moved her towards the young bereaved husband. Besides, were not all feuds on the point of being made up by the excellent device concocted between her brother and her niece?

Meantime, Philip was in raptures with the kindness of the beautiful Madame de Selinville. He, whom the Mistresses Walsingham treated as a mere clumsy boy, was promoted by her manner to be a man and a cavalier. He blushed up to the roots of his hair and looked sheepish whenever one of her entrancing smiles lit upon him; but then she inquired after his brother so cordially, she told him so openly how brilliant had been Berenger's career at the Court, she regretted so heartily their present danger and detention, and promised so warmly to use her interest with Queen Catherine, that in the delight of being so talked to, he forgot his awkwardness, and spoke freely and confidentially, may be too confidentially, for he caught Berenger frowning at him, and made a sudden halt in his narrative, disconcerted but very angry with his brother for his distrust.

When the ladies had ridden away to the convent in the summer evening, and the two brothers had returned to their prison, Philip would have begun to rave about Madame de Selinville, but his mouth was stopped at once with, "Don't be such a fool, Phil!" and when Berenger shut his eyes, leant back, and folded his arms together, there was no more use in talking to him.

This exceeding dejection continued for a day or two, while Berenger's whole spirit chafed in agony at his helplessness, and like demons there ever haunted him the thoughts of what might betide Eustacie, young, fair, forsaken, and believing herself a widow. Proudly defiant as he showed himself to all eyes beyond his tower, he seemed to be fast gnawing and pining himself away in the anguish he suffered through these long days of captivity.

Perhaps it was Philip's excitement about any chance of meeting Madame de Selinville, that first roused him from the contemplation of his own misery. It struck him that if he did not rouse himself to exert his influence, the boy, left to no companionship save what he could make for himself, might be led away by intercourse with the gendarmes, or by the blandishments of Diane, whatever might be her game. He must be watched over, and returned to Sir Marmaduke the same true-hearted honest lad who had left home. Nor had Berenger lain so long under Cecily St. John's tender watching without bearing away some notes of patience, trust, and dutifulness that returned upon him as his mind recovered tone after the first shock. The whispers that had bidden him tarry the Lord's leisure, be strong, and commit his way to Him who could bring it to pass, and could save Eustacie as she had already been saved, returned to him once more: he chid himself for his faintness of heart, rallied his powers, and determined that cheerfulness, dutifulness, and care for Philip should no longer fail.

So he reviewed his resources, and in the first place arranged for a brief daily worship with his two English fellow-prisoners, corresponding to the home hours of chapel service. Then he proposed to Philip to spend an hour every day over the study of the Latin Bible; and when Philip showed himself reluctant to give up his habit of staring over the battlements, he represented that an attack on their faith was not so improbable but that they ought to be prepared for it.

"I'm quite prepared," quoth Philip; "I shall not listen to a word they say."

However, he submitted to this, but was far more contumacious as to Berenger's other proposal of profiting by Sidney's copy of Virgil. Here at least he was away from Mr. Adderley and study, and it passed endurance to have Latin and captivity both at once. He was more obliged for Berenger's offer to impart to him the instruction in fencing he had received during his first visit to Paris; the Chevalier made no difficulty about lending them foils, and their little court became the scene of numerous encounters, as well as of other games and exercises. More sedentary sports were at their service, chess, tables, dice, or cards, but Philip detested these, and they were only played in the evening, or on a rainy afternoon, by Berenger and the Chevalier.

It was clearly no part of the old gentleman's plan to break their health or spirits. He insisted on taking them out riding frequently, though always with four gendarmes with loaded arquebuses, so as to preclude all attempt at escape, or conversation with the peasants. The rides were hateful to both youths, but Berenger knew that so many hours of tedium were thus disposed of, and hoped also to acquire some knowledge of the country; indeed, he looked at every cottage and every peasant with affectionate eyes, as probably having sheltered Eustacie; and Philip, after one visit paid to the convent at Bellaise, was always in hopes of making such another. His boyish admiration of Madame de Selinville was his chief distraction, coming on in accesses whenever there was a hope of seeing her, and often diverting Berenger by its absurdities, even though at other times he feared that the lad might be led away by it, or dissension sown between them. Meetings were rare—now and then Madame de Selinville would appear at dinner or at supper as her father's guest; and more rarely, the Chevalier would turn his horse's head in the direction of Bellaise, and the three gentlemen would be received in the unpartitioned parlour, and there treated to such lemon cakes as had been the ruin of La Sablerie; but in general the castle and the convent had little intercourse, or only just enough to whet the appetite of the prisoners for what constituted their only variety.

Six weeks had lagged by before any answer from Paris was received, and then there was no reply from Walsingham, who had, it appeared, returned home immediately after King Charles's funeral. The letter from the Council bore that the Queen-mother was ready to accept the Baron de Ribaumont's excuses in good part, and to consider his youth; and she had no doubt of his being treated with the like indulgence by the King, provided he would prove himself a loyal subject, by embracing the Catholic faith, renouncing all his illegitimate claims to the estates of Nid-de-Merle, and, in pledge of his sincerity, wedding his cousin, the Countess de Selinville, so soon as a dispensation should have been procured. On no other consideration could he be pardoned or set at liberty.

"Then," said Berenger slowly, "a prisoner I must remain until it be the will of Heaven to open the doors."

"Fair nephew!" exclaimed the Chevalier, "make no rash replies. Bethink you to what you expose yourself by obstinacy. I may no longer be able to protect you when the King returns." And he further went on to represent that, by renouncing voluntarily all possible claims on the Nid-de-Merle estates, the Baron would save the honour of poor

Eustacie (which indeed equally concerned the rest of the family), since they then would gladly drop all dispute of the validity of the marriage; and the lands of Selinville would be an ample equivalent for these, as well as for all expectations in England.

"Sir, it is impossible!" said Berenger. "My wife lives."

"*Comment?* when you wear mourning for her."

"I wear black because I have been able to procure nothing else since I have been convinced that she did not perish at La Sablerie. I was on my way to seek her when I was seized and detained here."

"Where would you have sought her, my poor cousin?" compassionately asked the Chevalier.

"That I know not. She may be in England by this time; but that she escaped from La Sablerie, I am well assured."

"Alas! my poor friend, you feed on delusion. I have surer evidence—you shall see the man yourself—one of my son's people, who was actually at the assault, and had strict orders to seek and save her. Would that I could feel the least hope left!"

"Is the man here? Let me see him," said Berenger, hastily.

He was at once sent for, and proved to be one of the stable servants, a rough, soldierly-looking man, who made no difficulty in telling that M. de Nid-de-Merle had bidden his own troop to use every effort to reach the Widow Laurent's house, and secure the lady. They had made for it, but missed the way, and met with various obstacles; and when they reached it, it was already in flames, and he had seen for a moment Mademoiselle de Nid-de-Merle, whom he well knew by sight, with an infant in her arms at an upper window. He had called to her by name, and was about to send for a ladder, when recognising the Ribaumont colours, she had turned back, and thrown herself and her child into the flames. M. de Nid-de-Merle was frantic when he heard of it, and they had searched for the remains among the ruins; but, bah! it was like a lime-kiln, nothing was to be found—all was calcined.

"No fragment left?" said Berenger; "not a corner of tile or beam?"

"Not so much wood as you could boil an egg with; I will swear it on the Mass."

"That is needless," said Berenger. "I have seen the spot myself. That is all I desired to ask."

The Chevalier would have taken his hand and condoled with him over the horrible story; but he drew back, repeating that he had seen Widow Laurent's house, and that he saw that some parts of the man's story were so much falsified that he could not believe the rest. Moreover, he knew tha Eustacie had not been in the town at the time of the siege.

Now the Chevalier *bonâ fide* believed the man's story, so far as that he never doubted that Eustacie had perished, and he looked on Berenger's refusal to accept the tale as the mournful last clinging to a vain hope. In his eyes, the actual sight of Eustacie, and the total destruction of the house, were mere matters of embellishment, possibly untrue, but not invalidating the main fact. He only said, "Well, my friend, I will not press you while the pain of this narration is still fresh."

"Thank you, sir; but this is not pain, for I believe not a word of it; therefore it is impossible for me to entertain the proposal, even if I could forsake my faith or my English kindred. You remember, sir, that I returned this same answer at Paris, when I had no hope that my wife survived."

"True, my fair cousin, but I fear time will convince you that this constancy is unhappily misplaced. You shall have time to consider; and when it is proved to you that my poor niece is out of the reach of your fidelity, and when you have become better acquainted with the claims of the Church to your allegiance, then may it only prove that your conversion does not come too late. I have the honour to take my leave."

"One moment more, sir. Is there no answer as to my brother?"

"None, cousin. As I told you, your country has at present no ambassador; but, of course, on your fulfilment of the conditions, he would be released with you."

"So," said Philip, when the old knight had quitted the room, "of course you cannot marry while Eustacie lives; but if——"

"Not another word, profane boy!" angrily cried Berenger.

"I was only going to say, it is a pity of one so goodly not to bring her over to the true faith, and take her to England."

"Much would she be beholden to you!" said Berenger. "So!" he added, sighing, "I had little hope but that it would be thus. I believe it is all a web of this old plotter's weaving, and that the Queen-mother acts in it at his request. He wants only to buy me off with his daughter's estates from asserting my claim to this castle and lands; and I trow he will never rise up here till—till——"

"Till when, Berry?"

"Till mayhap my grandfather can move the Queen to do something for us; or till Madame de Selinville sees a face she likes better than her brother's carving; or, what can I tell? till malice is tired out, and Heaven's will sets us free! May Eustacie only have reached home! But I'm sorry for you, my poor Phil."

"Never heed, brother," said Philip; "what is prison to me, so that I can now and then see those lovely eyes?"

And the languishing air of the clumsy lad was so comical as to beguile Berenger into a laugh. Yet Berenger's own feeling would go back to his first meeting with Diane; and as he thought of the eyes then fixed on him, he felt that he was under a trial that might become more severe.

CHAPTER XXXI.

THE DARK POOL OF THE FUTURE.

"Triumph, triumph, only she
That knit his bonds can set him free."
SOUTHEY.

No change was made in the life of the captives of Nid-de-Merle after the answer from Paris, except that Père Bonami, who had already once or twice dined at the Chevalier's table, was requested to make formal exposition of the errors of the Reformers and of the tenets of his own Church to the Baron de Ribaumont.

Philip took such good care not to be deluded that, though he sat by to see fair play, yet it was always with his elbows on the table and his fingers in his ears, regardless of appearing to the priest in the character of the deaf adder. After all, he was not the object, and good Père Bonami at first thought the day his own, when he found that almost all his arguments against Calvinism were equally impressed upon Berenger's mind, but the differences soon revealed themselves; and the priest, though a good man, was not a very happily-chosen champion, for he was one of the old-fashioned, scantily-instructed country-priests, who were more numerous before the Jesuit revival of learning, and knew nothing of controversy save that adapted to the doctrines of Calvin; so that in dealing with an Anglican of the school of Ridley and Hooker, it was like bow and arrow against sword. And in those days of change, controversial reading was one of the primary studies even of young laymen, and Lord Walwyn, with a view to his grandson's peculiar position, had taken care that he should be well instructed, so that he was not at all unequal to the contest. Moreover, apart from argument, he clung as a point of honour to the Church as to the wife that he had accepted in his childhood; and often tried to recall the sketch that Philip Sidney had once given him of a tale that a friend of his designed to turn into a poem, like Ariosto's, in *terza rima*, of a Red Cross knight separated from his Una as the true faith, and tempted by a treacherous Duessa, who impersonated at once Falsehood and Rome. And he knew so well that the least relaxation of his almost terrified resistance would make him so entirely succumb to Diane's beauty and brilliancy, that he kept himself stiffly frigid and reserved.

Diane never openly alluded to the terms on which he stood, but he often found gifts from unknown hands placed in his room. The books which he had found there were changed when he had had time to study them; and marks were placed in some of the most striking passages. They were of the class that turned the brain of the Knight of La Mancha, but with a predominance of the pastoral, such as the Diana of George of Montemayor and his numerous imitators—which Philip thought horrible stuff—enduring nothing but a few of the combats of Amadis de Gaul or Palmerin of England, until he found that Madame de Selinville prodigiously admired the "silly swains more silly than their sheep," and was very anxious that M. le Baron should be touched by their beauties; whereupon honest Philip made desperate efforts to swallow them in his brother's stead, but was always found fast asleep in the very middle of arguments between Damon and Thrysis upon the *devoirs* of love, or the mournings of some disconsolate nymph over her jealousies of a favoured rival.

One day, a beautiful ivory box, exhaling sweet perfume, appeared in the prison chamber, and therewith a sealed letter in verse, containing an affecting description of how Corydon had been cruelly torn by the lions in endeavouring to bear away Sylvie from her cavern, how Sylvie had been rent from him and lost, and how vainly he continued to bewail her, and disregard the loving lament of Daphné, who had ever mourned and pined for him as she kept her flock, made the rivulets, the brooks, the mountains re-echo with her sighs and plaints, and had wandered through the hills and valleys, gathering simples wherewith she had compounded a balsam that might do away with the scars that the claws of the lions had left, so that he might again appear with the glowing cheeks and radiant locks that had excited the envy of the god of day.

Berenger burst out laughing over the practical part of this poetical performance, and laughed the more at Philip's hurt, injured air at his mirth. Philip, who would have been the first to see the absurdity in any other Daphné, thought this a passing pleasant device, and considered it very unkind in his brother not even to make experiment of the balsam of simples, but to declare that he had much rather keep his scars for Eustacie's sake than wear a smooth face to please Diane.

Still Berenger's natural courtesy stood in his way. He could not help being respectful and attentive to the old Chevalier, when their terms were, apparently at least, those of host and guest; and to a lady he *could* not be rude and repellent, though he could be reserved. So, when the kinsfolk met, no stranger would have discovered that one was a prisoner and the others his captors.

One August day, when Madame de Selinville and her lady attendants were supping at the castle at the early hour of six, a servant brought in word that an Italian pedlar craved leave to display his wares. He was welcome, both for need's sake and for amusement, and was readily admitted. He was a handsome olive-faced Italian, and was followed by a little boy with a skin of almost Moorish dye—and great was the display at once made on the tables, of

> "Lawn as white as driven snow,
> Cyprus, black as e'er was crow;
> Gloves as sweet as fragrant posies,
> Masks for faces and for noses;"

and there was a good deal of the eager, desultory bargaining that naturally took place where purchasing was an unusual excitement and novelty, and was to form a whole evening's amusement. Berenger, while supplying the defects of his scanty travelling wardrobe, was trying to make out whether he had seen the man before, wondering if he were the same whom he had met in the forest of Montpipeau, though a few differences in dress, hair, and beard made him somewhat doubtful.

"Perfumes? Yes, lady, I have store of perfumes: ambergris and violet dew, and the Turkish essence distilled from roses; yea, and the finest spirit of the Venus myrtle-tree, the secret known to the Roman dames of old, whereby they secured perpetual beauty and love—though truly Madame should need no such essence. That which nature has bestowed on her secures to her all hearts—and one valued more than all."

"Enough," said Diane, blushing somewhat, though with an effort at laughing off his words; "these are the tricks of your trade."

"Madame is incredulous; yet, Lady, I have been in the East. Yonder boy comes from the land where there are spells that make known the secrets of lives."

The old Chevalier, who had hitherto been taken up with the abstruse calculation—derived from his past days of economy—how much ribbon would be needed to retrim his murrey *just-au-corps*, here began to lend an ear, though saying nothing. Philip looked on in open-eyed wonder, and nudged his brother, who muttered in return, "Jugglery!"

"Ah, the fair company are all slow to believe," said the pedlar. "Hola, Alessio!" and taking a glove that Philip had left on the table, he held it to the boy. A few unintelligible words passed between them; then the boy pointed direct to Philip, and waved his hand northwards. "He says the gentleman who owns this glove comes from the North, from far away," interpreted the Italian; then as the boy made the gesture of walking in chains, "that he is a captive."

"Ay," cried Philip, "right, lad; and can he tell how long I shall be so?"

"Things yet to come," said the mountebank, "are only revealed after long preparation. For them must he gaze into the dark pool of the future. The present and the past he can divine by the mere touch of what has belonged to the person."

"It is passing strange," said Philip to Madame de Selinville. "You credit it, Madame?"

"Ah, have we not seen the wonders come to pass that a like diviner foretold to the Queen-mother?" said Diane: "her sons should be all kings—that was told to her when the eldest was yet Dauphin."

"And there is only one yet to come," said Philip, awestruck. "But see, what has he now?"

"Véronique's kerchief," returned Madame de Selinville, as the Italian began to interpret the boy's gesture.

"Pretty maidens, he says, serve fair ladies—bear tokens for them. This damsel has once been the bearer of a bouquet of heather of the pink and white, whose bells were to ring hope."

"Eh, eh, Madame, it is true!" cried Véronique, crimson with surprise and alarm. "M. le Baron knows it is true."

Berenger had started at this revelation, and uttered an inarticulate exclamation; but at that moment the boy, in whose hand his master had placed a crown from the money newly paid, began to make vehement gestures, which the man interpreted. "*Le Balafré*, he says, pardon me, gentlemen, *le Balafré* could reveal even a deeper scar of the heart than of the visage"—and the boy's brown hand was pressed on his heart—"yet truly there is yet hope (*espérance*) to be found. Yes"—as the boy put his hand to his neck—"he bears a pearl, parted from its sister pearls. Where they are, there is hope. Who can miss Hope, who has sought it at a royal death-bed?"

"Ah, where is it?" Berenger could not help exclaiming.

"Sir," said the pedlar, "as I told Messieurs and Mesdames before, the spirits that cast the lights of the future on the dark pool need invocation. Ere he can answer M. le Baron's demands, he and I must have time and seclusion. If Monsieur le Chevalier will grant us an empty room, there will we answer all queries on which the spirits will throw light."

"And how am I to know that you will not bring the devil to shatter the castle, my friend?" demanded the Chevalier. "Or more likely still, that you are not laughing all the time at these credulous boys and ladies?"

"Of that, sir, you may here convince yourself," said the mountebank, putting into his hand a sort of credential in

Italian, signed by Renato di Milano, the Queen's perfumer, testifying to the skill of his compatriot Ercole Stizzito both in perfumery, cosmetics, and in the secrets of occult sciences.

The Chevalier was no Italian scholar, and his daughter interpreted the scroll to him, in a rapid low voice, adding, "I have had many dealings with René of Milan, father. I know he speaks sooth. There can be no harm in letting the poor man play out his play—all the castle servants will be frantic to have their fortunes told."

"I must speak with the fellow first, daughter," said the Chevalier. "He must satisfy me that he has no unlawful dealings that could bring the Church down on us." And he looked meaningly at the mountebank, who replied by a whole muster-roll of ecclesiastics, male and female, who had heard and approved his predictions.

"A few more words with thee, fellow," said the Chevalier, pointing the way to one of the rooms opening out of the hall. "As master of the house I must be convinced of his honesty," he added. "If I am satisfied, then who will may seek to hear their fortune."

Chevalier, man and boy disappeared, and Philip was the first to exclaim, "A strange fellow! What will he tell us? Madame, shall you hear him?"

"That depends on my father's report," she said. "And yet," sadly and pensively, "my future is dark and void enough. Why should I vex myself with hearing it?"

"Nay, it may brighten," said Philip.

"Scarcely, while hearts are hard," she murmured with a slight shake of the head, that Philip thought indescribably touching; but Berenger was gathering his purchases together, and did not see. "And you, brother," said Philip, "you mean to prove him?"

"No," said Berenger. "Have you forgotten, Phil, the anger we met with, when we dealt with the gipsy at Hurst Fair?"

"Pshaw, Berry, we are past flogging now."

"Out of reach, Phil, of the rod, but scarce of the teaching it struck into us."

"What?" said Philip sulkily.

"That divining is either cozening man or forsaking God, Phil. Either it is falsehood, or it is a lying wonder of the devil."

"But, Berry, this man is no cheat."

"Then he is worse."

"Only, turn not away, brother. How should he have known things that even I know not?—the heather."

"No marvel in that," said Berenger. "This is the very man I bought Annora's fan from; he was prowling round Montpipeau, and my heather was given to Véronique with little secrecy. And as to the royal deathbed, it was René, his master, who met me there."

"Then you think it mere cozening? If so, we should find it out."

"I don't reckon myself keener than an accomplished Italian mountebank," said Berenger, drily.

Further conference was cut short by the return of the Chevalier, saying, in his paternal genial way, "Well, children, I have examined the fellow and his credentials, and for those who have enough youth and hope to care to have the future made known to them, bah! it is well."

"Is it sorcery, sir?" asked Philip, anxiously.

The Chevalier shrugged his shoulders. "What know I?" he said. "For those who have a fine nose for brimstone there may be, but he assures me it is but the white magic practised in Egypt, and the boy is Christian!"

"Did you try his secrets, father?" inquired Madame de Selinville.

"I, my daughter? An old man's fortune is in his children. What have I to ask?"

"I—I scarcely like to be the first!" said the lady, eager but hesitating. "Véronique, you would have your fortune told?"

"I will be the first," said Philip, stepping forward manfully. "I will prove him for you, lady, and tell you whether he be a cozener or not; or if his magic be fit for you to deal with."

And confident in the inherent intuition of a plain Englishman, as well as satisfied to exercise his resolution for once in opposition to Berenger's opinion, Master Thistlewood stepped towards the closet where the Italian awaited his clients, and Berenger knew that it would be worse than useless to endeavour to withhold him. He only chafed at the smile which passed between father and daughter at this doughty self-assertion.

There was a long silence. Berenger sat with his eyes fixed on the window where the twilight horizon was still soft and bright with the pearly gold of the late sunset, thinking with an intensity of yearning what it would be could he truly become certain of Eustacie's present doings; questioning whether he would try to satisfy that longing by the doubtful auguries of the diviner, and then, recollecting how he had heard from wrecked sailors that to seek to delude their thirst with sea-water did but aggravate their misery. He knew that whatever he might hear would be unworthy of confidence. Either it might have been prompted by the Chevalier, or it might be merely framed to soothe and please him—or, were it a genuine oracle, he had no faith in the instinct that was to perceive it, but what he *had* faith in was the Divine protection over his lost ones. "No," he thought to himself, "I will not by a presumptuous sin, in my own impatience, risk incurring woes on them that deal with familiar spirits and wizards that peep and mutter. If ever I am to hear of Eustacie again, it shall be by God's will, not the devil's."

Diane de Selinville had been watching his face all the time, and now said, with that almost timid air of gaiety that she wore when addressing him: "You too, cousin, are awaiting Monsieur Philippe's report to decide whether to look into the pool of mystery."

"Not at all, madame," said Berenger, gravely. "I do not understand white magic."

"Our good cousin has been too well bred among the Reformers to condescend to our little wickednesses, daughter," said the Chevalier; and the sneer—much like that which would await a person now who scrupled at joining in table-turning or any form of spiritualism—purpled Berenger's scar, now his only manner of blushing; but he instantly perceived that it was the Chevalier's desire that he should consult the conjurer, and therefore became the more resolved against running into a trap.

"I am sure," said Madame de Selinville, earnestly, though with an affectation of lightness, "a little wickedness is fair when there is a great deal at stake. For my part, I would not hesitate long, to find out how soon the King will relent towards my fair cousin here!"

"That, Madame," said Berenger, with the same grave dryness, "is likely to be better known to other persons than this wandering Greek boy."

Here Philip's step was heard returning hastily. He was pale, and looked a good deal excited, so that Madame de Selinville uttered a little cry, and exclaimed, "Ah! is it so dreadful then?"

"No, no, madame," said Philip, turning round, with a fervour and confidence he had never before shown. "On my word, there is nothing formidable. You see nothing—nothing but the Italian and the boy. The boy gazes into a vessel of some black liquid, and sees—sees there all you would have revealed. Ah!"

"Then you believe?" asked Madame de Selinville.

"It cannot be false," answered Philip; "he told me everything. Things he could not have known. My very home, my father's house, passed in review before that strange little blackamoor's eyes; where I—though I would have given worlds to see it—beheld only the lamp mirrored in the dark pool."

"How do you know it was your father's house?" said Berenger.

"I could not doubt. Just to test the fellow, I bade him ask for my native place. The little boy gazed, smiled, babbled his gibberish, pointed. The man said he spoke of a fair mansion among green fields and hills, 'a grand *cavalier embonpoint*,'—those were his very words,—at the door, with a tankard in one hand. Ah! my dear father, why could not I see him too? But who could mistake him or the manor?"

"And did he speak of future as well as past?" said Diane.

"Yes, yes, yes," said Philip, with more agitation. "Lady, that will you know for yourself."

"It was not dreadful?" she said, rising.

"Oh no;" and Philip had become crimson, and hesitated; "certes, not dreadful. But——I must not say more."

"Save good-night," said Berenger, rising. "See, our gendarmes are again looking as if we had long exceeded their patience. It is an hour later than we are wont to retire."

"If it be your desire to consult this mysterious fellow now you have heard your brother's report, my dear Baron," said the Chevalier, "the gendarmes may devour their impatience a little longer."

"Thanks, sir," said Berenger; "but I am not tempted," and he gave the usual signal to the gendarmes, who, during meals, used to stand as sentries at the great door of the hall.

"It might settle your mind," muttered Philip, hesitating. "And yet—yet——"

But he used no persuasions, and permitted himself to be escorted with his brother along the passages to their own chamber, where he threw himself into a chair with a long sigh, and did not speak. Berenger meantime opened the Bible, glanced over the few verses he meant to read, found the place in the Prayer-book, and was going to the stairs to call Humfrey, when Philip broke forth: "Wait, Berry; don't be in such haste."

"What, you want time to lose the taste of your dealings with the devil?" said Berenger, smiling.

"Pshaw! no devil in the matter," testily said Philip. "No, I was only wishing you had not had a Puritan fit, and seen and heard for yourself. Then I should not have had to tell you," and he sighed.

"I have no desire to be told," said Berenger, who had become more fixed in the conviction that it was an imposture.

"No desire! Ah! I had none when I knew what it was. But you ought to know."

"Well," said Berenger, "you will burst anon if I open not my ears."

"Dear Berry, speak not thus. It will be the worse for you when you do hear. Alack, Berenger, all ours have been vain hopes. I asked for *her*—and the boy fell well-nigh into convulsions of terror as he gazed; spoke of flames and falling houses. That was wherefore I pressed you not again—it would have wrung your heart too much. The boy fairly wept and writhed himself, crying out in his tongue for pity on the fair lady and the little babe in the burning house. Alack! brother," said Philip, a little hurt that his brother had not changed countenance.

"This is the lying tale of the man-at-arms which our own eyes contradicted," said Berenger; "and no doubt was likewise inspired by the Chevalier."

"See the boy, brother! How should he have heard the Chevalier? Nay, you might hug your own belief, but it is hard that we should both be in durance for your mere dream that she lives."

"Come, Phil, it will be the devil indeed that sows dissension between us," said Berenger. "You know well enough that were it indeed with my poor Eustacie as they would fain have us believe, rather than give up her fair name I would rot in prison for life. Or would you have me renounce my faith, or wed Madame de Selinville upon the witness of a pool of ink that I am a widower?" he added, almost laughing.

"For that matter," muttered Philip, a good deal ashamed and half affronted, "you know I value the Protestant faith so that I never heard a word from the wily old priest. Nevertheless, the boy, when I asked of our release, saw the gates set open by Love."

"What did Love look like in the pool? Had he wings like the Cupids in the ballets at the Louvre?" asked Berenger provokingly.

"I tell you I saw nothing," said Philip tartly: "this was the Italian's interpretation of the boy's gesture. It was to be by means of love, he said, and of a lady who—— He made it plain enough who she was," added the boy, colouring.

"No doubt, as the Chevalier had taught him."

"You have prejudged, and are deaf to all," said Philip.

"What, could the Chevalier have instructed him to say that I—I—" he hesitated, "that my—my love—I mean that he saw my shield per pale with the field fretty and the sable leopard."

"Oh! it is to be my daughter, is it?" said Berenger, laughing; "I am very happy to entertain your proposals for her."

"Berenger, what mocking fiend has possessed you?" cried Philip, half angrily, half pitifully. "How can you so speak of that poor child?"

"Because the more they try to force on me the story of her fate, the plainer it is to me that they do not believe it. I shall find her yet, and then, Phil, you shall have the first chance."

Philip growled.

"Well, Phil," said his brother, good-humouredly, "any way, till this Love comes that is to let us out, don't let Moor or fiend come between us. Let me keep my credence for the honest Bailli's daughters at Luçon; and remember I would give my life to free you, but I cannot give away my faith." Philip bent his head. He was of too stubborn a mould to express contrition or affection, but he mused for five minutes, then called Humfrey, and at the last moment, as the heavy tread came upstairs, he turned round and said, "You're in the right on't there, Berry. Hap what hap, the foul fiend may carry off the conjurer before I murmur at you again! Still I wish you had seen him. You would know 'tis sooth."

While Berenger, in his prison chamber, with the lamplight beaming on his high white brow and clear eye, stood before his two comrades in captivity, their true-hearted faces composed to reverence, and as he read, "I have hated them that hold of superstitious vanities, and my trust hath been in the

Lord. I will be glad and rejoice in Thy mercy, for Thou hast considered my trouble and hast known my soul in adversities," feeling that here was the oracle by which he was willing to abide—Diane de Selinville was entering the cabinet where the secrets of the future were to be unveiled.

There she stood—the beautiful Court lady—her lace coif (of the Mary of Scotland type) well framed the beautiful oval of her face, and set off the clear olive of her complexion, softened by short jetty curls at the temples, and lighted by splendid dark eyes, and by the smiles of a perfect pair of lips. A transparent veil hung back over the ruff like frostwork-formed fairy wings, and over the white silk bodice and sleeves laced with violet, and the violet skirt that fell in ample folds on the ground; only, however, in the dim light revealing by an occasional gleam that it was not black. It was a stately presence, yet withal there was a tremor, a quiver of the downcast eyelids, and a trembling of the fair hand, as though she were ill at ease; even though it was by no means the first time she had trafficked with the dealers in mysterious arts who swarmed around Catherine de Medicis. There were words lately uttered that weighed with her in their simplicity, and she could not forget them in that gloomy light, as she gazed on the brown face of the Italian, Ercole, faultless in outline as a classical mask, but the black depths of the eyes sparkling with intensity of observation, as if they were everywhere at once and gazed through and through. He wore his national dress, with the short cloak over one shoulder; but the little boy, who stood at the table, had been fantastically arrayed in a sort of semi-Albanian garb, a red cap with a long tassel, a dark, gold-embroidered velvet jacket sitting close to his body, and a white kilt over his legs, bare except for buskins stiff with gold. The poor little fellow looked pale in spite of his tawny hue, his enormous black eyes were heavy and weary, and he seemed to be trying to keep aloof from the small brazen vessel formed by the coils of two serpents that held the inky liquid of which Philip had spoken.

No doubt of the veritable nature of the charm crossed Diane; her doubt was of its lawfulness, her dread of the supernatural region she was invading. She hesitated before she ventured on her first question, and started as the Italian first spoke,—"What would the Eccellentissima? Ladies often hesitate to speak the question nearest their hearts. Yet is it ever the same. But the lady must be pleased to form it herself in words, or the lad will not see her vision."

"Where, then, is my brother?" said Diane, still reluctant to come direct to the point.

The boy gazed intently into the black pool, his great eyes dilating till they seemed like black wells, and after a long time, that Diane could have counted by the throbs of her heart, he began to close his fingers, perform the action over the other arm of one playing on the lute, throw his head back, close his eyes, and appear to be singing a lullaby. Then he spoke a few words to his master quickly.

"He sees," said Ercole, "a gentleman touching the lute, seated in a bedroom, where lies, on a rich pillow, another gentleman,"—and as the boy stroked his face, and pointed to his hands—"wearing a mask and gloves. It is, he says, in my own land, in Italy," and as the boy made the action of rowing, "in the territory of Venice."

"It is well," said Madame de Selinville, who knew that nothing was more probable than that her brother should be playing the King to his sleep in the medicated mask and gloves that cherished the royal complexion, and, moreover, that Henry was lingering to take his pastime in Italy to the great inconvenience of his kingdom.

Her next question came nearer her heart—"You saw the gentleman with a scar. Will he leave this castle?"

The boy gazed, then made gestures of throwing his arms wide, and of passing out; and as he added his few words, the master explained: "He sees the gentleman leaving the castle, through open gate, in full day, on horseback; and—and it is Madame who is with them," he added, as the lad pointed decidedly to her, "it is Madame who opens their prison."

Diane's face lighted with gladness for a moment; then she said, faltering (most women of her day would not have been even thus reserved), "Then I shall marry again?"

The boy gazed and knitted his brow; then, without any pantomime, looked up and spoke. "The Eccellentissima shall be a bride once more, he says," explained the man, "but after a sort he cannot understand. It is exhausting, lady, thus to gaze into the invisible future; the boy becomes confused and exhausted ere long."

"Once more—I will only ask of the past. My cousin, is he married or a widower?"

The boy clasped his hands and looked imploringly, shaking his head at the dark pool, as he murmured an entreating word to his master. "Ah! Madame," said the Italian, "that question hath already been demanded by the young Inglese. The poor child has been so terrified by the scene it called up, that he implores he may not see it again. A sacked and burning town, a lady in a flaming house——"

"Enough, enough," said Diane; "I could as little bear to hear as he to see. It is what we have ever known and feared. And now"—she blushed as she spoke—"sir, you will leave me one of those potions that Signor Renato is wont to compound."

"*Capisco!*" said Ercole, with a rapid motion of his head.

"It must be such," added Diane, "as can be disguised in sherbet or milk. All hitherto have failed, as the person in question tastes no wine."

"It will take a more refined preparation—a subtler essence," returned Ercole; "but the Eccellentissima shall be obeyed if she will supply the means, for the expense will be heavy."

The bargain was agreed upon, and a considerable sum advanced for a philtre, compounded of strange Eastern plants and mystic jewels; and then Diane, with a shudder of relief, passed into the full light of the hall, bade her father good-night, and was handed by him into the litter that had long been awaiting her at the door.

The Chevalier, then, with care on his brow, bent his steps towards the apartment where the Italian still remained counting the money he had received.

"So!" he said as he entered, "so, fellow, I have not hindered your gains, and you have been true to your agreement?"

"Illustrissimo, yes. The pool of vision mirrored the flames, but nothing beyond—nothing—nothing."

"They asked you then no more of those words you threw out of Espérance?"

"Only the English youth, sir; and there were plenty of other hopes to dance before the eyes of such a lad! With M. le Baron it will be needful to be more guarded."

"M. le Baron shall not have the opportunity," said the Chevalier. "He may abide by his decision, and what the younger one may tell him. Fear not, good man, it shall be made good to you, if you obey my commands. I have other work for you. But first repeat to me more fully what you told me before. Where was it that you saw this unhappy girl under the name of Espérance?"

"At a hostel, sir, at Charente, where she was attending on an old heretic teacher of the name of Gardon, who had fallen sick there, being pinched by the fiend with rheumatic pains after his deserts. She bore the name of Espéranco Gardon, and passed for his son's widow."

"And by what means did you know her not to be the mean creature she pretended?" said the Chevalier, with a gesture of scornful horror.

"Illustrissimo, I never forget a face. I had seen this lady with M. le Baron when they made purchases of various trinkets at Montpipeau; and I saw her fully again. I had the honour to purchase from her certain jewels, that the Eccellenza will probably redeem; and even—pardon, sir—I cut off and bought of her, her hair."

"Her hair!" exclaimed the Chevalier, in horror. "The miserable girl to have fallen so low! Is it with you, fellow?"

"Surely, Illustrissimo. Such tresses—so shining, so silky, so well-kept,—I reserved to adorn the heads of Signor Renato's most princely customers," said the man, unpacking from the inmost recesses of one of his most ingeniously arranged packages, a parcel which contained the rich mass of beautiful black tresses. "Ah! her head looked so noble," he added, "that I felt it profane to let my scissors touch those locks; but she said that she could never wear them openly more, and that they did but take up her time, and were useless to her child and her father—as she called him; and she much needed the medicaments for the old man that I gave her in exchange."

"Heavens! A daughter of Ribaumont!" sighed the Chevalier, clenching his hand. "And now, man, let me see the jewels with which the besotted child parted."

The jewels were not many, nor remarkable. No one but a member of the family would have identified them, and not one of the pearls was there; and the Chevalier refrained from inquiring after them, lest, by putting the Italian on the scent of anything so exceptionally valuable, he should defeat his own object, and lead to the man's securing the pearls and running away with them. But Ercole understood his glance, with the quickness of a man whose trade forced him to read countenances. "The Eccellenza is looking for the pearls of Ribaumont? The lady made no offer of them to me."

"Do you believe that she has them still?"

"I am certain of it, sir. I know that she has jewels—though she said not what they were—which she preserved at the expense of her hair. It was thus. The old man had, it seems, been for weeks on the rack with pains caught by a chill when they fled from La Sablerie, and, though the fever had left him, he was still so stiff in the joints as to be unable to move. I prescribed for him unguents of balm and Indian spice, which, as the Eccellenza knows, are worth far more than their weight in gold; nor did these jewels make up the cost of these, together with the warm cloak for him, and the linen for her child that she had been purchasing. I tell you, sir, the babe must have no linen but the finest fabric of Cambrai—yes, and even carnation-coloured ribbons—though, for herself, I saw the homespun she was sewing. As she mused over what she could throw back, I asked if she had no other gauds to make up the price, and she said, almost within herself, 'They are my child's, not mine.' Then remembering that I had been buying the hair of the peasant maidens, she suddenly offered me her tresses. But I could yet secure the pearls, if Eccellenza would."

"Do you then believe her to be in any positive want or distress?" said the Chevalier.

"Signor, no. The heretical households among whom she travels gladly support the families of their teachers, and at Catholic inns they pay their way. I understood them to be on their way to a synod of Satan at that nest of heretics,

Montauban, where doubtless the old miscreant would obtain an appointment to some village."

"When did you thus fall in with them?"

"It was on one of the days of the week of Pentecost," said Ercole. "It is at that time I frequent fairs in those parts, to gather my little harvest on the maiden's heads."

"*Parbleu!* class not my niece with those sordid beings, man," said the Chevalier, angrily. "Here is your price"—tossing a heavy purse on the table—"and as much more shall await you when you bring me sure intelligence where to find my niece. You understand; and mark, not one word of the gentleman you saw here. You say she believes him dead?"

"The Illustrissimo must remember that she never dropped her disguise with me, but I fully think that she supposes herself a widow. And I understand the Eccellenza, she is still to think so. I may be depended on."

"You understand," repeated the Chevalier, "this sum shall reward you when you have informed me where to find her—as a man like you can easily trace her from Montauban. If you have any traffickings with her, it shall be made worth your while to secure the pearls for the family; but, remember, the first object is herself, and that she should be ignorant of the existence of him whom she fancied her husband."

"I see, Signor; and not a word, of course, of my having come from you. I will discover her, and leave her noble family to deal with her. Has the Illustrissimo any further commands?"

"None," began the Chevalier; then, suddenly, "This unhappy infant—is it healthy? Did it need any of your treatment?"

"Signor, no. It was a fair, healthy bambina of a year old, and I heard the mother boasting that it had never had a day's illness."

"Ah, the less a child has to do in the world, the more is it bent on living," said the Chevalier with a sigh; and then, with a parting greeting, he dismissed the Italian, but only to sup under the careful surveillance of the steward, and then to be conveyed by early morning light beyond the territory where the affairs of Ribaumont were interesting.

But the Chevalier went through a sleepless night. Long did he pace up and down his chamber, grind his teeth, clench his fists and point them at his head, and make gestures of tearing his thin grey locks; and many a military oath did he swear under his breath as he thought to what a pass things had come. His brother's daughter waiting on an old Huguenot *bourgeois*, making sugar-cakes, selling her hair! and what next? Here was she alive after all, alive and disgracing herself; alive—yes, both she and her husband —to perplex the Chevalier, and force him either to new crimes or to beggar his son! Why could not the one have really died on the St. Bartholomew, or the other at La Sablerie, instead of putting the poor Chevalier in the wrong by coming to life again?

What had he done to be thus forced to peril his soul at his age? Ah, had he but known what he should bring on himself when he wrote the unlucky letter, pretending that the silly little child wished to dissolve the marriage! How should he have known that the lad would come meddling over? And then, when he had dexterously brought about that each should be offended with the other, and consent to the separation, why must royalty step in and throw them together again? Yes, and he surely had a right to feel ill-used, since it was in ignorance of the ratification of the marriage that he had arranged the frustration of the elopement, and that he had forced on the wedding with Narcisse, so as to drive Eustacie to flight from the convent—in ignorance again of her life that he had imprisoned Berenger, and tried to buy off his claims to Nid-de-Merle with Diane's hand. Circumstances had used him cruelly, and he shrank from fairly contemplating the next step.

He knew well enough what it must be. Without loss of time a letter must be sent to Rome, backed by strong interest, so as to make it appear that the ceremony at Montpipeau, irregular, and between a Huguenot and Catholic, had been a defiance of the Papal decree, and must therefore be nullified. This would probably be attainable, though he did not feel absolutely secure of it. Pending this, Eustacie must be secluded in a convent; and, while still believing herself a widow, must, immediately on the arrival of the decree and dispensation, be forced into the marriage with Narcisse before she heard of Berenger's being still alive. And then Berenger would have no longer any excuse for holding out. His claims would be disposed of, and he might be either sent to England, or he might be won upon by Madame de Selinville's constancy.

And this, as the Chevalier believed, was the only chance of saving a life that he was unwilling to sacrifice, for his captive's patience and courtesy had gained so much upon his heart that he was resolved to do all that shuffling and temporizing could do to save the lad from Narcisse's hatred and to secure him Diane's love.

As to telling the truth and arranging his escape, that scarcely ever crossed the old man's mind. It would have been to resign the lands of Nid-de-Merle, to return to the makeshift life he knew but too well, and, what was worse, to ruin and degrade his son, and incur his resentment. It would probably be easy to obtain a promise from Berenger, in his first joy and gratitude, of yielding up all pretensions of his own or his wife's; but, however honourably meant, such a promise would be worth very little, and would be utterly scorned by Narcisse. Besides, how could he thwart the love of his daughter and the ambition of his son both at once?

No; the only security for the possession of Nid-de-Merle lay in either the death of the young baron and his child, or else in his acquiescence in the invalidity of his marriage, and therefore in the illegitimacy of the child.

And it was within the bounds of possibility that, in his seclusion, he might at length learn to believe in the story of the destruction at La Sablerie, and, wearying of captivity, might yield at length to the persuasions of Diane and her father, and become so far involved with them as to be unable to draw back, or else be so stung by Eustacie's desertion as to accept her rival willingly.

It was a forlorn hope, but it was the only medium that lay between either the death or the release of the captive; and therefore the old man clung to it as almost praiseworthy, and did his best to bring it about by keeping his daughter ignorant that Eustacie lived, and writing to his son that the Baron was on the point of becoming a Catholic and marrying his sister: and thus that all family danger and scandal would be avoided, provided the matter were properly represented at Rome.

CHAPTER XXXII.

"JAM SATIS."

> "You may go walk, and give me leave awhile,
> My lessons make no music in three parts."
>
> *Taming of the Shrew.*

WHETHER the dark pool really showed Sir Marmaduke Thistlewood or not, at the moment that his son desired that his image should be called up, the good knight was, in effect, sitting nodding over the tankard of sack with which his supper was always concluded, while the rest of the family, lured out of the sunny hall by the charms of a fresh summer evening, had dispersed into the gardens or hall.

Presently a movement in the neighbourhood made him think it incumbent on him to open his eyes wide, and exclaim, "I'm not asleep."

"Oh no! you never are asleep when there's anything you ought to see!" returned Dame Annora, who was standing by him with her hand on his chair.

"How now? Any tidings of the lads?" he exclaimed.

"Of the lads? No, indeed; but there will be bad tidings for the lads if you do not see to it! Where do you think your daughter is, Sir Duke?"

"Where? How should I know? She went out to give her sisters some strawberries, I thought."

"See here," said Lady Thistlewood, leading the way to the north end of the hall, where a door opened into what was called the Yew-tree Grove. This consisted of five rows of yew-trees, planted at regular intervals, and their natural mode of growth so interfered with by constant cutting, that their ruddy trunks had been obliged to rise branchless, till about twelve feet above ground they had been allowed to spread out their limbs in the form of ordinary forest-trees; and, altogether, their foliage became a thick, unbroken, dark, evergreen roof, impervious to sunshine, and almost impervious to rain, while below their trunks were like columns forming five arcades, floored only by that dark red crusty earth and green lichen growth that seems peculiar to the shelter of yew-trees. The depth of the shade and the stillness of the place made it something peculiarly soothing and quiet, more especially when, as now, the sunset light came below the branches, richly tinted the russet pillars, cast long shadows, and gleamed into all the recesses of the interlacing boughs and polished leafage above.

"Do you see, Sir Duke?" demanded his lady.

"I see my little maids making a rare feast under the trees upon their strawberries set out on leaves. Bless their little hearts! what a pretty fairy feast they've made of it, with the dogs looking on as grave as judges! It makes me young again to get a smack of the haut-bois your mother brought from Chelsea Gardens."

"Haut-bois! He'd never see if the house were afire overhead. What's that beyond?"

"No fire, my dear, but the sky all aglow with sunset, and the red cow standing up against the light, chewing her cud, and looking as well pleased as though she knew there wasn't her match in Dorset."

Lady Thistlewood fairly stamped, and pointed with her

fan, like a pistol, down a side aisle of the grove, where two figures were slowly moving along.

"Eh! what? Lucy with her apron full of rose-leaves, letting them float away while she cons the children's lesson for the morrow with Merrycourt? They be no great loss, when the place is full of roses. Or why could you not call to the wench to take better heed to them, instead of making all this pother?"

"A pretty sort of lesson it is like to be! A pretty sort of return for my poor son, unless you take the better heed!"

"Would that I saw any return at all for either of the poor dear lads," sighed the knight wearily; "but what you may be driving at I cannot perceive."

"What! When 'tis before your very eyes, how yonder smooth-tongued French impostor, after luring him back to his ruin beyond seas, is supplanting him even here, and your daughter giving herself over to the wily viper!"

"The man is a popish priest," said Sir Marmaduke; "no more given to love than Mr. Adderley or Friar Rogers."

The dame gave a snort of derision: "Prithee, how many popish priests be now wedded parsons? Nor, indeed, even if his story be true, do I believe he is a priest at all. I have seen many a young abbé, as they call themselves, clerk only in name, loitering at court, free to throw off the cassock any moment they chose, and as insolent as the rest. Why, the Abbé de Lorraine, cardinal that is now, said of my complexion——"

"No vows, quotha!" muttered Sir Marmaduke, well aware of the Cardinal de Lorraine's opinion of his lady's complexion. "So much the better; he is too good a young fellow to be forced to mope single, and yet I hate men's breaking their word."

"And that's all you have to say!" angrily cried her ladyship. "No one save myself ever thinks how it is to be with my poor dear wounded, heart-broken son, when he comes home, to find himself so scurvily used by that faithless girl of yours, ready——"

"Hold, madam," said Sir Marmaduke, with real sternness; "nothing rash against my daughter. How should she be faithless to a man who has been wedded ever since she knew him?"

"He is free now," said Lady Thistlewood, beginning to cry (for the last letters received from Berenger had been those from Paris, while he still believed Eustacie to have perished at La Sablerie); "and I do say it is very hard that just when he is rid of the French baggage, the bane of his life, and is coming home, may be with a child upon his hands, and all wounded, scarred, and blurred, the only wench he would or should have married should throw herself away on a French vagabond beggar, and you aiding and abetting."

"Come, come, Dame Nan," said Sir Marmaduke, "who told you I was aiding and abetting?"

"Tell me not, Sir Duke, you that see them a courting under your very eyes, and will not stir a finger to hinder it. If you like to see your daughter take up with a foreign adventurer, why, she's no child of mine, thank Heaven! and I've nought to do with it."

"Pshaw, Dame, there's no taking up in the case; and if there were, sure it is not you that should be hard on Lucy."

Whereupon Annora fell into such a flood of tears at the cruelty of casting such things up to her, that Sir Marmaduke was fain in his blundering way to declare that he only meant that an honest Englishman had no chance where a Frenchman once came in, and then very nearly to surrender at discretion. At any rate, he escaped from her tears by going out at the door, and calling to Lucy to mind her rose-leaves; then, as she gazed round, dismayed at the pink track along the ground, he asked her what she had been doing. Whereto she answered with bright face and honest eyes, that Mr. Méricour had been going over with her the ode "*Jam satis*," of Horatius, wherewith to prepare little Nan for him to-morrow, and then she ran hurriedly away to secure the remainder of the rose-leaves, while her companion was already on his knees picking up the petals she had dropped.

"Master Merrycourt," said Sir Marmaduke, a little gruffly, "never heed the flower-leaves. I want a word with you."

Claude de Méricour rose hastily, as if somewhat struck by the tone.

"The matter is this," said the knight, leading him from the house, and signing back the little girls who had sprung towards them—"It has been brought to my mind that you are but a youth, and, pardon me, my young master, but when lads and lasses have their heads together over one book, tongues wag."

The colour rushed hotly into young Méricour's face, and he answered quickly, "My rank—I mean my order—should answer that."

"Stay, young man, we are not in France; your order, be it what it may, has not hindered many a marriage in England; though, look you, no man should ever wed with my consent who broke his word to God in so doing; but they tell me your vows are not always made at your age."

"Nor are they," exclaimed Méricour, in a low voice, but with a sudden light on his countenance. "The tonsure was given me as a child, but no vow of celibacy has passed my lips."

Sir Marmaduke exclaimed, "Oh!—" with a prolongation of the sound that lasted till Méricour began again.

"But, sir, let tongues wag as they will, it is for nought. Your fair daughter was but as ever preparing beforehand with me the tasks with which she so kindly indoctrinates her little sisters. I never thought of myself as aught but a religious, and should never dream of human love."

"I thought so! I said so!" said Sir Marmaduke, highly gratified. "I knew you were an honourable man that would never speak of love to my daughter by stealth, nor without means to maintain her after her birth."

The word "birth" brought the blood into the face of the son of the peer of France, but he merely bowed with considerable stiffness and pride, saying, "You did me justice, sir."

"Come, don't be hurt, man," said Sir Marmaduke, putting his hand on his shoulder. "I told you I knew you for an honourable man! You'll be over here to-morrow to hear the little maids their *Jam satis*, or whatever you call it, and dine with us, after to taste Lucy's handiwork in jam cranberry, a better thing as I take it."

Méricour had recovered himself, smiled, shook the good Sir Marmaduke's proffered hand, and, begging to excuse himself from bidding good-night to the ladies on the score of lateness, he walked away to cross the downs on his return to Combe Walwyn, where he was still resident, according to the arrangement by which he was there to await Berenger's return, now deferred so much beyond all reasonable expectation.

Sir Marmaduke, with a free heart, betook himself to the house, dreading to find that Lucy had fallen under the objurgations of her stepmother, but feeling impelled to stand her protector, and guided to the spot by the high key of Dame Annora's voice.

He found Lucy—who, on the rare occasions when good-natured Lady Thistlewood was really angry with her, usually cowered meekly—now standing her ground, and while the dame was pausing for breath, he heard her gentle voice answering steadily, "No, madam, to him I could never owe faith, nor troth, nor love, save such as I have for Philip."

"Then it is very unfeeling and ungrateful of you. Nor did you think so once, but it is all his scars and——"

By this time Sir Marmaduke had come near enough to put his arm round his daughter, and say, "No such thing, Dame. It had been unseemly in the lass had it been otherwise. She is a good girl and a discreet; and the Frenchman, if he has made none of their vows, feels as bound as though he had. He's an honest fellow, thinking of his studies and not of ladies or any such trumpery. So give me a kiss, Lucy girl, and thou shalt study *Jam satis*, or any other jam he pleases, without more to vex thee."

Lucy, now that the warfare was over, had begun to weep so profusely that so soon as her father released her, she turned, made a mute gesture to ask permission to depart, and hurried away; while Lady Thistlewood, who disliked above all that her husband should think her harsh to her step-children, began to relate the exceeding tenderness of the remonstrance which had been followed with such disproportionate floods of tears.

Poor Sir Marmaduke hoped at least that the veil of night had put an end to the subject which harassed him at a time when he felt less capable than usual of bearing vexation, for he was yearning sadly after his only son. The youths had been absent ten months, and had not been heard of for more than three, when they were just leaving Paris in search of the infant. Sir Francis Walsingham, whose embassy had ended with the death of Charles IX., knew nothing of them, and great apprehensions respecting them were beginning to prevail, and, to Sir Marmaduke especially, seemed to be eating out the peace and joy of his life. Philip, always at his father's side ever since he could run alone, was missed at every visit to stable or kennel; the ring of his cheery voice was wanting to the house; and the absence of his merry whistle seemed to make Sir Marmaduke's heart sink like lead as he donned his heavy boots, and went forth in the silver dew of the summer morning to judge which of his cornfields would soonest be ready for the sickle. Until this expedition of his sons he had, for more than fourteen years, never been alone in those morning rounds on his farm; and much as he loved his daughters, they seemed to weigh very light in the scale compared with the sturdy heir who loved every acre with his own ancestral love. Indeed, perhaps, Sir Marmaduke had a deeper, fonder affection for the children of his first marriage, because he had barely been able to give his full heart to their mother before she was taken from him, and he had felt almost double tenderness to be due to them, when he at length obtained his first and only true love. Now, as he looked over the shining billows of the waving barley, his heart was very sore with longing for Philip's gladsome shout at the harvest-field, and he thought with surprise and compunction how he had seen Lucy leave him struggling with a flood of tears. While he was still thus gazing, a head appeared in the narrow path that led across the fields, and presently he recognised the slender, upright form of the young Frenchman.

"A fair good morrow to you, Master Merrycourt! You come right early to look after your ode?"

"Sir," said Méricour, gravely saluting him, "I come to make you my confession. I find that I did not deal truly with you last night, but it was all unwittingly."

"How?" exclaimed Sir Marmaduke, recollecting Lucy's

tears and looking much startled. "You have not——" and there he broke off, seeing Méricour eager to speak.

"Sir," he said, "I was bred as one set apart from love. I had never learnt to think it possible to me,—I thought so even when I replied to you last evening; but, sir, the words you then spoke, the question you asked me set my heart burning, and my senses whirling——" And between agitation and confusion he stammered and clasped his hands passionately, trying to continue what he was saying, but muttering nothing intelligible.

Sir Marmaduke filled up the interval with a long whistle of perplexity; but, too kind not to pity the youth's distress, he laid his hand on his shoulder, saying, "You found out you were but a hot-blooded youth after all, but an honest one. For, as I well trust, my lass knows nought of this."

"How should she know, sir, what I knew not myself?"

"Ha! ha!" chuckled Sir Duke to himself, "so 'twas all Dame Nan's doing that the flame has been lighted! Ho! ho! But what is to come next is the question?" and he eyed the French youth from head to foot with the same considering look with which he was wont to study a bullock.

"Sir, sir," cried Méricour, absolutely flinging himself on his knee before him with national vehemence, "do give me hope! Oh! I will bless you, I will——"

"Get up, man," said the knight, hastily; "no fooling of this sort. The milkmaids will be coming. Hope—why, what sort of hope can be given you in the matter?" he continued; "you are a very good lad, and I like you well enough, but you are not the sort of stuff one gives one's daughter to. Ay, ay, I know you are a great man in your own country, but what are you here?"

"A miserable fugitive and beggar, I know that," said Méricour, vehemently, "but let me have but hope, and there is nothing I will not be!"

"Pish!" said Sir Marmaduke.

"Hear me," entreated the youth, recalled to common sense: "you know that I have lingered at the chateau yonder, partly to study divinity and settle my mind, and partly because my friend Ribaumont begged me to await his return. I will be no longer idle; my mind is fixed. To France I cannot return, while she gives me no choice between such doctrine and practice as I saw at court, and such as the Huguenots would have imposed on me. I had already chosen England as my country before—before this wild hope had awakened in me. Here, I know my nobility counts for nothing, though, truly, sir, few names in France are prouder. But it shall be no hindrance. I will become one of your men of the robe. I have heard that they can enrich themselves and intermarry with your country *noblesse*."

"True, true," said Sir Marmaduke, "there is more sense in that notion than there seemed to be in you at first. My poor brother Phil was to have been a lawyer if he had lived, but it seems to me you are a long way off from that yet! Why, our Templars be mostly Oxford scholars."

"So it was explained to me," said Méricour, "but for some weeks past the Lady Burnet, to whose sons, as you know, I have been teaching French, has been praying me to take the charge of them at Oxford, by which means I should at least be there maintained, and perchance obtain the means for carrying on my studies at the Temple."

"Not ill thought of," said the knight; "a fair course enough for you; but look you, you must have good luck indeed to be in a state to marry within ten or fifteen years, —very likely not then—having nothing of your own, and my wench but little, for Lucy's portion cannot be made equal to her sisters', her mother having been no heiress like Dame Nan. And would you have me keep the maid unwedded till she be thirty or thirty-five years old, waiting for your fortune?"

Méricour looked terribly disconcerted at this.

"Moreover," added the knight, "they will all be at me, so soon as those poor lads come home—Heaven grant they do —to give her to Berenger."

"Sir," said Méricour, looking up with a sudden smile, "all that I would ask is, what you are too good a father to do, that you would not put any force on her inclinations."

"How now? you said you had never courted her!"

"Nor have I, sir. But I see the force of your words. Should she love another man, my dreams were, of course, utterly vain, but if not——" He broke off.

"Well, well, I am no man to force a girl to a match against her will; but never trust to that man. I know what women are; and let a fantastic stranger come across them, there's an end of old friends. But yours is an honest purpose, and you are a good youth; and if you had anything to keep her with, you should have Lucy to-morrow, with all my heart."

Then came the further question whether Méricour should be allowed an interview with Lucy. Sir Marmaduke was simple enough to fancy that she need not be made aware of the cause of Méricour's new arrangement, and decided against it. The young man sorrowfully acquiesced, but whether such a secret could be kept was another thing. To him it would have been impossible to renew their former terms of intercourse without betraying his feelings, and he therefore absented himself. Lady Thistlewood triumphed openly in Sir Marmaduke's having found him out and banished him from the house; Lucy looked white and shed silent tears.

Her father's soft heart was moved, and one Sunday evening he whispered into her ear that Dame Nan was all wrong, and Méricour only kept away because he was an honourable man. Then Lucy smiled and brightened, and Sir Duke fondly asked her if she were fool enough to fancy herself in love with the man.

"Oh no, how should she, when he had never named love to her? She was only glad her father esteemed him."

So then foolish, fond Sir Marmaduke told her all that had passed, and if it had not been too late, he would have sent for Méricour from Lady Burnet's; but his own story did almost as well in bringing back Lucy's soft pink colour. She crept up into Cecily's room one day, and found that she knew all about it, and was as kind and sympathising as she could be—when a vocation had been given up, though no vows had been taken. She did not quite understand it, but she would take it on trust.

CHAPTER XXXIII.

THE SCANDAL OF THE SYNOD OF MONTAUBAN.

"O ye, wha are sae guid yoursel,
Sae pious and sae holy,
Ye've naught to do but mark and tell
Your neebour's fauts and folly."

BURNS.

THE old city of Montauban, once famous as the home of Ariosto's Rinaldo and his brethren, known to French romance as "Les Quatre Fils Aymon," acquired in later times a very diverse species of fame,—that, namely, of being one of the chief strongholds of the Reformed. The Bishop Jean de Lettes, after leading a scandalous life, had professed a sort of Calvinism, had married, and retired to Geneva, and his successor had not found it possible to live at Montauban from the enmity of the inhabitants. Strongly situated, with a peculiar municipal constitution of its own, and used to Provençal independence both of thought and deed, the inhabitants had been so unanimous in their Calvinism, and had offered such efficient resistance, as to have wrung from Government reluctant sanction for the open observance of the Reformed worship, and for the maintenance of a college for the education of their ministry.

There then was convoked the National Synod, answering to the Scottish General Assembly, excepting that the persecuted French presbyterians met in a different place every year. Delegated pastors there gathered from every quarter. From Northern France came men used to live in constant hazard of their lives; from Paris, confessors such as Merlin, the chaplain who, léaving Coligny's bedside, had been hidden for three days in a hayloft, feeding on the eggs that a hen daily laid beside him; army-chaplains were there who had passionately led battle-psalms ere their colleagues charged the foe, and had striven with vain endeavours to render their soldiers saints; while other pastors came from Pyrenean villages where their generation had never seen flames lighted against heresy, nor knew what it was to disperse a congregation in haste and secrecy for fear of the enemy.

The audience was large and sympathising. Montauban had become the refuge of many Huguenot families who could nowhere else profess their faith without constant danger; and a large proportion of these were ladies, wives of gentlemen in the army kept up by La Noue, or widows who feared that their children might be taken from them to be brought up by their Catholic relations, elderly dames who longed for tranquillity after having lost husbands or sons by civil war. Thickly they lodged in the strangely named *gasches* and *vertiers*, as the divisions and subdivisions of the city were termed, occupying floors or apartments of the tall old houses; walking abroad in the streets in grave attire, stiff hat, crimped ruff, and huge fan, and forming a society in themselves, close-packed, punctilious and dignified, rigidly devout but strictly censorious, and altogether as unlike their typical countryfolks of Paris as if they had belonged to a different nation. And the sourest and most severe of all were such as had lived farthest south, and personally suffered the least peril and alarm.

Dancing was an unheard-of enormity; cards and dice were

prohibited; any stronger expletive than the elegant ones invented for the special use of the King of Navarre was expiated either by the purse or the skin; Marot's psalmody was the only music, black or sad colour the only wear; and, a few years later, the wife of one of the most distinguished statesmen and councillors of Henri of Navarre was excommunicated for the enormity of wearing her hair curled.

To such a community it was a delightful festival to receive a national assembly of ministers ready to regale them on daily sermons for a whole month, and to retail in private the points of discipline debated in the public assembly; and, apart from mere eagerness for novelty, many a discreet heart beat with gladness at the meeting with the hunted pastor of her native home, who had been the first to strike the spiritual chord, and awake her mind to religion.

Every family had their honoured guest, every reception-room was in turn the scene of some pious little assembly that drank *eau sucrée*, and rejoiced in its favourite pastor; and each little congress indulged in gentle scandal against its rival coterie. But there was one point on which all the ladies agreed,—namely, that good Maître Isaac Gardon had fallen into an almost doting state of blindness to the vanities of his daughter-in-law, and that she was a disgrace to the community, and ought to be publicly reprimanded.

Isaac Gardon, long reported to have been martyred—some said at Paris, others averred at La Sablerie—had indeed been welcomed with enthusiastic joy and veneration, when he made his appearance at Montauban, pale, aged, bent, leaning on a staff, and showing the dire effect of the rheumatic fever which had prostrated him after the night of drenching and exposure during the escape from La Sablerie. Crowded as the city was, there was a perfect competition among the tradesfolk for the honour of entertaining him and the young widow and child of a St. Bartholomew martyr. A cordwainer of the street of the *Soubirous Hauts* obtained this honour, and the wife, though speaking only the sweet Provençal tongue, soon established the most friendly relations with M. Gardon's daughter-in-law.

Two or three more pastors likewise lodged in the same house, and ready aid was given by Mademoiselle Gardon, as all called Eustacie, in the domestic cares thus entailed, while her filial attention to her father-in-law and her sweet tenderness to her child struck all this home circle with admiration. Children of that age were seldom seen at home among the better classes in towns. Then, as now, they were universally consigned to country-nurses, who only brought them home at three or four years old, fresh from a squalid, neglected cottage life: and Eustacie's little moonbeam, *la petite Rayonette*, as she loved to call her, was quite an unusual spectacle; and from having lived entirely with grown people, and enjoyed the most tender and dainty care, she was intelligent and brightly docile to a degree that appeared marvellous to those who only saw children stupified by a contrary system. She was a lovely little thing, exquisitely fair, and her plump white limbs small but perfectly moulded; she was always happy, because always healthy, and living in an atmosphere of love; and she was the pet and wonder of all the household, from the grinning apprentice to the grave young candidate who hoped to be elected pastor to the Duke de Quinet's village in the Cévennes.

And yet it was *la petite Rayonette* who first brought her mother into trouble. Since her emancipation from swaddling-clothes she had been equipped in a little grey woollen frock, such as Eustacie had learnt to knit among the peasants, and varied with broad white stripes which gave it something of the moonbeam effect; but the mother had not been able to resist the pleasure of drawing up the bosom and tying it with a knot of the very carnation colour that Berenger used to call her own. That knot was discussed all up and down the Rue Soubirous Hauts, and even through the Carriera Major! The widow of an old friend of Maître Gardon had remonstrated on the improprieties of such gay vanities, and Mdlle. Gardon had actually replied, reddening with insolence, that her husband had loved to see her wear the colour.

Now, if the brethren at Paris had indulged their daughters in such backslidings, see what had come of it! But that poor Théodore Gardon should have admired his bride in such unhallowed adornments, was an evident calumny; and many a head was shaken over it in grave and pious assembly.

Worse still; when she had been invited to a supper at the excellent Madame Fargeau's, the presumptuous little *bourgeoise* had evidently not known her place, but had seated herself as if she were a noble lady, a *fille de qualité*, instead of a mere minister's widow and a watchmaker's daughter. Pretend ignorance that precedence was to be here observed! That was another Parisian piece of impudence, above all in one who showed such ridiculous airs as to wipe her face with her own handkerchief instead of the table-cloth, and to be reluctant to help herself from the general dish of *potage* with her own spoon. Even that might have been overlooked if she would have regaled them with a full and particular account of her own rescue from the massacre at Paris; but she merely coloured up, and said that she had been so ill as to know scarcely anything about it; and when they pressed her further, she shortly said, "They locked me up;" and, before she could be cross-examined as to who was this "they," Maître Gardon interfered, saying that she had suffered so much that he requested the subject might never be mentioned to her. Nor would he be more explicit, and there was evidently some mystery, and he was becoming blindly indulgent and besotted by the blandishments of an artful woman.

Eustacie was saved from hearing the gossip by her ignorance of the Provençal, which was the only language of all but the highest and most cultivated classes. The hostess had very little *langue d'oui*, and never ventured on any complicated discourse; and Isaac Gardon, who could speak both the *oc* and *oui*, was not a person whom it was easy to beset with mere hearsay or petty remonstrance, but enough reached him at last to make him one day say mildly, "My dear child, might not the little one dispense with her ribbon while we are here?"

"Eh, father? At the bidding of those impertinents?"

"Take care, daughter; you were perfect with the tradesfolk and peasants, but you cannot comport yourself as successfully with this *petite noblesse*, or the pastors' wives."

"They are insolent, father. I, in my own true person, would treat no one as these petty dames treat me," said Eustacie. "I would not meddle between a peasant woman and her child, nor ask questions that must needs wring her heart."

"Ah, child! humility is a bitter lesson; and even this world needs it now from you. We shall have suspicions; and I heard to-day that the King is in Dauphiny, and with him M. de Nid-de-Merle. Be not alarmed; he has no force with him, and the peace still subsists; but we must avoid suspicion. There is a *prêche* at the Moustier to-day, in French; it would be well if you were to attend it."

"I understand as little of French sermons as of Provençal," murmured Eustacie; but it was only a murmur.

Maître Gardon had soon found out that his charge had not head enough to be made a thorough-going controversial

Calvinist. Clever, intelligent, and full of resources as she was, she had no capacity for argument, and could not enter into theoretical religion. Circumstances had driven her from her original Church and alienated her from those who had practised such personal cruelties on her and hers, but the mould of her mind remained what it had been previously; she clung to the Huguenots because they protected her from those who would have forced an abhorrent marriage on her and snatched her child from her; and, personally, she loved and venerated Isaac Gardon with ardent, self-sacrificing filial love and gratitude, accepted as truth all that came from his lips, read the Scriptures, sang and prayed with him, and obeyed him as dutifully as ever the true Espérance could have done; but, except the merest external objections against the grossest and most palpable popular corruptions and fallacies, she really never entered into the matter. She had been left too ignorant of her own system to perceive its true claims upon her; and though she could not help preferring High Mass to a Calvinist assembly, and shrinking with instinctive pain and horror at the many profanations she witnessed, the really spiritual leadings of her own individual father-like leader had opened so much that was new and precious to her, so full of truth, so full of comfort, giving so much moral strength, that, unaware that all the foundations had been laid by Mère Monique, the resolute, high-spirited little thing, out of sheer constancy and constitutional courage, would have laid down her life as a Calvinist martyr, in profound ignorance that she was not in the least a Calvinist all the time.

Hitherto, her wandering life amid the persecuted Huguenots of the West had prevented her from hearing any preaching but good Isaac's own, which had been rather in the way of comfort and encouragement than of controversy, but in this great gathering it was impossible that there should not be plenty of vehement polemical oratory, such as was sure to fly over that weary little head. After a specimen or two, the chances of the sermon being in Provençal, and the necessity of attending to her child, had been Eustacie's excuse for usually offering to attend to the *ménage*, and set her hostess free to be present at the preachings.

However, Rayonette was considered as no valid excuse; for did not whole circles of black-eyed children sit on the floor in sleepy stolidity at the feet of their mothers or nurses, and was it not a mere worldly folly to pretend that a child of sixteen months could not be brought to church? It was another instance of the mother's frivolity and the grandfather's idolatry.

The Moustier, or minster, the monastic church of Montauban, built on Mont Auriol in honour of St. Théodore, had, twelve years before, been plundered and sacked by the Calvinists, not only out of zeal for iconoclasm, but from long-standing hatred and jealousy against the monks. Catherine de Médicis had, in 1546, carried off two of the jasper columns from its chief doorway to the Louvre; and, after some years more, it was entirely destroyed. The grounds of the Auriol Mountain Monastery have been desolate down to the present day, when they have been formed into public gardens. When Eustacie walked through them, carrying her little girl in her arms, a rose in her bosom to console her for the loss of her bright breast-knot, they were in raw fresh dreariness, with tottering, blackened cloisters, garden flowers run wild, images that she had never ceased to regard as sacred lying broken and defiled among the grass and weeds.

Up the broad path was pacing the municipal procession, headed by the three Consuls, each with a serjeant bearing a white rod in front and a scarlet mantle, and the Consuls themselves in long robes with wide sleeves of quartered black and scarlet, followed by six halberdiers, likewise in scarlet, blazoned with the shield of the city — gules, a golden willow-tree, pollarded and shedding its branches, a chief azure with the three fleur-de-lys of royalty. As little Rayonette gleefully pointed at the brilliant pageant, Eustacie could not help saying, rather bitterly, that these *messieurs* seemed to wish to engross all the gay colours from heaven and earth for themselves; and Maître Isaac could not help thinking she had some right on her side as he entered the church once gorgeous with jaspers, marbles, and mosaics, glowing with painted glass, resplendent with gold and jewels, rich with paintings and draperies of the most brilliant dyes; but now, all that was not an essential part of the fabric utterly gone, and all that was, soiled, dulled, defaced; the whole building, even up to the end of the chancel, was closely fitted with benches occupied by the "sad-coloured" congregation. Isaac was obliged by a strenuous effort of memory to recall "Nehushtan" and the golden calves, before he could clear from his mind, "Now they break down all the carved work thereof with axes and with hammers." But, then, did not the thorough-going Reformers think Master Isaac a very weak and backsliding brother?

Nevertheless, in right of his age, his former reputation, and his sufferings, his place was full in the midst of the square-capped, black-robed ministers who sat herded on a sort of platform together, to address the Almighty and the congregation in prayers and discourses, interspersed with psalms sung by the whole assembly. There was no want of piety, depth, force, or fervour. These were men refined by persecution, who had struggled to the light that had been darkened by the popular system, and, having once been forced into foregoing their scruples as to breaking the unity of the Church, regarded themselves even as apostles of the truth. Listening to them, Isaac Gardon felt himself rapt into the hopes of cleansing, the aspirations of universal re-integration that had shone before his early youth, ere the Church had shown herself deaf, and the Reformers in losing patience had lost purity, and disappointment had crushed him into an aged man.

He was recalled by the echo of a gay, little inarticulate cry —those baby tones that had become such music to his ears that he hardly realized that they were not indeed from his grandchild. In a moment's glance he saw how it was. A little bird had flown in at one of the empty windows, and was fluttering over the heads of the congregation, and a small, plump, white arm and hand was stretched out and pointing—a rosy, fair, smiling face upturned; a little grey figure had scrambled up on the knee of one of the still, black-hooded women; and the shout of irrepressible delight was breaking on the decorum of the congregation, in spite of hushes, in spite of the uplifted rod of a scarlet serjeant on his way down the aisle to quell the disturbance; nay, as the bird came nearer, the exulting voice, proud of the achievement of a new word, shouted "*Moineau, moineau.*" Angered by defiance to authority, down came the rod, not indeed with great force, but with enough to make the arms clasp round the mother's neck, the face hide itself on it, a loud, terrified wail ring through the church, and tempestuous sobbing follow it up. Then uprose the black-hooded figure, the child tightly clasped, and her mantle drawn round it, while the other hand motioned the official aside, and down the aisle, even to the door, she swept with the lofty carriage, high-drawn neck, and swelling bosom of an offended princess.

Maître Gardon heard little more of the discourse, indeed

he would have followed at once had he not feared to increase the sensation and the scandal. He came home to find Rayonette's tears long ago dried, but her mother furious. She would leave Montauban that minute, she would never set foot in a heretic conventicle again, to have her fatherless child, daughter of all the Ribaumonts, struck by base *canaille*. Even her uncle could not have done worse; he at least would have respected her blood.

Maître Gardon did not know that his charge could be in such a passion, as, her eyes flashing through tears, she insisted on being taken away at once. No, she would hear nothing. She seemed to feel resentment due to the honour of all the Ribaumonts, and he was obliged peremptorily to refuse to quit Montauban till his business at the Synod should be completed, and then to leave her in a flood of angry tears and reproaches for exposing her child to such usage, and approving it.

Poor little thing, he found her meek and penitent for her unjust anger towards himself. Whatever he desired she would do, she would stay or go with him anywhere except to a sermon at the Moustier, and she did not think that in her heart her good father desired little infants to be beaten—least of all, Berenger's little one. And with Rayonette already on his knee, stealing his spectacles, peace was made.

Peace with him, but not with the congregation! Were people to stalk out of church in a rage, and make no reparation? Was Maître Isaac to talk of orphans, only children, and maternal love, as if weak human affection did not need chastisement? Was this saucy Parisienne to play the offended, and say that if the child were not suffered at church she must stay at home with it? The ladies agitated to have the obnoxious young widow reprimanded in open Synod, but, to their still greater disgust, not a pastor would consent to perform the office. Some said that Maître Gardon ought to rule his own household, others that they respected him too much to interfere, and there were others abandoned enough to assert that if any one needed a reprimand it was the serjeant.

Of these was the young candidate, Samuel Macé, who had been educated at the expense of the Dowager Duchess de Quinet, and hoped that her influence would obtain his election to the pastorate of a certain peaceful little village deep in the Cévennes. She had intimated that what he wanted was a wife to teach and improve the wives of the peasant farmers, and where could a more eligible one be found than Espérance Gardon? Her cookery he tasted, her industry he saw, her tenderness to her child, her attention to her father, were his daily admiration; and her soft velvet eyes and sweet smile went so deep in his heart that he would have bought her ells upon ells of pink ribbon, when once out of sight of the old ladies; would have given a father's love to her little daughter, and a son's duty and veneration to Isaac Gardon.

His patroness did not deny her approval. The gossip had indeed reached her, but she had a high esteem for Isaac Gardon, believed in Samuel Macé's good sense, and heeded Montauban scandal very little. Her *protégé* would be much better married to a spirited woman who had seen the world than to a mere farmer's daughter who had never looked beyond her cheese. Old Gardon would be an admirable adviser, and if he were taken into the *ménage* she would add to the endowment another arable field, and grass for two more cows. If she liked the young woman on inspection, the marriage should take place in her own august presence.

What! had Maître Gardon refused? Forbidden that the subject should be mentioned to his daughter? Impossible!

Either Macé had managed matters foolishly, or the old man had some doubt of him which she could remove, or else it was foolish reluctance to part with his daughter-in-law. Or the gossips were right after all, and he knew her to be too light-minded, if not worse, to be the wife of any pious young minister. Or there was some mystery. Any way, Madame la Duchesse would see him, and bring him to his senses, make him give the girl a good husband if she were worthy, or devote her to condign punishment if she were unworthy.

CHAPTER XXXIV.

MADAME LA DUCHESSE.

"He found an ancient dame in dim brocade."

TENNYSON.

MADAME LA DUCHESSE DE QUINET had been a great heiress and a personal friend and favourite of Queen Jeanne d'Albret. She had been left a widow after five years' marriage, and for forty subsequent years had reigned despotically in her own name and that of *mon fils.* Busied with the support of the Huguenot cause, sometimes by arms, but more usually by politics, and constantly occupied by the hereditary government of one of the lesser counties of France, the Duke was all the better son for relinquishing to her the home administration, as well as the education of his two motherless boys; and their confidence and affection were perfect, though he was almost as seldom at home as she was abroad. At times, indeed, she had visited Queen Jeanne at Nérac; but since the good Queen's death, she only left the great chateau of Quinet to make a royal progress of inspection through the family towns, castles, and estates, sometimes to winter in her beautiful hereditary *hôtel* at Montauban, and as at present to attend any great assembly of the Reformed.

Very seldom was her will not law. Strong sense and judgment, backed by the learning that Queen Marguerite of

Navarre had introduced among the companions of her daughter, had rendered her superior to most of those with whom she came in contact: and the Huguenot ministers, who were much more dependent on their laity than the Catholic priesthood, for the most part treated her as not only a devout and honourable woman, an elect lady, but as a sort of State authority. That she had the right-mindedness to respect and esteem such men as Théodore Beza, Merlin, &c. who treated her with great regard, but never cringed, had not become known to the rest. Let her have once pronounced against poor little Espérance Gardon, and public disgrace would be a matter of certainty.

There she sat in her wainscoted walnut cabinet, a small woman by her inches, but stately enough to seem of majestic stature, and with grey eyes, of inexpressible keenness, which she fixed upon the halting, broken form of Isaac Gardon, and his grave, venerable face, as she half rose and made a slight acknowledgment of his low bow.

"Sit, Maître Gardon, you are lame," she said, with a wave of her hand. "I gave you the incommodity of coming to see me here, because I imagined that there were matters you would not openly discuss *en pleine salle.*"

"Madame is considerate," said Isaac, civilly, but with an open-eyed look and air that at once showed her that she had not to deal with one of the ministers who never forgot their low birth in intercourse with her.

"I understand," said she, coming to the point at once, "that you decline the proposals of Samuel Macé for your daughter-in-law. Now I wish you to know that Macé is a very good youth, whom I have known from his birth"—and she went on in his praise, Isaac bowing at each pause, until she had exhausted both Macé's history and her own beneficent intentions for him. Then he said, "Madame is very good, and the young man appeared to me excellent. Nevertheless, this thing may not be. My daughter-in-law has resolved not to marry again."

"Nay, but this is mere folly," said the Duchess. "We hold not Catholic tenets on merit in abstaining, but rather go by St. Paul's advice that the younger widows should marry, rather than wax wanton. And, to tell you the truth, Maître Gardon, this daughter of yours does seem to have set tongues in motion."

"Not by her own fault, Madame."

"Stay, my good friend; I never found a man—minister or lay—who was a fair judge in these matters. You old men are no better than the young—rather worse—because you do not distrust yourselves. Now, I say no harm of the young woman, and I know an angel would be abused at Montauban for not wearing sad-coloured wings; but she needs a man's care—you are frail, you cannot live for ever—and how is it to be with her and her child?"

"I hope to bestow them among her kindred ere I die, Madame," said Isaac.

"No kindred can serve a woman like a sensible husband! Besides, I thought all perished at Paris. Listen, Isaac Gardon: I tell you plainly that scandal is afloat. You are blamed for culpable indifference to alleged levities—I say not that it is true—but I see this, that unless you can bestow your daughter-in-law on a good, honest man, able to silence the whispers of malice, there will be measures taken that will do shame both to your own grey hairs and to the memory of your dead son, as well as expose the poor young woman herself. You are one who has a true tongue, Isaac Gardon; and if you can assure me that she is a faithful, good woman, as poor Macé thinks her, and will give her to him in testimony thereof, then shall not a mouth open against her. If not, in spite of all my esteem for you, the discipline of the Reformed must take its course."

"And for what?" said Isaac, with a grave tone, almost of reproof. "What discipline can punish a woman for letting her infant wear a coloured ribbon, and shielding it from a blow?"

"That is not all, Master Isaac," said the Duchess, seriously. "In spite of your much-respected name, evil and censorious tongues will have it that matters ought to be investigated; that there is some mystery; that the young woman does not give a satisfactory account of herself, and that the child does not resemble either her or your son—in short, that you may be deceived by an impostor, perhaps a Catholic spy. Mind, I say not that I credit all this, only I would show you what reports you must guard against."

"*La pauvre petite!*" said Isaac, under his breath, as if appalled; then collecting himself, he said, "Madame, these are well-nigh threats. I had come hither nearly resolved to confide in you without them."

"Then there is a mystery?"

"Yes, Madame, but the deception is solely in the name. She is, in very truth, a widow of a martyr of the St.-Barthélemy, but that martyr was not my son, whose wife was happy in dying with him."

"And who, then, is she?"

"Madame la Duchesse has heard of the family of Ribaumont."

"Ha! M. de Ribaumont! A gay comrade of King Henry II., but who had his eyes opened to the truth by M. l'Amiral, though he lacked courage for an open profession. Yes, the very last pageant I beheld at Court, was the wedding of his little son to the Count de Ribaumont's daughter. It was said that the youth was one of our victims at Paris."

"Even so, Madame; and this poor child is the little one whom you saw wedded to him." And then, in answer to the Duchess's astonished inquiry, he proceeded to relate how Eustacie had been forced to fly from her kindred, and how he had first encountered her at his own lurking-place, and had accepted her as a charge imposed on him by Providence; then explained how, at La Sablerie, she had been recognised by a young gentleman whom she had known at Paris, but who professed to be fleeing to England, there to study the Protestant controversy; and how she had confided to him a letter to her husband's mother, who was married in England, begging her to send for her and her daughter, the latter being heiress to certain English estates, as well as French.

"Madame," added Gardon, "Heaven forgive me, if I do the youth injustice by suspecting him, but no answer ever arrived to that letter; and while we still expected one, a good and kindly citizen, who I trust has long been received into glory, sent me notice that a detachment of Monsieur's army was on its way from La Rochelle, under command of M. de Nid-de-Merle, to search out this poor lady in La Sablerie. He, good man, deemed that, were we gone, he could make terms for the place, and we therefore quitted it. Alas! Madame knows how it fared with the pious friends we left. Little deeming how they would be dealt with, we took our way along the Sables d'Olonne, where alone we could be safe, since, as Madame knows, they are for miles impracticable for troops. But we had another enemy there—the tide; and there was a time when we truly deemed that the mercy granted us had been that we had fallen into the hand of the Lord instead of the hand of cruel man. Yes, Madame, and even for that did she give thanks, as she stood, never even trembling, on the low sandbank, with her babe in her bosom, and the sea creeping up on all sides. She only turned to me with a smile, saying, 'She is asleep, she will not feel it, or know anything till she wakes up in Paradise, and sees her father.' Never saw I a woman, either through nature or grace, so devoid of fear. We were rescued at last, by the mercy of Heaven, which sent a fisherman, who bore us to his boat when benumbed with cold, and scarce able to move. He took us to a good priest's, Colombeau of Nissard, a man who, as Madame may know, is one of those veritable saints who still are sustained by the truth within their Church, and is full of charity and mercy. He asked me no questions, but fed, warmed, sheltered us, and sped us on our way. Perhaps, however, I was over-confident in myself, as the guardian of the poor child, for it was Heaven's will that the cold and wet of our night on the sands — though those tender young frames did not suffer therefrom—should bring on an illness which has made an old man of me. I struggled on as long as I could, hoping to attain to a safe resting-place for her, but the winter cold completed the work; and then, Madame—oh that I could tell you the blessing she was to me!—her patience, her watchfulness, her tenderness, through all the long weeks that I lay helpless alike in mind and body at Charente. Ah! Madame, had my own daughter lived, she could not have been more to me than that noble lady; and her cheerful love did even more for me than her tender care."

"I must see her," ejaculated the Duchess; then added, "But was it this illness that hindered you from placing her in safety in England?"

"In part, Madame; nay, I may say, wholly. We learnt that the assembly was to take place here, and I had my poor testimony to deliver, and to give notice of my intention to my brethren before going to a foreign land, whence perhaps I may never return."

"She ought to be in England," said Madame de Quinet; "she will never be safe from these kinsmen in this country."

"M. de Nid-de-Merle has been all the spring in Poland with the King," said the minister, "and the poor lady is thought to have perished at La Sablerie. Thus the danger has been less pressing, but I would have taken her to England at once, if I could have made sure of her reception, and besides——" he faltered.

"The means?" demanded the Duchess, guessing at the meaning.

"Madame is right. She had brought away some money and jewels with her, but alas, Madame, during my illness, without my knowledge, the dear child absolutely sold them to procure comforts for me. Nay"— his eyes filled with tears—"she whom they blame for vanities, sold the very hair from her head to purchase unguents to ease the old man's pains; nor did I know it for many a day after. From day to day we can live, for our own people willingly support a pastor and his family; and in every house my daughter has been loved,—everywhere but in this harsh-judging town. But for the expense of a voyage, even were we at Bordeaux or La Rochelle, we have nothing, save by parting with the only jewels that remain to her, and those—those, she says, are heirlooms; and, poor child, she guards them almost as jealously as her infant, around whom she has fastened them beneath her clothes. She will not even as yet hear of leaving them in pledge, to be redeemed by the family. She says they would hardly know her without them. And truly, Madame, I scarce venture to take her to England, ere I know what reception would await her. Should her husband's family disown or cast her off, I could take better care of her here than in a strange land."

"You are right, Maître Gardon," said the Duchess; "the risk might be great. I would see this lady. She must be a rare creature. Bear her my greetings, my friend, and pray her to do me the honour of a visit this afternoon. Tell her I would come myself to her, but that I understand she does not wish to attract notice."

"Madame," said Isaac, rising, and with a strange manner, between a smile and a tear of earnestness, "allow me to bespeak your goodness for my daughter. The poor little thing is scarcely more than a child. She is but eighteen even now, and it is not always easy to tell whether she will be an angel of noble goodness, or, pardon me, a half-petulant child."

"I understand:" Madame de Quinet laughed, and she probably did understand more than reluctant, anxious Isaac Gardon thought she did, of his winning, gracious, yet haughty, headstrong, little charge, so humbly helpful one moment, so self-asserting and childish the next, so dear to him, yet so unlike anything in his experience.

"Child," he said, as he found her in the sunny window engaged in plaiting the deep folds of his starched ruffs, "you have something to forgive me."

"Fathers do not ask their children's pardon," said Eustacie, brightly, but then, with sudden dismay, "Ah! you have not said I should go to that Moustier again."

"No, daughter; but Madame de Quinet entreats—these are her words—that you will do her the honour of calling on her. She would come to you, but that she fears to attract notice to us."

"You have told her!" exclaimed Eustacie.

"I was compelled, but I had already thought of asking your consent, and she is a true and generous lady, with whom your secret will be safe, and who can hush the idle tongues here. So, daughter," he added restlessly, "don your hood; that ruff will serve for another day."

"Another day, when the morrow is Sunday, and my father's ruff is to put to shame all the other pastors'," said Eustacie, her quick fingers still moving. "No, he shall not go ill-starched for any Duchess in France. Nor am I in any haste to be lectured by Madame de Quinet, as they say she lectured the Dame de Soubrera the other day."

"My child, you will go; much depends on it."

"Oh yes, I am going; only if Madame de Quinet knows who I am, she will not expect me to hurry at her beck and call the first moment. Here, Rayonette, my bird, my beauty, thou must have a clean cap; ay, and these flaxen curls combed."

"Would you take the child?"

"Would I go without Mademoiselle de Ribaumont? She is all her mother is, and more. There, now she is a true rose-bud, ready to perch on my arm. No, no, *bon père.* So great a girl is too much for you to carry. Don't be afraid, my darling, we are not going to a sermon, no one will beat her; oh no, and if the insolent retainers and pert lacqueys laugh at her mother, no one will hurt her."

"Nay, child," said Maître Gardon; "this is a well-ordered household, where contempt and scorn are not suffered. Only, dear, dear daughter, let me pray you to be your true self with the Duchess."

Eustacie shrugged her shoulders, and had mischief enough in her to enjoy keeping her good father in some doubt and dread as he went halting wearily by her side along the much-decorated streets that marked the grand Gasche of Tarn and Tarascon. The Hôtel de Quinet stretched out its broad stone steps, covered with vaultings, absolutely across the street, affording a welcome shade, and no obstruction where wheeled carriages never came.

All was, as Maître Isaac had said, decorum itself. A couple of armed retainers, rigid as sentinels, waited on the steps; a grave porter, maimed in the wars, opened the great door; half a dozen *laquais* in sober though rich liveries sat on a bench in the hall, and had somewhat the air of having been set to con a lesson. Two of them coming respectfully forward, ushered Maître Gardon and his companion to an ante-room, where various gentlemen, or pastors, or candidates—among them Samuel Macé—were awaiting a summons to the Duchess, or merely using it as a place of assembly. A page of high birth, but well schooled in steadiness of demeanour, went at once to announce the arrival; and Gardon and his companion had not been many moments in conversation with their acquaintance among the ministers, before a grave gentleman returned, apparently from his audience, and the page, coming to Eustacie, intimated that she was to follow him to Madame la Duchesse's presence.

He conducted her across a great tapestry-hung saloon, where twelve or fourteen ladies of all ages—from seventy to fifteen—sat at work: some at tapestry, some spinning, some making coarse garments for the poor. A great throne-like chair, with a canopy over it, a footstool, a desk and a small table before it, was vacant, and the work—a poor child's knitted cap—laid down; but an elderly minister, seated at a carved desk, had not discontinued reading from a great black book, and did not even cease while the strangers crossed the room, merely making a slight inclination with his head, while the ladies half rose, rustled a slight reverence with their black, grey or russet skirts, but hardly lifted their eyes. Eustacie thought the Louvre had never been half so formidable or impressive.

The page lifted a heavy green curtain behind the canopy, knocked at a door, and, as it opened, Eustacie was conscious of a dignified presence, that, in spite of her previous petulance, caused her instinctively to bend in such a reverence as had formerly been natural to her; but, at the same moment, a low and magnificent curtsey was made to her, a hand was held out, a stately kiss was on her brow, and a voice of dignified courtesy said, "Pardon me, Madame la Baronne, for giving you this trouble. I feared that otherwise we could not safely meet."

"Madame is very good. My Rayonette, make thy reverence; kiss thy hand to the lady, my lamb." And the little one obeyed, gazing with her blue eyes full opened, and clinging to her mother.

"Ah! Madame la Baronne makes herself obeyed," said Madame de Quinet, well pleased. "Is it then a girl?"

"Yes, Madame, I could scarcely forgive her at first; but she has made herself all the dearer to me."

"It is a pity," said Madame de Quinet, "for yours is an ancient stem."

"Did Madame know my parents?" asked Eustacie, drawn from her spirit of defiance by the equality of the manner with which she was treated.

"Scarcely," replied the Duchess; but, with a smile, "I had the honour to see you married."

"Ah, then,"—Eustacie glowed, almost smiled, though a tear was in her eyes—"you can see how like my little one is to her father,—a true White Ribaumont."

The Duchess had not the most distinct recollection of the complexion of the little bridegroom; but Rayonette's fairness was incontestable, and the old lady complimented it so as to draw on the young mother into confidence on the pet moonbeam appellation which she used in dread of exciting suspicion by using the true name of Bérangère, with all the why and wherefore.

It was what the Duchess wanted. Imperious as some thought her, she would on no account have appeared to cross-examine any one whose essential nobleness of nature struck her as did little Eustacie's at the first moment she saw her; and yet she had decided, before the young woman arrived, that her own good opinion and assistance should depend on the correspondence of Madame de Ribaumont's history of herself with Maître Gardon's.

Eustacie had, for a year and a half, lived with peasants; and, indeed, since the trials of her life had really begun, she had never been with a woman of her own station to whom she could give confidence, or from whom she could look for sympathy. And thus a very few inquiries and tokens of interest from the old lady drew out the whole story, and more than once filled Madame de Quinet's eyes with tears.

There was only one discrepancy; Eustacie could not believe that the Abbé de Méricour had been a faithless messenger. Oh, no! Either those savage-looking sailors had played him false, or else her *belle-mère* would not send for her. "My mother-in-law never loved me," said Eustacie; "I know she never did. And now she has children by her second marriage, and no doubt would not see my little one preferred to them. I will not be *her* suppliant."

"And what then would you do?" said Madame de Quinet with a more severe tone.

"Never leave my dear father," said Eustacie, with a flash of eagerness; "Maître Isaac, I mean. He has been more to me than any—any one I ever knew—save ——"

"You have much cause for gratitude to him," said Madame de Quinet. "I honour your filial love to him. Yet, you have duties to this little one. You have no right to keep her from her position. You ought to write to England again. I am sure Maître Isaac tells you so."

Eustacie would have pouted, but the grave, kind authority of the manner prevented her from being childish, and she said, "If I wrote, it should be to my husband's grandfather, who brought him up, designated him as his heir, and whom he loved with all his heart. But, oh, Madame, he has one of those English names! So dreadful! It sounds like Vol-au-vent, but it is not that precisely."

Madame de Quinet smiled, but she was a woman of resources. "See, my friend," she said, "the pursuivant of the consuls here has the rolls of the herald's visitations throughout the kingdom. The arms and name of the Baron de Ribaumont's wife will there be entered; and from my house at Quinet you shall write, and I, too, will write; my son shall take care that the letters be forwarded safely, and you shall await their arrival under my protection. That will be more fitting than running the country with an old pastor, *hein?*"

"Madame, nothing shall induce me to quit him!" exclaimed Eustacie, vehemently.

"Hear me out, child," said the Duchess. "He goes with us to assist my chaplain; he is not much fitter for wandering than you, or less so. And you, Madame, must, I fear me, still remain his daughter-in-law in my household; or if you bore your own name and rank, this uncle and cousin of yours might learn that you were still living; and did they claim you——"

"Oh, Madame, rather let me be your meanest kitchen-girl!"

"To be—what do they call you?—Espérance Gardon will be quite enough. I have various women here—widows, wives, daughters of sufferers for the truth's sake, who either are glad of rest, or are trained up to lead a godly life in the discipline of my household. Among them you can live without suspicion, provided," the old lady added, smiling, "you can abstain from turning the heads of our poor young candidates."

"Madame," said Eustacie, gravely, "I shall never turn any one's head. There was only one who was obliged to love me, and happily I am not fair enough to win any one else."

"*Tenez*, child. Is this true simplicity? Did Gardon, truly, never tell you of poor Samuel Macé?"

Eustacie's face expressed such genuine amazement and consternation, that the Duchess could not help touching her on the cheek, and saying, "Ah! simple as a *pensionnaire*, as we used to say when no one else was innocent. But it is true, my dear, that to poor Samuel we owe our meeting. I will send him off, the poor fellow, at once to Bourg-le-Roy to preach his three sermons; and when they have driven you a little out of his head, he shall have Mariette there—a good girl, who will make him an excellent wife. She is ugly enough, but it will be all the same to him just then! I will see him, and let him know that I have reasons. He lodges in your house, does he? Then you had better come to me at once. So will evil tongues best be silenced."

"But hold," the Duchess said, smiling. "You will think me a foolish old woman, but is it true that you have saved the Pearls of Ribaumont, of which good Canon Froissart tells?"

Eustacie lifted her child on her knee, untied the little grey frock, and showed them fastened beneath, well out of sight. "I thought my treasures should guard one another," she said. "One I sent as a token to my mother-in-law. For the rest, they are not mine, but hers; her father lent them to me, not gave: so she wears them thus; and anything but *her* life should go rather than *they* should."

"*Hein*, a fine guardian for them!" was all the Duchess said in answer.

CHAPTER XXXV.

THE ITALIAN PEDLAR.

"This caitiff monk for gold did swear,
That by his drugs my rival fair
A saint in heaven should be."
SCOTT.

A GRAND cavalcade bore the house of Quinet from Montauban—coaches, wagons, outriders, gendarmes—it was a perfect court progress, and so slow and cumbrous that it was a whole week in reaching a grand old castle standing on a hill-side among chestnut woods, with an avenue a mile long leading up to it; and battlemented towers fit to stand a siege.

Eustacie was ranked among the Duchess's gentlewomen. She was so far acknowledged as a lady of birth, that she was usually called Madame Espérance; and though no one was supposed to doubt her being Théodore Gardon's widow, she was regarded as being a person of rank who had made a misalliance by marrying him. This Madame de Quinet had allowed the household to infer, thinking that the whole bearing of her guest was too unlike that of a Paris *bourgeoise* not to excite suspicion, but she deemed it wiser to refrain from treating her with either intimacy or distinction that might excite jealousy or suspicion. Even as it was, the consciousness of a secret, or the remnants of Montauban gossip, prevented any familiarity between Eustacie and the good ladies who surrounded her; they were very civil to each other, but their only connecting link was the delight that every one took in petting pretty little Rayonette, and the wonder that was made of her signs of intelligence and attempts at talking. Even when she toddled fearlessly up to the stately Duchess on her canopied throne, and held out her entreating hands, and lisped the word "*montre*," Madame would pause in her avocations, take her on her knee, and display that wonderful gold and enamel creature which cried tic-tic, and still remained an unapproachable mystery to M. le Marquis and M. le Vicomte, her grandsons.

Pale, formal stiff boys they looked, twelve and ten years old, and under the dominion of a very learned tutor, who taught them Latin, Greek and Hebrew, alternately with an equally precise, stiff old esquire, who trained them in martial exercises, which seemed to be as much matters of rote with them as their tasks, and to be quite as uninteresting. It did not seem as if they ever played, or thought of playing; and if they were ever to be gay, witty Frenchmen, a wonderful change must come over them.

The elder was already betrothed to a Béarnese damsel, of an unimpeachably ancient and Calvinistic family; and the whole establishment had for the last three years been employed on tapestry hangings for a whole suite of rooms, that were to be fitted up and hung with the histories of Ruth, of Abigail, of the Shunammite, and of Esther, which their diligent needles might hope to complete by the time the marriage should take place, three years later! The Duchess, who really was not unlike "that great woman" the Shunammite, in her dignified content with "dwelling among her own people," and her desire to "receive a prophet in the name of a prophet," generally sat presiding over the work while some one, chaplain, grandson, or young maiden, read aloud from carefully assorted books; religious treatises at certain hours, and at others, history. Often, however, Madame was called away into her cabinet, where she gave audience to intendants, notaries from her estates, pastors from the villages, captains of little garrisons, soldiers offering service, farmers, women, shepherds, foresters, peasants, who came either on her business or with their own needs—for all of which she was ready with the beneficence and decision of an autocrat.

The chapel had been "purified," and made bare of all altar or image. It was filled with benches and a desk, whence Isaac Gardon, the chaplain, any pastor on a visit, or sometimes a candidate for his promotion, would expound, and offer prayers, shortly in the week, more at length on Sunday; and there, too, classes were held for the instruction of the peasants.

There was a great garden full of medicinal plants, and decoctions and distilleries were the chief variety enjoyed by the gentlewomen. The Duchess had studied much in quaint Latin and French medical books, and, having great experience and good sense, was probably as good a doctor as any one in the kingdom except Ambroise Paré and his pupils; and she required her ladies to practise under her upon the numerous ailments that the peasants were continually bringing for her treatment. "No one could tell," she said, "how soon they might be dealing with gun-shot wounds, and all ought to know how to sew up a gash, or cure an ague."

This department suited Eustacie much better than the stitching, and best of all she liked to be sent with Maître Isaac to some cottage where solace for soul and body were needed, and the inmate was too ill to be brought to Madame la Duchesse. She was learning much and improving too in the orderly household, but her wanderings had made her something of a little gipsy. She now and then was intolerably weary, and felt as if she had been entirely spoilt for her natural post. "What would become of her," she said to Maître Isaac, "if she were too grand to dress Rayonette?"

She was not greatly distressed that the Montauban pursuivant turned out to have only the records of the Provençal nobility, and was forced to communicate with his brethren at Bordeaux before he could bring down the Ribaumont genealogy to the actual generation; and so slow was communication, so tardy the mode of doing everything, that the chestnut leaves were falling and autumn becoming winter before the blazoned letter showed Ribaumont, de Picardie—"Gules, fretty or, a canton of the last, a leopard, sable. Eustache Béranger, m. Annora, daughter and heiress of Villiam, Baron of Valvem, in the county of Dorisette, England, who beareth, azure, a syren regardant in a mirror proper." The syren was drawn in all her propriety impaled with the leopard, and she was so much more comprehensible than the names, to both Madame de Quinet and Eustacie, that it was a pity they could not direct their letters to her rather than to "Le Baron de Valvem," whose cruel W's perplexed them so much. However, the address was the least of Eustacie's troubles; she should be only too glad when she got to that, and she was sitting in Maître Isaac's room, trying to make him dictate her sentences and asking him how to spell every third word, when the dinner bell rang, and the whole household dropped down from *salon*, library, study, or chamber to the huge hall, with its pavement of black and white marble, and its long tables, for Madame de Quinet was no woman to discard wholesome old practices.

Then, as Eustacie, with Rayonette trotting at her side, and Maître Isaac leaning on her arm, slowly made her way to that high table where dined Madame la Duchesse, her grandsons, the ministers, the gentlemen in waiting, and some three or four women besides herself, she saw that the lower end of the great hall was full of silks, cloths, and ribbons heaped together; and, passing by the lengthy rank of retainers, she received a bow and look of recognition from a dark, acute-looking visage which she remembered to belong to the pedlar she had met at Charente.

The Duchess, at the head of her table, was not in the best of humours. Her son had sent home letters by a courier whom he had picked up for himself and she never liked nor trusted, and he required an immediate reply when she particularly resented being hurried. It was a *galimafré*, literally a hash, she said; for indeed most matters where she was not consulted, did become a *galimafré* with her. Moreover, under favour of the courier, her porters had admitted this pedlar, and the Duchess greatly disliked pedlars. All her household stores were bought at shops of good repute in Montauban, and no one ought to be so improvident as to require dealings with these mountebank vagabonds, who dangled vanities before the eyes of silly girls, and filled their heads with Paris fashions, if they did not do still worse, and excite them to the purchase of cosmetics and love-charms.

Yet the excitement caused by the approach of a pedlar was invincible, even by Madame la Duchesse. It was inevitable that the crying need of glove, kerchief, needle, or the like, should be discovered as soon as he came within ken, and, once in the hall, there was no being rid of him except by a flagrant act of inhospitality. This time, it was worst of all, for M. le Marquis himself must needs be the first to spy him, bring him in, and be in want of a silver chain for his hawk; and his brother the Vicomte must follow him up with all manner of wants inspired by the mere sight of the pack.

Every one with the smallest sum of money must buy, every one without inspect and assist in bargaining; and all dinner time, eyes, thoughts, and words were wandering to the gay pile in the corner, or reckoning up needs and means. The pedlar, too, knew what a Calvinist household was, and had been extremely discreet, producing nothing that could reasonably be objected to; and the Duchess, seeing that the stream was too strong for her, wisely tried to steer her bark through it safely instead of directly opposing it.

As soon as grace was over, she called her maître d'hôtel, and bade him look after that *galimafré*, and see that none of these fools were unreasonably cheated, and that there was no attempt at gulling the young ones with charms or fortune-telling, as well as to conclude the matter so as to give no excuse for the Italian fellow lingering to sup and sleep. She then retired to her cabinet to prepare her despatches, which were to include a letter to Lord Walwyn. Though a nominal friendship subsisted between Elizabeth and the French court, the Huguenot chiefs always maintained a correspondence with England, and there was little danger but that the Duke de Quinet would be able to get a letter, sooner or later, conveyed to any man of mark. In the course of her letter, Madame de Quinet found it necessary to refer to Eustacie. She rang her little silver handbell for the little foot-page, who usually waited outside her door. He appeared not. She rang again, and receiving no answer, opened her door and sallied forth, a wrathful dame, into the hall. There, of course, Master Page had been engulfed in the *galimafré*, and not only forming one of the swarm around the pedlar, but was actually aping courtly grimaces as he tried a delicate lace ruffle on the hand of a silly little smirking maiden, no older than himself! But this little episode was, like many others, overlooked by Madame de Quinet, as her eye fell upon the little figure of Rayonette standing on the table, with her mother and two or three ladies besides coaxing her to open her mouth, and show the swollen gums that had of late been troubling her, while the pedlar was evidently expending his blandishments upon her.

The maître d'hôtel was the first to perceive his mistress, and, as he approached, received a sharp rebuke from her for allowing the fellow to produce his quack medicines; and, at the same time, she desired him to request Madame Espérance to come to her immediately on business. Eustacie, who always had a certain self-willed sense of opposition when the Duchess showed herself peremptory towards her, at first began to make answer that she would come as soon as her business was concluded; but the steward made a gesture towards the great lady sailing up and down as she paced the daïs in stately impatience. "Good fellow," she said, "I will return quickly, and see you again, though I am now interrupted. Stay there, little one, with good Mademoiselle Perrot; mother will soon be back."

Rayonette, in her tooth-fretfulness, was far from enduring to be forsaken so near a strange man, and her cry made it necessary for Eustacie to take her in arms, and carry her to the daïs where the Duchess was waiting.

"So!" said the lady, "I suspected that the fellow was a quack as well as a cheat."

"Madame," said Eustacie, with spirit, "he sold me unguents that greatly relieved my father last spring."

"And because rubbing relieved an old man's rheumatics, you would let a vagabond cheat drug and sicken this poor child for what is no ailment at all—and the teeth will relieve in a few days. Or, if she were feverish, have not we decoctions brewed from heaven's own pure herbs in the garden, with no unknown ingredient?"

"Madame," said Eustacie, ruffling into fierceness, "you are very good to me; but I must keep the management of my daughter to myself."

The Duchess looked at her from head to foot. Perhaps it was with an impulse to treat her impertinence as she would have done that of a dependant; but the old lady never forgot herself: she only shrugged her shoulders and said, with studied politeness, "When I unfortunately interrupted your consultation with this eminent physician, it was to ask you a question regarding this English family. Will you do me the honour to enter my cabinet?"

And whereas no one was looking, the old lady showed her displeasure by ushering Madame de Ribaumont into her cabinet like a true noble stranger guest; so that Eustacie felt disconcerted.

The Duchess then began to read aloud her own letter to Lord Walwyn, pausing at every clause, so that Eustacie felt the delay and discussion growing interminable, and the Duchess then requested to have Madame de Ribaumont's own letter at once, as she wished to inclose it, make up her packet, and send it without delay. Opening a secret door in her cabinet, she showed Eustacie a stair by which she might reach Maître Gardon's room without crossing the hall. Eustacie hoped to find him there and tell him how intolerable was the Duchess; but, though she found him, it was in company with the tutor, who was spending an afternoon on Plato with him. She could only take up her letter and retreat to Madame's cabinet, where she had left her child. She finished it as best she might, addressed it after the herald's spelling of the title, bound it with some of the

Duchess's black floss silk—wondering meanwhile, but little guessing that the pedlar knew, where was the tress that had bound her last attempt at correspondence, guessing least of all that that tress lay on a heart still living and throbbing for her. All this had made her a little forget her haste to assert her liberty of action by returning to the pedlar; but, behold, when she came back to the hall, it had resumed its pristine soberness, and merely a few lingering figures were to be seen, packing up their purchases.

While she was still looking round in dismay, Mademoiselle Perrot came up to her and said, "Ah! Madame, you may well wonder! I never saw Maître Benoît there so cross; the poor man did but offer to sell little Fanchon the elixir that secures a good husband, and old Benoît descended on him like a griffin enraged, would scarce give him time to compute his charges or pack his wares, but hustled him forth like a mere thief! And I missed my bargain for that muffler that had so taken my fancy. But, Madame, he spoke to me apart, and said you were an old customer of his, and that rather than the little angel should suffer with her teeth, which surely threaten convulsions, he would leave with you this sovereign remedy of sweet syrup—a spoonful to be given each night."

Eustacie took the little flask. She was much inclined to give the syrup by way of precaution, as well as to assure herself that she was not under the Duchess's dominion; but some strong instinct of the truth of the lady's words that the child was safer and healthier undoctored, made her resolve at least to defer it until the little one showed any perilous symptom. And as happily Rayonette only showed two little white teeth, and much greater good humour, the syrup was nearly forgotten, when, a fortnight after, the Duchess received a despatch from her son which filled her with the utmost indignation. The courier had indeed arrived, but the packet had proved to be filled with hay and waste paper. And upon close examination, under the lash, the courier had been forced to confess to having allowed himself to be overtaken by the pedlar, and treated by him to a supper at a *cabaret*. No doubt, while he was afterwards asleep, the contents of his packet had been abstracted. There had been important documents for the Duke besides Eustacie's letters, and the affair greatly annoyed the Duchess, though she had the compensation of having been proved perfectly right in her prejudice against pedlars, and her dislike of her son's courier. She sent for Eustacie to tell her privately of the loss, and of course the young mother at once turned pale and exclaimed, "The wicked one! Ah! what a blessing that I gave my little darling none of his dose!"

"*Hein?* You had some from him then!" demanded the Duchess with displeasure.

"No, Madame, thanks, thanks to you. Oh! I never will be self-willed and naughty again. Forgive me, Madame." And down she dropped on her knee, with clasped hands and glistening eyes.

"Forgive you, silly child, for what?" said Madame de Quinet, nearly laughing.

"Ah! for the angry, passionate thoughts I had! Ah! Madame, I was all but giving the stuff to my little angel in very spite—and then——" Eustacie's voice was drowned in a passion of tears, and she devoured the old lady's hand with her kisses.

"Come, come," said the Duchess, "let us be reasonable. A man may be a thief, but it does not follow that he is a poisoner."

"Nay, that will we see," cried Eustacie. "He was

resolved that the little lamb should not escape, and he left a flask for her with Mademoiselle Perrot. I will fetch it, if Madame will give me leave. Oh, the great mercy of Heaven that made her so well that I gave her none!"

Madame de Quinet's analytic powers did not go very far, and would probably have decided against the syrup if it had been nothing but virgin honey. She was one who fully believed that her dear Queen Jeanne had been poisoned with a pair of gloves, and she had unlimited faith in the powers of evil possessed by René of Milan. Of course, she detected the presence of a slow poison, whose effects would have been attributed to the ailment it was meant to cure; and though her evidence was insufficient, she probably did Ercole no injustice. She declined testing the compound on any unfortunate dog or cat, but sealed it up in the presence of Gardon, Eustacie, and Mademoiselle Perrot, to be produced against the pedlar if ever he should be caught.

Then she asked Eustacie if there was any reason to suspect that he recognised her. Eustacie related the former dealings with him, when she had sold him her jewels and her hair, but she had no notion of his being the same person whom she had seen when at Montpipeau. Indeed, he had altered his appearance so much that he had been only discovered at Nid-de-Merle by eyes sharpened by distrust of his pretensions to magic arts.

Madame de Quinet, however, concluded that Eustacie had been known, or else that her jewels had betrayed her, and that the man must have been employed by her enemies. If it had not been the depth of winter, she would have provided for the persecuted lady's immediate transmission to England; but the storms of the Bay of Biscay would have made this impossible in the state of French navigation, even if Isaac Gardon had been in a condition to move; for the first return of cold had brought back severe rheumatic pains, and with them came a shortness of breath, which even the Duchess did not know to be the token of heart complaint. He was confined to his room, and it was kneeling by his bedside that Eustacie poured out her thankfulness for her child's preservation, and her own repentance for the passing fit of self-will and petulance. The thought of Rayonette's safety seemed absolutely to extinguish the fresh anxiety that had arisen since it had become evident that her enemies no longer supposed her dead, but were probably upon her traces. Somehow, danger had become almost a natural element to her, and having once expressed her firm resolution that nothing should separate her from her adopted father, to whom indeed her care became constantly more necessary, she seemed to occupy herself very little with the matter; she nursed him as cheerfully and fondly, and played with Rayonette as merrily as ever, and left to him and Madame de Quinet the grave consultations as to what was to be done for her security. There was a sort of natural buoyancy about her that never realized a danger till it came, and then her spirit was roused to meet it.

CHAPTER XXXVI.

SPELL AND POTION.

> "Churl, upon thy eyes I throw
> All the power this charm doth owe."
>
> *Midsummer Night's Dream.*

HER rival lived! The tidings could not but be communicated to Diane de Selinville, when her father set out *en grande tenue* to demand his niece from the Duke de Quinet. This, however, was not till spring was advancing; for the pedlar had not been able to take a direct route back to Nid-de-Merle, since his first measure had necessarily been to escape into a province where the abstraction of a Huguenot nobleman's despatches would be considered as a meritorious action. Winter weather, and the practice of his profession likewise, delayed Ercole so much that it was nearly Easter before he brought his certain intelligence to the Chevalier, and to the lady an elixir of love, clear and colourless as crystal, and infallible as an inspirer of affection.

Should she administer it, now that she knew her cousin not to be the lawful object of affection she had so long esteemed him, but, as he persisted in considering himself, a married man? Diane had more scruples than she would have had a year before, for she had not so long watched and loved one so true and conscientious as Berenger de Ribaumont without having her perceptions elevated; but at the same time the passion of love had become intensified, both by long continuance and by resistance. She had attached herself, believing him free, and her affections could not be disentangled by learning that he was bound—rather the contrary.

Besides, there was plenty of sophistry. Her father had always assured her of the invalidity of the marriage, without thinking it necessary to dwell on his own arrangements for making it invalid, so that was no reasonable ground of objection; and a lady of Diane's period, living in the world where she had lived, would have had no notion of objecting to her lover for a previous amour, and as such was she bidden to rank Berenger's relations with Eustacie. And there was the less scruple on Eustacie's account, because the Chevalier, knowing that the Duchess had a son and two grandsons, had conceived a great terror that she meant to give his niece to one of them; and this would be infinitely worse, both for the interests of the family and of their party, than even her reunion with the young Baron. Even Narcisse, who on his return had written to Paris a grudging consent to the experiment of his father and sister, had allowed that the preservation of Berenger's life was needful till Eustacie should be in their power so as to prevent such a marriage as that! To Diane, the very suggestion became certainty: she already saw Eustacie's shallow little heart consoled and her vanity excited by these magnificent prospects, and she looked forward to the triumph of her own constancy, when Berenger should find the image so long enshrined in his heart crumble in its sacred niche.

Yet a little while then would she be patient, even though nearly a year had passed and still she saw no effect upon her prisoners, unless, indeed, Philip had drunk of one of her potions by mistake and his clumsy admiration was the consequence. The two youths went on exactly in the same manner, without a complaint, without a request, occupying themselves as best they might—Berenger courteously attentive to her father, and coldly courteous to herself. He had entirely recovered his health, and the athletic powers displayed by the two brothers when wrestling, fencing, or snow-balling in the courtyard, were the amazement and envy of their guard. Twice in the course of the winter there had been an alarm of wolves, and in their eagerness and excitement about this new sport, they had accepted the Chevalier's offer of taking their parole for the hunt. They had then gone forth with a huge posse of villagers, who beat the woods with their dogs till the beast was aroused from its lair and driven into the alleys, where waited gentlemen, gendarmes, and gamekeepers with their guns. These two chases were chiefly memorable to Berenger, because in the universal intermingling of shouting peasants he was able in the first to have some conversation with Eustacie's faithful protector Martin, who told him the incidents of her wanderings, with tears in his eyes, and blessed him for his faith that she was not dead; and in the second, he actually found himself in the ravine of the Grange du Temple. No need to ask, every voice was shouting the name, and though the gendarmes were round him and he durst not speak to Rotrou, still he could reply with significative earnestness to the low bow with which the farmer bent to evident certainty that here was the imprisoned Protestant husband of the poor lady. Berenger wore his black vizard mask as had been required of him, but the man's eyes followed him, as though learning by heart the outline of his tall figure. The object of the Chevalier's journey was, of course, a secret from the prisoners, who merely felt its effects by having their meals served to them in their own tower; and when he returned after about a month's absence thought him looking harassed, aged, and so much out of humour that he could scarcely preserve his usual politeness. In effect he was greatly chagrined.

"That she is in their hands is certain, the hypocrites!" he said to his daughter and sister; "and no less so that they have designs on her; but I let them know that these could be easily traversed."

"But where is she, the unhappy apostate child?" said the Abbess. "They durst not refuse her to you."

"I tell you they denied all present knowledge of her. The Duke himself had the face to make as though he never heard of her. He had no concern with his mother's household and guests forsooth! I do not believe he has; the poor fellow stands in awe of that terrible old heretic dragon, and keeps aloof from her as much as he can. But he is, after all, a *beau jeune homme;* nor should I be surprised if he were the girl's gay bridegroom by this time, though I gave him a hint that there was an entanglement about the child's first marriage which, by French law, would invalidate any other without a dispensation from the Pope."

"A hard nut that for a heretic," laughed the Abbess.

"He acted the ignorant—knew nothing about the young lady; but had the civility to give me a guide and an escort to go to Quinet. *Ma foi!* I believe they were given to hinder me—take me by indirect roads, make me lose time at chateaux. When I arrived at the grim old chateau—a true dungeon, precise as a convent—there was the dame, playing the Queen Jeanne as well as she could, and having the insolence to tell me that it was true that Madame la Baronne de Ribaumont, as she was pleased to call her, had honoured her residence for some months, but that she had now quitted it, and she flatly refused to answer any question whither she was gone! The hag! she might at least have had the decorum to deny all knowledge of her, but nothing is more impertinent than the hypocritical sincerity of the heretics."

"But her people," exclaimed the Abbess; "surely some of them knew, and could be brought to speak."

"All the servants I came in contact with played the incorruptible; but still I have done something. There were some fellows in the village who are not at their ease under that rule. I caused my people to inquire them out. They knew nothing more than that the old heretic Gardon with his family had gone away in Madame la Duchesse's litter, but whither they could not tell. But the *cabaretier* there is furious secretly with the Quinets for having spoilt his trade by destroying the shrine at the holy well, and I have made him understand that it will be for his profit to send me off intelligence so soon as there is any communication between them and the lady. I made the same arrangement with a couple of gendarmes of the escort the Duke gave me. So at least we are safe for intelligence such as would hinder a marriage."

"But they will be off to England!" said the Abbess.

"I wager they will again write to make sure of a reception. Moreover, I have set that fellow Ercole and others of his trade to keep a strict watch on all the roads leading to the ports, and give me due notice of their passing thither. We have law on our side, and, did I once claim her, no one could resist my right. Or should the war break out, as is probable, then could my son sweep their whole province with his troops. This time she cannot escape us."

The scene that her father's words and her own imagination conjured up, of Eustacie attracting the handsome widower-duke, removed all remaining scruples from Madame de Selinville. For his own sake, the Baron must be made to fulfil the prophecy of the ink-pool, and allow his prison doors to be opened by love. Many and many a tender art did Diane rehearse; numerous were her sighs; wakeful, languishing, and restless her nights and days; and yet, whatever her determination to practise upon her cousin the witcheries that she had learnt in the *Escadron de la Reine-mère*, and seen played off effectually where there was not one grain of love to inspire them, her powers and her courage always failed her in the presence of him whom she sought to attract. His quiet reserve and simplicity always disconcerted her, and any attempt at blandishment that he could not mistake was always treated by him as necessarily an accidental error, as if any other supposition would render her despicable; and yet there was now and then a something that made her detect an effort in his restraint, as if it were less distaste than self-command. Her brother had contemptuously acquiesced in the experiment made by herself and her father, and allowed that so long as there was any danger of the Quinet marriage, the Baron's existence was needful. He would not come to Nid-de-Merle, nor did they want him there, knowing that he could hardly have kept his hands off his rival. But when the war broke out again in the summer of 1575 he joined that detachment of Guise's army which hovered about the Loire, and kept watch on the Huguenot cities and provinces of Western France. The Chevalier made seveaal expeditions to confer with his son, and to keep up his relations with the network of spies whom he had spread over the Quinet provinces. The prisoners were so much separated from all intercourse with the dependants that they were entirely ignorant of the object of his absence from home. On these occasions they never left their tower and its court, and had no enlivenment save an occasional gift of dainties or message of inquiry from the ladies at Bellaise. These were brought by a handsome but slight, pale lad called Aimé de Selinville, a relative of the late Count, as he told them, who had come to act as a gentleman attendant upon the widowed countess. The brothers rather wondered how he was disposed of at the convent, but all there was so contrary to their preconceived notions that they acquiesced. The first time he arrived it was on a long, hot summer day, and he then brought them a cool iced sherbet in two separate flasks, that for Philip being mixed with wine, which was omitted for Berenger; and the youth stood lingering and watching, anxious, he said, to be able to tell his lady how the drinks were approved. Both were excellent, and to that effect the prisoners replied; but no sooner was the messenger gone than Berenger said smilingly, "That was a love potion, Phil."

"And you drank it!" cried Philip, in horror.

"I did not think of it till I saw how the boy's eyes were gazing curiously at me as I swallowed it. You look at me as curiously, Phil. Are you expecting it to work? Shall I be at the fair lady's feet next time we meet?"

"How can you defy it, Berry?"

"Nay, Phil; holy wedded love is not to be dispelled by a mountebank's decoction."

"But suppose it were poisonous, Berry, what can be done?" cried Philip, starting up in dismay.

"Then you would go home, Phil, and this would be over. But"—seeing his brother's terror—"there is no fear of that. She is not like to wish to poison me."

And the potion proved equally ineffective on mind and body, as indeed did all the manipulations exercised upon a little waxen image that was supposed to represent M. le Baron. Another figure was offered to Diane, in feminine form, with black beads for eyes and a black plaster for hair, which, when stuck full of pins and roasted before the fire, was to cause Eustacie to peak and pine correspondingly. But from this measure Diane shrank. If aught was done against her rival it must be by her father and brother, not by herself; and she would not feel herself directly injuring her little cousin, nor sinking herself below him whom she loved. Once his wife, she would be good for ever, held up by his strength.

Meantime Berenger had received a greater shock than she or her father understood in the looking over of some of the family parchments kept in store at the castle. The Chevalier, in showing them to him, had chiefly desired to glorify the family by demonstrating how its honours had been won, but Berenger was startled at finding that Nid-de-Merle had been, as it appeared to him, arbitrarily and unjustly declared to be forfeited by the Sieur de Bellaise, who had been thrown into prison by Louis XI. for some demonstration in favour of the poor Duke de Berri, and granted to the favourite Ribaumont. The original grant was there, and to his surprise he found it was to male heirs—the male heirs alone of the direct line of the Ribaumont—to whom the grant was made. How, then, came it to Eustacie? The disposal had, with almost equal injustice, been changed by King Henry II. and the late Count de Ribaumont in favour of the little daughter whose union with the heir of the elder line was to conclude all family feuds. Only now did Berenger understand what his father had said on his death-bed of flagrant injustice committed in his days of darkness. He felt that he was reaping the reward of the injuries committed against the Chevalier and his son on behalf of the two unconscious children. He would willingly at once have given up all claim to the Nid-de-Merle estate—and he was now of age; two birthdays had passed in his captivity and brought him to years of discretion—but he had no more power than before to dispose of what was the property of Eustacie and her child; and the whole question of the validity of his marriage would be given up by his yielding even the posthumous claim that might have devolved on him in case of Eustacie's death. This would be giving up her honour, a thing impossible.

"Alas!" he sighed, "my poor father might well say he had bound a heavy burthen round my neck."

And from that time his hopes sank lower as the sense of the justice of his cause left him. He could neither deny his religion nor his marriage, and therefore could do nothing for his own deliverance; and he knew himself to be suffering as the cause of a great injustice; indeed, to be bringing suffering on the still more innocent Philip.

The once proudly indifferent youth was flagging now; was losing appetite, flesh, and colour; was unwilling to talk or to take exercise; and had a wan and drooping air that was most painful to watch. It seemed as if the return of summer brought a sense of the length and weariness of the captivity, and that the sunshine and gaiety of the landscape had become such a contrast to the captives' deadness of spirit that they could hardly bear to behold them, and felt the dull prison walls more congenial to their feelings than the gaiety of the summer hay and harvest-fields.

CHAPTER XXXVII.

BEATING AGAINST THE BARS.

> "My horse is weary of the stall,
> And I am sick of captive thrall."
>
> *Lady of the Lake.*

LETTERS! They were hailed like drops of water in a thirsty land. No doubt they had been long on the way, ere they had reached the hands of the Chevalier de Ribaumont, and it was quite possible that they had been read and selected; but, as Berenger said, he defied any Frenchman to imitate either Lord Walwyn's style or Sir Marmaduke's, and when late in the autumn the packet was delivered to him, the two captives gloated over the very outsides before they opened them.

The first intelligence that greeted them made them give a cry of amusement and surprise. Lady Thistlewood, whose regrets that each of her girls was not a boy had passed into a proverb, had at length, in Dolly's seventh year, given birth to a son on Midsummer Day.

"Well," said Philip, sighing, "we must drink his health to-night! It is well, if we are to rot here, that some one should make it up to them!"

"And join Walwyn and Hurst!" said Berenger; and then both faces grew much graver, as by these letters, dated three months since, they understood how many they must have missed, and likewise that nothing had been heard of themselves since they had left Paris sixteen months ago. Their letters, both to their relations and to Sir Francis Walsingham, had evidently been suppressed; and Lord North, who had succeeded Walsingham as ambassador, had probably been misled by design, either by Narcisse de Nid-de-Merle himself, or by some of his agents, for Lord Walwyn had heard from him that the young men were loitering among the castles and garrisons of Anjou, leading a gay and dissipated life, and that it was universally believed that the Baron de Ribaumont had embraced the Catholic faith, and would shortly be presented to Henry III. to receive the grant of the Selinville honours, upon his marriage with his cousin, the widow of the last of the line. With much earnestness and sorrow did good old Lord Walwyn write to his grandson, conjuring him to bethink himself of his home, his pure faith, his loving friends, and the hopes of his youth: and, at least, if he himself had been led away by the allurements of the other party, to remember that Philip had been entrusted to him in full confidence, and to return him to his home. "It was grief and shame to him," said the good old man, "to look at Sir Marmaduke, who had risked his son in the charge of one hitherto deemed trustworthy; and even if Berenger had indeed forgotten and cast away those whom he had once seemed to regard with love and duty, he commanded him to send home Philip, who owed an obedience to his father that could not be gainsayed." Lord Walwyn further bade his grandson remember that the arrangements respecting his inheritance had been made in confidence that his heir was English in heart and faith, and that neither the Queen nor his own conscience would allow him to let his inheritance pass into French or Papist hands. There was scarcely a direct reproach, but the shaken, altered handwriting showed how stricken the aged man must be; and after his signature was added one still more trembling line, "An ye return not speedily, ye will never see the old grandsire more."

Berenger scarcely finished the letter through his burning tears of agony, and then, casting it from him, began to pace the room in fierce agitation, bursting out into incoherent exclamations, grasping at his hair, even launching himself against the massive window with such frenzied gestures and wild words that Philip, who had read through all with his usual silent obtuseness, became dismayed, and, laying hold of him, said, "Prithee, brother, do not thus! What serves such passion?"

Berenger burst into a strange loud laugh at the matter-of-fact tone. "What serves it! what serves anything!" he cried, "but to make me feel what a miserable wretch I am? But he will die, Philip—he will die—not having believed me! How shall we keep ourselves from the smooth-tongued villain's throat? That I should be thus judged a traitor by my grandfather——"

And with a cry as of bodily anguish, he hid his face on the table, and groaned as he felt the utter helplessness of his strong youth in bonds.

"It can't be helped," was the next of the unconsolatory platitudes uttered by Philip, who always grew sullen and dogged when his brother's French temperament broke forth under any sudden stroke. "If they will believe such things, let them! You have not heard what my father says to it."

"It will be all the same," groaned Berenger.

"Nay! now that's a foul slander, and you should be ashamed of doing my father such wrong," said Philip. "Listen;" and he read: "I will believe no ill of the lad no more than of thee, Phil. It is but a wild-goose chase, and the poor young woman is scarce like to be above ground; but, as I daily tell them, 'tis hard a man should forfeit his land for seeking his wife. My Lord North sends rumours that he is under Papist guiding, and sworn brother with the Black Ribaumonts; and my lady, his grandmother, is like to break her heart, and my lord credits them more than he ought, and never a line as a token comes from you. Then there's Dame Annora, as proud of the babe as though neither she nor woman born ever had a son before, and plains over him, that both his brothers should be endowed and he but a younger son. What will be the end on't I cannot tell. I will stand up for the right as best man may do, and never forget that Berry is her first-born, and that his child may be living; but the matter is none of mine, and my lord is very aged, nor can a man meddle between his wife and her father. So this I tell you that you may make your brother lay it to heart. The sooner he is here the better, if he be still, as I verily believe and maintain him to be, an honest English heart that snaps his fingers at French papistry." "There," concluded Philip, triumphantly, "he knows an honest man! He's friend and good father to you as much as ever. Heed none of the rest. He'll never let this little rogue stand in your light."

"As if I cared for that!" said Berenger, beginning his caged-tiger walk again, and, though he tried to repress his anguish, breaking out at times into fierce revilings of the cruel toils that beset him, and despairing lamentations over those beloved ones at home, with sobs, groans, and tears, such as Philip could not brook to witness, both because they were so violent and mournful, and because he thought them womanish, though in effect no woman's grief could have had half that despairing force. The *fierté* of the French noble, however, came to his aid. At the first sound of the great supper bell he dashed away his tears, composed his features, washed his face, and demanded haughtily of Philip, whether there were any traces in his looks that the cruel hypocrite, their jailer, could gloat over.

And with proud step and indifferent air he marched into the hall, answered the Chevalier's polite inquiry whether the letter had brought good tidings by coolly thanking him and saying that all at home were well; and when he met the old man's inquiring glance out of the little keen black bead in the puckered, withered eyelid, he put a perfectly stony unmeaningness into his own gaze, till his eyes looked like the blue porcelain from China so much prized by the Abbess. He even played at chess all the evening with such concentrated attention as to be uniformly victorious.

Yet half the night Philip heard suppressed moans and sobs—then knew that he was on his knees—then, after long and comparatively silent weeping, he lay down again, and from the hour when he awoke in the morning, he returned no more to the letters; and though for some little time more sad and dispirited, he seemed to have come to regard the misjudgment at home as a part of the burthen he was already bearing.

That burthen was, however, pressing more heavily. The temperaments of the two brothers so differed that while the French one was prostrated by the agony of a stroke, and then rallied patiently to endure the effects, the English character opposed a passive resistance to the blow, gave no sign of grief or pain, and from that very determination suffered a sort of exhaustion that made the effects of the evil more and more felt. Thus, from the time Philip's somewhat tardy imagination had been made to realize his home, his father, and his sisters, the home-sickness, and weariness of his captivity, which had already begun to undermine his health and spirits, took increasing effect.

He made no complaint—he never expressed a wish—but, in the words of the prophet, he seemed "pining away on his feet." He did not sleep, and though, to avoid remark, he never failed to appear at meals, he scarcely tasted food. He never willingly stirred from cowering over the fire, and was so surly and ill-tempered that only Berenger's unfailing good humour could have endured it. Even a wolf hunt did not stir him. He only said he hated outlandish beasts, and that it was not like chasing the hare in Dorset. His calf-love for Madame de Selinville had entirely faded away in his yearnings after home. She was only one of the tediously recurring sights of his captivity, and was loathed like all the rest. The regulation rides with the Chevalier were more detestable than ever, and by and by they caused such fatigue that Berenger perceived that his strength must be waning, and became so seriously alarmed that one evening, when Philip had barely dragged himself to the hall, tasted nothing but a few drops of wine, and then dropped into an uneasy slumber in his chair, he could not but turn to the Chevalier an appealing, indignant countenance, as he said, in a low but quivering voice, "You see, sir, how he is altered!"

"Alas! fair nephew, it is but too plain. He is just of the age when such restraint tells severely upon the health."

Then Berenger spoke out upon the foul iniquity of the boy's detention. For himself, he observed, he had nothing to say; he knew the terms of his release, and had not accepted them; but Philip, innocent of all damage to the Ribaumont interests, the heir of an honourable family, what had he done to incur the cruel imprisonment that was eating away his life?

"I tell you, sir," said Berenger, with eyes filled with tears, "that his liberty is more precious to me than my own. Were he but restored to our home, full half the weight would be gone from my spirit."

"Fair nephew," said the Chevalier, "you speak as though I had any power in the matter, and were not merely standing between you and the King."

"Then if so," said Berenger, "let the King do as he will with me, but let Philip's case be known to our Ambassador."

"My poor cousin," said the Chevalier, "you know not what you ask. Did I grant your desire, you would only learn how implacable King Henri is to those who have personally offended him—above all, to heretics. Nor could the Ambassador do anything for one who resisted by force of arms the King's justice. Leave it to me; put yourself in my hands, and deliverance shall come for him first, then for you."

"How, sir?"

"One token of concession—one attendance at mass—one pledge that the alliance shall take place when the formalities have been complied with—then can I report you our own; give you almost freedom at once; despatch our young friend to England without loss of time; so will brotherly affection conquer those chivalrous scruples, most honourable in you, but which, carried too far, become cruel obstinacy."

Berenger looked at Philip; saw how faded and wan was the ruddy sun-burnt complexion, how lank and bony the sturdy form, how listless and wasted the hands. Then arose, bursting within him, the devoted generosity of the French nature, which would even accept sin and ruin for self, that so the friend may be saved; and after all, had he not gone to mass out of mere curiosity?—did he not believe that there was salvation in the Gallican Church? Was it not possible that, with Philip free to tell his story at home, his own deliverance might come before he should be irrevocably committed to Madame de Selinville? If Eustacie were living, her claims must overthrow that which her rival was forcing upon him at her own peril. Nay, how else could he obtain tidings of her? And for those at home, did they deserve that he should sacrifice all, Philip included, for their sake? The thoughts, long floating round his brain, now surged upon him in one flood, and seemed to overwhelm in those moments of confusion all his powers of calling up the other side of the argument; he only had an instinct remaining that it would be a lie to God and man alike. "God help me!" he sighed to himself; and there was sufficient consideration and perplexity expressed in his countenance to cause the Chevalier to feel his cause almost gained; and rising eagerly, with tears in his eyes, he exclaimed, "Embrace me, my dear, dear son! The thing is done! Oh! what peace, what joy!"

The instinct of recoil came stronger now. He stepped back with folded arms, saying again, "God help me! God forbid that I should be a traitor!"

"My son, hear me; these are but easily removed points of honour," began the Chevalier; but at that moment Philip suddenly started from, or in his slumber, leapt on his feet, and called out, "Avaunt, Satan!" then opened his eyes, and looked, as if barely recalling where he was.

"Philip!" exclaimed Berenger, "did you hear?"

"I—I don't know," he said, half-bewildered. "Was I dreaming that the fiend was parleying with us in the voice of M. le Chevalier there to sell our souls for one hour of home?"

He spoke English, but Berenger replied in French.

"You were not wrong, Philip. Sir, he dreamt that the devil was tempting me in your voice while you were promising me his liberty on my fulfilling your first condition."

"What?" said Philip, now fully awake, and gathering the state of things, as he remembered the words that had doubtless been the cause of his dream. "And if you did, Berenger, I give you warning they should never see me at home. What! could I show my face there with such tidings? No! I should go straight to La Noue, or to the Low Countries, and kill every Papist I could for having debauched you!"

"Hush! hush! Philip," said Berenger, "I could not break my faith to Heaven or my wife even for your sake, and my cousin sees how little beholden you would be to me for so doing. With your leave, Monsieur, we will retire."

The Chevalier detained Berenger for a moment to whisper, "What I see is so noble a heart that I know you cannot sacrifice him to your punctilio."

Philip was so angry with Berenger, so excited, and so determined to show that nothing ailed him, that for a short time he was roused, and seemed to be recovering; but in a few days he flagged again, only, if possible, with more gruffness, moodiness, and pertinacity in not allowing that anything was amiss. It was the bitterest drop of all in Berenger's cup, when in the end of January he looked back at what Philip had been only a month before, and saw how he had wasted away and lost strength; the impulse rather to ruin himself than destroy his brother came with such force that he could scarcely escape it by his ever-recurring cry for help to withstand it. And then Diane, in her splendid beauty and witchery, would rise before him, so that he knew how a relaxation of the lengthened weary effort would make his whole self break its bonds and go out to her. Dreams of felicity and liberty, and not with Eustacie, would even come over him, and he would awaken to disappointment before he came to a sense of relief and thankfulness that he was still his own. The dislike, distaste, and dread that came so easily in his time of pain and weakness were less easy to maintain in his full health and forced inactivity. Occupation of mind and hope seemed the only chance of enabling either of the two to weather this most dreary desert period; and Berenger, setting his thoughts resolutely to consider what would be the best means of rousing Philip, decided at length that any endeavour to escape, however arduous and desperate, would be better than his present apathetic languor, even if it led to nothing. After the first examination of their prison, Berenger had had no thought of escape; he was then still weak and unenterprising. He had for many months lived in hopes of interference from home; and, besides, the likelihood that so English a party as his own would be quickly pursued and recaptured, where they did not know their road and had no passports, had deterred him lest they should fall into still straiter imprisonment. But he had since gained, in the course of his rides, and by observation from the top of the tower, a much fuller knowledge of the country. He knew the way to the Grange du Temple, and to the chief towns in the neighbourhood. Philip and Humfrey had both lost something of their intensely national look and speech, and, moreover, war having broken out again, there was hope of falling in with Huguenot partisans even nearer than at La Rochelle. But whether successful or not, some enterprise was absolutely needed to save Philip from his despondent apathy; and Berenger, who in these eighteen months had grown into the strength and vigour of manhood, felt as if he had force and power for almost any effort save this hopeless waiting.

He held council with Humfrey, who suggested that it might be well to examine the vaults below the keep. He had a few days before, while going after some of the firewood, stored below the ground-floor chamber, observed a door, locked, but with such rusty iron hinges that they might possibly yield to vigorous efforts with a stone; and who could tell where the underground passages might come out?

Berenger eagerly seized the idea. Philip's mood of contradiction prompted him to pronounce it useless folly, and he vouchsafed no interest in the arrangements for securing light, by selecting all the bits of firewood fittest for torches, and saving all the oil possible from the two lamps they were allowed. The chief difficulty was that Guibert was not trusted, so that all had to be done out of his sight; and on the first day Berenger was obliged to make the exploration alone, since Humfrey was forced to engross Guibert in some occupation out of sight, and Philip had refused to have anything to do with it, or be like a rat routing in the corners of his trap.

However, Berenger had only just ascertained that the ironwork was so entirely rusted away as to offer no impediment, when Philip came languidly roaming into the cellar, saying, "Here! I'll hold the torch! You'll be losing yourself in this wolf's mouth of a place if you go alone."

The investigation justified Philip's predictions of its uselessness. Nothing was detected but rats, and vaults, and cobwebs; it was cold, earthy, and damp; and when they thought they must have penetrated far beyond the precincts of the keep, they heard Humfrey's voice close to them, warning them that it was nearly dinner-time.

The next day brought them a more promising discovery, namely of a long straight passage, with a gleam of light at the end of it; and this for the first time excited Philip's interest or curiosity. He would have hastened along it at once, but for the warning summons from Humfrey; and in the excitement of even this grain of interest, he ate more heartily at supper than he had done for weeks, and was afterwards more eager to prove to Berenger that night was the best time to pursue their researches.

And Berenger, when convinced that Guibert was sound asleep, thought so too, and accompanied by Humfrey, they descended into the passage. The light, of course, was no longer visible, but the form of the crypt, through which they now passed, was less antique than that under the keep, and it was plain they were beneath a later portion of the Castle. The gallery concluded in a wall, with a small barred, unglazed window, perfectly dark, so that Berenger, who alone could reach to the bottom of it, could not guess where it looked out.

"We must return by daylight; then, may-be, we may judge," sighed Philip.

"Hark!" exclaimed Berenger.

"Rats," said Philip.

"No—listen—a voice! Take care!" he added, in a lower tone, "we may be close on some of the servants."

But, much nearer than he expected, a voice on his right hand demanded, "Does any good Christian hear me?"

"Who is there?" exclaimed Philip.

"Ah! good sir, do I hear the voice of a companion in misery? Or, if you be free, would you but send tidings to my poor father?"

"It is a Norman accent!" cried Berenger. "Ah! ah! can it be poor Landry Osbert?"

"I am—I am that wretch. Oh, would that M. le Baron could know!"

"My dear, faithful foster-brother! They deceived me," cried Berenger, in great agitation, as an absolute howl came from the other side of the wall: "M. le Baron come to this! Woe worth the day!" and Berenger with difficulty mitigated his affectionate servant's lamentations enough to learn from him how he had been seized almost at the gates of Bellaise, closely interrogated, deprived of the letter to Madame la Baronne, and thrown into this dungeon. The Chevalier, not an unmerciful man, according to the time, had probably meant to release him as soon as the marriage between his son and niece should have rendered it superfluous to detain this witness to Berenger's existence. There, then, the poor fellow had lain for three years, and his work during this weary time had been the scraping with a potsherd at the stone of his wall, and his pertinacious perseverance had succeeded in forming a hole just large enough to enable him to see the light of the torch carried by the gentlemen. On his side, he said, there was nothing but a strong iron door, and a heavily-barred window, looking, like that in the passage, into the fosse within the walled garden; but, on the other hand, if he could enlarge his hole sufficiently to creep through it, he could escape with them in case of their finding a subterranean outlet. The opening within his cell was, of course, much larger than the very small space he had made by loosening a stone towards the passage, but he was obliged always to build up each side of his burrow at the hours of his jailer's visit, lest his work should be detected, and to stamp the rubbish into his floor. But while they talked, Humfrey and Philip, with their knives, scraped so diligently that two more stones could be displaced; and, looking down the widening hole through the prodigious mass of wall, they could see a ghastly, ragged, long-bearded scarecrow, with an almost piteous expression of joy on his face, at once again seeing familiar faces. And when, at his earnest entreaty, Berenger stood so as to allow his countenance to be as visible as the torch could make it through the "wall's-hole," the vault echoed with the poor fellow's delighted cry. "I am happy! M. le Baron is himself again. The assassin's cruel work is gone! Ah! thanks to the saints! Blessed be St. Lucie, it was not in vain that I entreated her!"

The torches were, however, waxing so low that the sight could not long be afforded poor Osbert; and, with a promise to return to him next day, the party returned to the upper air, where they warmed themselves over the fire, and held council over measures for the present relief of the captive. Berenger grieved that he had given him up so entirely for lost as to have made no exertions on his behalf, and declared his resolution of entreating that he might be allowed to enjoy comparative comfort with them in the keep. It was a risk, but the Chevalier might fairly suppose that the knowledge of Osbert's situation had oozed out through the servants, and gratitude and humanity alike impelled Berenger to run some risk for his foster-brother's sake. He was greatly touched at the poor fellow's devotion, and somewhat amused, though with an almost tearful smile at the joy with which he had proclaimed—what Berenger was quite unaware of, since the keep furnished no mirrors—the disappearance of his scars. "'Tis even so," said Philip, "though I never heeded it. You are as white from crown to beard as one of the statues at Paris; but the great red gash is a mere seam, save when yon old Satan angers you, and then it blushes for all the rest of your face."

"And the cheek-wound is hidden, I suppose," said Berenger, feeling under the long fair moustache and the beard, which was developing into respectable proportions.

"Hidden? ay, entirely. No one would think your bald crown had only twenty-one years over it; but you are a personable fellow still, quite enough to please Daphné," said Philip.

"Pshaw!" replied Berenger, pleased nevertheless to hear the shadow of a jest again from Philip.

It was quite true. These months of quiescence—enforced though they were—had given his health and constitution time to rally after the terrible shock they had sustained. The severe bleedings had, indeed, rendered his complexion perfectly colourless; but there was something in this, as well as in the height which the loss of hair gave his brow, which, added to the depth and loftiness of countenance that this long period of patience and resolution had impressed on his naturally fine features, without taking away that open candour that had first attracted Diane when he was a rosy lad. His frame had strengthened at the same time, and assumed the proportions of manhood; so that, instead of being the overgrown maypole that Narcisse used to sneer at, he was now broad-shouldered and robust, exceedingly powerful, and so well made that his height, upwards of six feet, was scarcely observed, except by comparison with the rest of the world.

And his character had not stood still. He had first come to Paris a good, honest, docile, though high-spirited boy; and though manly affections, cares, and sorrows had been thrust on him, he had met them like the boy that he was, hardly conscious how deep they went. Then had come the long dream of physical suffering, with only one thought pertinaciously held throughout—that of constancy to his lost wife; and from this he had only thoroughly wakened in his captivity, the resolution still holding fast, but with more of reflection and principle, less of mere instinct, than when his powers were lost or distracted in the effort of constant endurance of pain and weakness. The charge of Philip, the endeavour both of educating him and keeping up his spirits, as well as the controversy with Père Bonami, had been no insignificant parts of the discipline of these months; and, little as the Chevalier had intended it, he had trained his young kinsman into a far more substantial and perilous adversary, both in body and mind, than when he had caged him in his castle of the Blackbird's Nest.

CHAPTER XXXVIII.

THE ENEMY IN PRESENCE.

"Then came and looked him in the face
An angel beautiful and bright,
And then he knew it was a fiend,
That miserable knight."
COLERIDGE.

"FATHER, dear father, what is it? What makes you look so ill, so haggard?" cried Diane de Selinville, when summoned the next morning to meet her father in the parlour of the convent.

"Ah, child! see here. Your brother will have us make an end of it. He has found her."

"Eustacie! Ah, and where?"

"That he will not say, but see here. This is all his billet tells me: 'The hare who has doubled so long is traced to her form. My dogs are on her, and in a week's time she will be ours. I request you, sir, to send me a good purse of crowns to reward my huntsmen; and in the meantime—one way or the other—that pet of my sister's must be disposed of. Kept too long, these beasts always become savage. Either let him be presented to the royal menagerie, or there is a still surer way.'"

"And that is all he says!" exclaimed Diane.

"All! He was always cautious. He mentions no names.

And now, child, what is to be done? To give him up to the King is, at the best, life-long imprisonment, yet, if he were still here when my son returns— Alas! alas! child, I have been ruined body and soul between you! How could you make me send after and imprison him? It was a mere assassination!" and the old man beat his head with grief and perplexity.

"Father!" cried Diane, tearfully, "I cannot see you thus. We meant it for the best. We shall yet save him."

"Save him! Ah, daughter, I tossed all night long thinking how to save him, so strong, so noble, so firm, so patient, so good even to the old man who has destroyed his hope—his life! Ah! I have thought till my brain whirls."

"Poor father! I knew you would love him," said Diane, tenderly. "Ah! we will save him yet. He shall be the best of sons to you. Look, it is only to tell him that she whom he calls his wife is already in my brother's hands, wedded to him."

"Daughter,"—and he pushed back his grey hair with a weary distressed gesture,—"I am tired of wiles; I am old; I can carry them out no longer."

"But this is very simple; it may already be true—at least it will soon be true. Only tell him that she is my brother's wife. Then will his generosity awaken, then will he see that to persist in the validity of his marriage would be misery, dishonour to her, then——"

"Child, you know not how hard he is in his sense of right. Even for his brother's sake he would not give way an inch, and the boy was as obstinate as he!"

"Ah! but this comes nearer. He will be stung; his generosity will be piqued. He will see that the kindest thing he can do will be to nullify his claim, and the child——"

The Chevalier groaned, struck his brow with his fist, and muttered, "That will concern no one—that has been provided for. Ah! ah! children, if I lose my own soul for you, you——"

"Father, my sweet father, say not these cruel things. Did not the Queen's confessor tell us that all means were lawful that brought a soul to the Church? and here are two."

"Two! Why, the youth's heresy is part of his point of honour. Child, child, the two will be murdered in my very house, and the guilt will be on my soul."

"No, father! We will—we will save him. See, only tell him this."

"This—what? My brain is confused. I have thought long—long."

"Only this, father, dear father. You shall not be tormented any more, if only you will tell him that my brother has made Eustacie his wife, then will I do all the rest."

Diane coaxed, soothed, and encouraged her father by her caresses, till he mounted his mule to return to the castle at dinner-time, and she promised to come early in the afternoon to follow up the stroke he was to give. She had never seen him falter before,—he had followed out his policy with a clear head and unsparing hand,—but now that Berenger's character was better known to him, and the crisis long-delayed had come so suddenly before his eyes, his whole powers seemed to reel under the alternative.

The dinner-bell clanged as he arrived at the castle, and the prisoners were marched into the hall, both intent upon making their request on Osbert's behalf, and therefore as impatient for the conclusion of the meal, and the absence of the servants, as was their host. His hands trembled so much that Berenger was obliged to carve for him; he made the merest feint of eating; and now and then raised his hand to his head as if to bring back scattered ideas.

The last servant quitted the room, when Berenger perceived that the old man was hardly in a state to attend to his request, and yet the miserable frost-bitten state of poor Landry seemed to compel him to speak.

"Sir," he began, "you could do me a great kindness."

The Chevalier looked up at him with glassy eyes.

"My son," he said, with an effort, "I also had something to say. Ah! let me think. I have had enough. Call my daughter," he added, feeling helplessly with his hands, so that Berenger started up in alarm, and received him in his arms just in time to prevent his sinking to the floor senseless.

"It is a stroke," exclaimed Berenger. "Call, Phil! Send the gendarmes."

The gendarmes might be used to the sight of death of their own causing, but they had a horror of that which came by Nature's hand. The purple face and loud gasps of the stricken man terrified them out of their senses. "*C'est un coup*," was the cry, and they went clattering off to the servants. These, all men but one old crone, came in a mass to the door, looked in, beheld their master rigid and prostrate on the floor, supported by the prisoner, and with fresh shrieks about "Mesdames! a priest! a doctor!" away they rushed. The two brothers were not in much less consternation, only they retained their senses. Berenger loosened the ruff and doublet, and bade Philip practise that art of letting blood which he had learnt for his benefit. When Madame de Selinville and her aunt, with their escort, having been met half-way from Bellaise, arrived sooner than could have been expected, they found every door open from hall to entrance gateway, not a person keeping watch, and the old man lying deathlike upon cushions in the hall, Philip bandaging his arm, and Berenger rubbing his temples with wine and the hottest spices on the table. "He is better—he is alive," said Berenger, as they entered; and as both ladies would have fallen on him with shrieks and sobs, he bade them listen, assured them that the only chance of life was in immediate care, and entreated that bedding might be brought down, and strong essences fetched to apply to the nose and temples. They obeyed, and brought the servants to obey; and by the time the priest and the sister infirmarer had arrived from the convent, he had opened his eyes, and, as he saw Berenger, tried to murmur something that sounded like "*Mon fils.*"

"He lives!—he speaks!—he can receive the sacraments!" was the immediate exclamation; and as preparations began to be made, the brothers saw that their presence was no longer needed, and returned to their own tower.

"So, sir," said the gendarme sergeant, as they walked down the passage, "you did not seize the moment for escape."

"I never thought of it," said Berenger.

"I hope, sir, you will not be the worse for it," said the sergeant. "An honourable gentleman you have ever proved yourself to me, and I will bear testimony that you did the poor old gentleman no hurt; but nobles will have it their own way, and pay little heed to a poor soldier."

"What do you mean, friend?"

"Why, you see, sir, it is unlucky that you two happened to be alone with M. le Chevalier. No one can tell what may be said when they seek an occasion against a person."

To the brothers, however, this suggestion sounded so horrible and unnatural, that they threw it from them. They applied themselves at every moment possible to enlarging Osbert's hole, and seeking an outlet from the dungeon; but this they had not been able to discover, and it was necessary to be constantly on their guard in visiting the vaults, lest their absence from their apartment should be detected. They believed that if Narcisse arrived at the castle, they should find in him a far less gentle jailer than the poor old man, for whose state their kindly young hearts could not but grieve.

They heard that he had recovered consciousness enough to have made a sort of confession; and Père Bonami brought them his formal request, as a dying man, for their pardon for all the injuries he had done them; but his speech was too much affected for any specification of what these were. The first thing they heard in early morning was that, in the course of the night, he had breathed his last; and all day the bells of all the churches round were answering one another with the slow, swinging, melancholy notes of the knell.

In the early twilight, Père Bonami brought a message that Madame de Selinville requested M. le Baron to come and speak with her, and he was accordingly conducted, with the gendarme behind him, to a small chamber opening into the hall—the same where the incantations of the Italian pedlar had been played off before Philip and Diane. The gendarme remained outside the door by which they entered the little dark room, only lighted by one little lamp.

"Here, daughter," said the priest, "is your cousin. He can answer the question you have so much at heart;" and with these words Père Bonami passed beneath the black curtain that covered the entrance into the hall, admitting as he raised it for a moment a flood of pure light from the wax tapers, and allowing the cadence of the chanting of the priests to fall on the ear. At first Berenger was scarcely able to discern the pale face that looked as if tears were all dried up, and even before his eyes had clearly perceived her in the gloom, she was standing before him with clasped hands, demanding, in a hoarse, breathless whisper, "Had he said anything to you?"

"Anything? No, cousin," said Berenger, in a kind tone. "He had seemed suffering and oppressed all dinner-time, and when the servants left us, he murmured a few confused words, then sank."

"Ah, ah, he spoke it not! Thank heaven! Ah! it is a load gone. Then neither will I speak it," sighed Diane, half aloud. "Ah! cousin, he loved you."

"He often was kind to us," said Berenger, impelled to speak as tenderly as he could of the enemy, who had certainly tortured him, but as if he loved him.

"He bade us save you," said Diane, her eyes shining with strange wild light in the gloom. "He laid it on my aunt and me to save you; you must let us. It must be done before my brother comes," she added, in hurried accents. "The messengers are gone; he may be here any moment. He must find you in the chapel—as—as my betrothed!"

"And you sent for me here to tempt me—close to such a chamber as that?" demanded Berenger, his gentleness becoming sternness, as much with his own worse self as with her.

"Listen. Ah! it is the only way. Listen, cousin. Do you know what killed my father? It was my brother's letter saying things must be brought to an end: either you must be given up to the King, or worse—worse. And now, without him to stand between you and my brother, you are lost. Oh! take pity on his poor soul that has left his body, and bring not your blood on his head."

"Nay," said Berenger, "if he repented, the after consequences to me will have no effect on him now."

"Have pity then on yourself—on your brother."

"I have," said Berenger. "He had rather die with me than see me a traitor."

"And least of all," she exclaimed, with choking grief, "have you compassion on me!—on me who have lost the only one who felt for me—on me who have loved you with every fibre of my heart—on me who have lived on the music of your hardest, coldest word—on me who would lay my life, my honour, in the dust for one grateful glance from you—and whom you condemn to the anguish of—your death! Aye, and for what? For the mere shadow of a little girl, who had no force to love you, of whom you know nothing—nothing! Oh! are you a crystal rock or are you a man? See, I kneel to you to save yourself and me."

There were hot tears dropping from Berenger's eyes as he caught Diane's hand, and held it forcibly to prevent her thus abasing herself. Her wild words and gestures thrilled him in every pulse and wrung his heart, and it was with a stifled, agitated voice that he said—

"God help you and me both, Diane! To do what you ask would—would be no saving of either. Nay, if you will kneel," as she struggled with him, "let it be to Him who alone can bring us through;" and releasing her hand, he dropped on his knees by her side, and covered his face with his hands, in an earnest supplication that the spirit of resistance which he almost felt slipping from him might be renewed. The action hushed and silenced her, and as he rose he spoke no other word, but silently drew back so much of the curtain that he could see into the hall, where the dead man still lay uncoffined upon the bed where his own hands had laid him, and the low, sweet requiem of kneeling priests floated round him. Rest, rest, and calm they breathed into one sorely tried living soul, and the perturbed heart was quelled by the sense how short the passage was to the world where captivity and longing would be ended. He beckoned to Père Bonami to return to Diane, and then, protected by his presence from any further demonstrations, kissed her hand and left her.

He told Philip as little as possible of this interview, but his brother remarked how much time he spent over the Psalms that evening.

The next day the brothers saw from their upper window the arrival of Narcisse, or, as he had called himself for the last three years, the Marquis de Nid-de-Merle, with many attendant gentlemen, and a band of fifty or sixty gendarmes. The court was filled with their horses, and rang with their calls for refreshment. And the captives judged it wise to remain in their upper room in case they should be called for.

They were proved to have been wise in so doing; for about an hour after their arrival there was a great clanging of steel boots, and Narcisse de Ribaumont, followed by a portly, heavily-armed gentleman, wearing a scarf of office, by two of the servants, and by two gendarmes, entered the room. It was the first time the cousins had met since *le baiser d'Eustacie* had been hissed into Berenger's ear. Narcisse looked older, sallower, and more worn than at that time; and Philip, seeing his enemy for the first time, contrasted him with the stately presence of Berenger, and felt as if a rat were strangling a noble steed.

Each young man punctiliously removed his hat, and Nid-de-Merle, without deigning further salutation, addressed his companion. "Sir, you are here on the part of the King, and to you I deliver up these prisoners who, having been detained here on a charge of carrying on a treasonable correspondence, and protected by my father out of consideration for the family, have requited his goodness by an attempt to strangle him, which has caused his death."

Philip actually made a leap of indignation; Berenger, better prepared, said to the officer, "Sir, I am happy to be placed in charge of a King's servant, who will no doubt see justice done, and shelter us from the private malice that could alone devise so monstrous an accusation. We are ready to clear ourselves upon oath over the corpse, and all the household and our own guards can bear witness."

"The witnesses are here," said Narcisse, pointing to the servants, ill-looking men, who immediately began to depose to having found their master purple-faced and struggling in the hands of the two young men, who had been left alone with him after dinner.

Berenger felt that there was little use in self-defence. It was a fabrication the more easily to secure his cousin's purpose of destroying him, and his best hope lay in passing into the hands of persons who were less directly interested in his ruin. He drew himself up to his full height, saying, "If there be justice in France, our innocence will be proved. I demand, sir, that you examine the abbess, the priest, the steward, the sergeant of gendarmes: they are impartial witnesses, and will serve the King's justice, if justice be his purpose. Or, if this be but M. de Nid-de-Merle's way of completing the work he left unfinished four years ago, I am ready. Only let my brother go free. He is heir to nothing here."

"Enough, sir. Words against the King's justice will be reckoned against you," said the officer. "I shall do myself the honour of attending the funeral the day after to-morrow, and then I shall convey you to Tours, to answer for this deed at your leisure. Monsieur le Marquis, are the prisoners secure here, or would you have them *gardés à vue.*"

"No need for that," said Narcisse, lightly; "had there been any exit they would have found it long ago. Your good fellows outside the door keep them safe enough. M. le Baron de Ribaumont, I have the honour to wish you a good morning."

Berenger returned his bow with one full of defiance, and the door was again locked upon the prisoners; while Philip exclaimed, "The cowardly villain, Berry; is it a hanging matter?"

"Not for noble blood," said Berenger. "We are more likely to be brought to no trial, but to lie prisoners for life;" then, as Philip grew white and shivered with a sick horror, he added bravely, "But they shall not have us, Philip. We know the vaults well enough to play at hide and seek with them there, and even if we find no egress we may hold out till they think us fled and leave open the doors!"

Philip's face lighted up again, and they did their best by way of preparation, collecting wood for torches, and putting aside food at their meals. It was a very forlorn hope, but the occupation it caused was effectual in keeping up Philip's spirits, and saving him from despondency.

CHAPTER XXXIX.

THE PEDLAR'S PREDICTION.

> " But if ne'er so close you wall him,
> Do the best that you may ;
> Blind Love, if so you call him,
> Will find out his way."
>
> *Old Song.*

"Too late," muttered Berenger to himself, as he stood by the fire in his prison-chamber. Humfrey and Philip were busy in the vaults, and he was taking his turn in waiting in the sitting-room to disarm suspicion. "It is too late now, and I thank God that so it is."

"Do you indeed, M. le Baron," said a low voice close beside him; and, as he turned in haste, he beheld, at the foot of the turret-stair, the youth Aimé de Selinville, holding a dark lantern in his hand, and veiling its light.

"Ha!" and he started to his feet. "Whence come you?"

"From my Lady," was the youth's answer. "She has sent me to ask whether you persist in what you replied to her the other day. For if not, she bids me say that it is not too late."

"And if I do persevere?"

"Then—ah! what do I know? Who can tell how far malice can go? And there are towers and bastilles where hope never enters. Moreover, your researches underground are known."

"Sir," said Berenger, the heartsinking quelled by the effort of resistance, "Madame de Selinville has my answer—I must take the consequences. Tell her, if she truly wishes me well, the honourable way of saving us would be to let our English friends know what has befallen us."

"You forget, M. le Baron, even if she could proclaim the dishonour of her family, interference from a foreign power might only lead to a surer mode of removing you," said Aimé, lowering his voice and shuddering.

"Even so, I should thank her. Then would the bitterest pang be taken away. Those at our home would not deem us faithless recreants."

"Thank her!" murmured the lad in an inward voice: "Very well, sir, I will carry her your decision. It is your final one. Disgrace, prison, death—rather than freedom, love, wealth!"

"The semblance of dishonour rather than the reality!" said Berenger, firmly.

The light-footed page disappeared, and in a few moments a very different tread came up from below, and Philip appeared.

"What is it, Berry? Methought I heard a voice."

"Forgive me, brother," said Berenger, holding out his hand; "I have thrown away another offer."

"Tush, the thing to pardon would be having accepted one. I only wish they would leave us in peace! What was it this time?"

"A message through young Selinville. Strange, to trust her secrets to that lad. But hush, here he is again, much sooner than I thought. What, sir, have you been with your Lady again?"

"Yes, sir," the youth said, with a trembling voice, and Berenger saw that his eyes were red with weeping; "she bids me tell you that she yields. She will save you even while you hate and despise her! There is only one thing——"

"And what is that?"

"You must encumber yourself with the poor Aimé. You must let me serve you instead of her. Listen, sir, it cannot be otherwise." Then with a brisker, more eager voice, he continued: "Monsieur knows that the family burial-place is Bellaise? Well, to-morrow, at ten o'clock, all the household, all the neighbourhood, will come and sprinkle holy water on the bier. The first requiem will be sung, and then will all repair to the convent. There will be the funeral mass, the banquet, the dole. Every creature in the castle—nay, in all the neighbourhood for twenty miles round—will be at the convent, for the Abbess has given out that the alms are to be double, and the bread of wheat. Not a soul will remain here, save the two gendarmes on guard at that door, and the poor Aimé, whom no one will miss, even if any person could be distinguished in their black cloaks. Madame la Comtesse has given him this key, which opens a door on the upper floor of the keep, unknown to the guards, who, for that matter, shall have a good tankard of spiced wine to console and occupy them. Then is the way clear to the castle-court, which is not overlooked by their window, the horses are in the stables, and we are off,—that is, if M. le Baron will save a poor youth from the wrath of M. de Nid-de-Merle."

"You are an honest fellow!" cried Philip, shaking him vehemently by the hand. "You shall go with us to England, and we will make a brave man of you."

"We shall owe you our lives," said Berenger, warmly, "and be ever bound to you. Tell your lady that *this* is magnanimity; that now I truly thank her as our preserver, and shall bless her all the days of the life she gives us. But my servants?"

"Guibert is a traitor," said Aimé; "he has been so ever since you were at Paris. Breathe no word to him; but he, as a Catholic, shall be invited to the funeral. Your stout Englishman should by all means be with us."

"My Norman, also," added Berenger,—"my dear foster-brother, who has languished in the dungeon for three years;" and when the explanation had been made, Aimé assented, though half-unwillingly, to the necessity, and presently quitted them to bear back their answer to his lady. Philip shook his hand violently again, patted him on the back, so as almost to take away his breath, and bade him never fear, they would be sworn brothers to him for ever; and then threw up his hat into the air, and was so near astonishing the donjon walls with a British hurrah, that Berenger had to put his hand over his mouth and strangle the shout in his very throat.

The chief of that night was spent in enlarging the hole in Osbert's wall, so as to admit of his creeping through it; and they also prepared their small baggage for departure. Their stock of money, though some had been spent on renewing their clothes, and some in needful gratuities to the servants and gendarmes, was sufficient for present needs, and they intended to wear their ordinary dress. They were unlikely to to meet any of the peasants in the neighbourhood; and, indeed, Berenger had so constantly ridden out in his black mask, that its absence, now that his scars were gone, was as complete a change as could be effected in one whose height was so unusual.

"There begins the knell," said Philip, standing at the window. "It's our joy-bell, Berry! Every clang seems to me to say, 'Home! home! home!'"

"For you, Phil," said Berenger; "but I must be satisfied of Eustacie's fate first. I shall go first to Nissard—whither we were bound when we were seized—then to La Rochelle, whence you may——"

"No more of that," burst out Philip. "What! would you have me leave you now, after all we have gone through together? Not that you will find her. I don't want to vex you, brother, on such a day as this, but yon conjurer's words are coming true in the other matter."

"How? What mean you, Phil?"

"What's the meaning of Aimé?" asked Philip. "Even I am French scholar enough for that. And who sends him?"

Meantime the court was already filling with swarms of persons of every rank and degree, but several anxious hours had passed before the procession was marshalled; and friars and monks, black, white, and grey,—priests in rich robes and tall caps,—black-cloaked gentlemen and men-at-arms,—all bearing huge wax tapers,—and peasants and beggars of every conceivable aspect,—filed out of the court, bearing with them the richly-emblazoned bier of the noble and puissant knight, the Beausire Charles Eustache de Ribaumont Nid-de-Merle, his son walking behind in a long black mantle, and all who counted kindred or friendship following two and two; then all the servants, every one who properly belonged to the castle, were counted out by the brothers from their windows, and Guibert among them.

"Messieurs," a low, anxious voice sounded in the room.

"We will only fetch Osbert."

It was a terrible only, as precious moments slipped away before there appeared in the lower chamber Berenger and Humfrey, dragging between them a squalid wretch, with a skin like stained parchment over a skeleton, tangled hair and beard, staring bewildered eyes, and fragments of garments, all dust, dirt, and rags.

"Leave me, leave me, dear master," said the object, stretching his whole person towards the fire as they let him sink down before it. "You would but ruin yourself."

"It is madness to take him," said Aimé, impatiently.

"I go not without him," said Berenger. "Give me the soup, Philip."

Some soup and wine had been placed by the fire, and likewise a shirt and a suit of Humfrey's clothes were spread before it. Aimé burst out into the yard, absolutely weeping with impatience, when, unheeding all his remonstrances, his three companions applied themselves to feeding, rubbing, and warming Osbert, and assuring him that the pains in his limbs would pass away with warmth and exercise. He had been valiant of heart in his dungeon; but his sudden plunge into upper air was like rising from the grave, and brought on all the effects of his dreary captivity, of which he had hardly been sensible when he had first listened to the voice of hope.

Dazzled, crippled, helpless, it seemed almost impossible that he should share the flight, but Berenger remained resolute; and when Aimé returned from his fourth frantic promenade, he was told that all was ready.

But for the strength of Berenger and Humfrey the poor fellow could never have been carried up and up, nearly to the top of the keep, then along a narrow gallery, then down again even to the castle-hall, now empty, though with the candlesticks still around where the bier had been. Aimé knelt for a moment where the head had been, hiding hi face; Osbert rested in a chair; and Philip looked wistfully up at his own sword hung over the chimney.

"Resume your swords, Messieurs," said Aimé, observing him; "Madame desires it; and take pistols also."

They gladly obeyed; and when, after this short delay, they proceeded, Osbert moved somewhat less painfully, but when they arrived at the stable only four horses stood there.

"Ah! this miserable!" cried Aimé, passionately, "he ruins all my arrangements."

"Leave me," again entreated Landry. "Once outside, I can act the beggar and cripple, and get back to Normandy."

"Better leave me," said Humfrey; "they cannot keep me when you are out of their clutches."

"Help me, Humfrey," said Berenger, beginning to lift his foster-brother to the saddle; but there the poor man wavered, cried out that his head swam, and he could not keep his seat, entreating almost in agony to be taken down.

"Lean on me," said Berenger, putting his arms round him. "There! you will be able to get to the Grange du Temple, where you will be in safe shelter."

"Sir, sir," cried Aimé, ready to tear his hair, "this is ruin! My lady meant you to make all speed to La Rochelle and there embark, and this is the contrary way!"

"That cannot be helped," said Berenger; "it is the only safe place for my foster-brother."

Aimé, with childish petulance, muttered something about ingratitude in crossing his lady's plans; but, as no one attended to him, he proceeded to unfasten his horse, and then exclaimed, half-crying, "Will no one help me?"

"Not able to saddle a horse! a pretty fellow for a cavalier!" exclaimed Philip, assisting, however, and in a few minutes they were all issuing from a low side gate, and looking back with bounding hearts at the drooping banner on the keep of Nid-de-Merle.

Only young Aimé went with bowed head and drooping look, as though pouting, and Berenger, putting Osbert's bridle into Humfrey's hand, stepped up to him, saying,

"Hark you, M. de Selinville, I am sorry if we seemed to neglect you. We owe you and your lady all gratitude, but I must be the judge of my own duty, and you can only be with me if you conform."

The youth seemed to be devouring his tears, but only said, "I was vexed to see my lady's plan marred, and your chance thrown away."

"Of that I must judge," said Berenger.

They were in a bye-lane, perfectly solitary. The whole country was at the funeral. Through the frosty air there came an occasional hum or murmur from Bellaise, or the tinkle of a cow-bell in the fields, but no human being was visible. It was certain, however, that the Rotrous, being Huguenots, and no vassals of Nid-de-Merle, would not be at the obsequies; and Berenger, walking with swift strides, supporting Osbert on his horse, continued to cheer him with promises of rest and relief there, and listened to no entreaties from Philip or Humfrey to take one of their horses. Had not Osbert borne him on his shoulders through the butchery at Paris, and endured three years of dungeon for his sake?

As for Philip, the slow pace of their ride was all insufficient for his glee. He made his horse caracole at every level space, till Berenger reminded him that they might have far to ride that night, and even then he was constantly breaking into attempts at shouting and whistling as often repressed, and springing up in his stirrups to look over the high hedges.

The Grange was so well concealed in its wooded ravine, that only, when close upon the gate, the party became aware that this farm-yard, usually so solitary, formed an exception to the general desertion of the country. There was a jingle and a stamp of horses in the court, which could hardly be daylight echoes of the Templars. Berenger feared that the Guisards might have descended upon Rotrou, and was stepping forward to reconnoitre, while young De Selinville, trembling, besought him not to run into danger, but to turn and hasten to La Rochelle. By this time, however, the party had been espied by two soldiers stationed at the gate, but not before Berenger had had time to remark that they did not wear either the gold *fleur de lys* like his late guards, or the white cross of Lorraine; nor had they the strange air of gay ferocity usual with the King's mercenaries. And almost by instinct, at a venture, he made the old Huguenot sign he had learnt from his father, and answered, "For God and the Religion."

The counter-sign was returned. "Béarn and Bourbon is the word to-day, comrade," replied the sentinel. "*Eh quoi!* have you had an encounter, that you bring a wounded man?"

"Not wounded, but nearly dead in a Guisard prison," said Berenger, with an unspeakable sense of relief and security, as the sentries admitted them into the large walled court, where horses were eating hay, being watered and rubbed down; soldiers snatching a hasty meal in corners; gentlemen in clanking breastplates coming in and out of the house, evidently taking orders from a young man in a grey and silver suit, whose brown eagle face, thin cheeks, arched nose, and black eyes of keenest fire, struck Berenger at once with a sense of recognition as well as of being under a glance that seemed to search out everybody and everything at once.

"More friends!" and the tone again recalled a flood of recollections. "I thank and welcome you. What! You have met the enemy—where is he?"

"My servant is not wounded, Sire," said Berenger,

removing his hat and bending low. "This is the effect of long captivity. We have but just escaped."

"Then we are in the same case! Pardon me, sir, I have seen you before, but for once I am at fault."

"When I call myself De Ribaumont, your Grace will not wonder."

"The dead alive! If I mistake not, it was in the Inferno itself that we last met! But we have broken through the gates at last! I remember poor King Charles was delighted to hear that you lived! But where have you been a captive?"

"At Nid-de-Merle, Sire; my kinsmen accused me of treason in order to hinder my search for my wife. We escaped even now during the funeral of the Chevalier."

"By favour of which we are making our way to Parthenay unsuspected, though, by my faith, we gather so like a snow-ball, that we could be a match for a few hundreds of Guisards. Who is with you, M. de Ribaumont?"

"Let me present to your Majesty my English brother, Philip Thistlewood," said Berenger, drawing the lad forward, making due obeisance, though entirely ignorant who was the plainly-dressed, travel-soiled stranger, so evidently a born lord of men.

"An Englishman is ever welcome," was his gracious reception.

"And," added Berenger, "let me also present the young De Selinville, to whom I owe my escape. Where is he, Philip?"

He seemed to be busy with the horses, and Berenger could not catch his eye.

"Selinville! I thought that good Huguenot house was extinct."

"This is a relation of the late Count de Selinville, my

cousin's husband, Sire. He arranged my evasion, and would be in danger at Nid-de-Merle. Call him, Philip."

Before this was done, however, the King's attention was otherwise claimed, and turning to one of his gentlemen he said, "Here, D'Aubigné, I present to you an acquaintance made in Tartarus. See to his entertainment ere we start for Parthenay."

Agrippa d'Aubigné, still young, but grave and serious looking, greeted M. de Ribaumont as men meet in hours when common interests make rapid friendships; and from him Berenger learnt, in a few words, that the King of Navarre's eyes had been opened at last to the treachery of the court, and his own dishonourable bondage. During a feverish attack, one night when D'Aubigné and D'Armagnac were sitting up with him, his resolution was taken; and on the first hunting day after his recovery, he, with these two, the Baron de Rosny and about thirty more of his suite, had galloped away, and had joined the Monsieur and the Prince of Condé at Alençon. He had abjured the Catholic faith, declared that nothing except ropes should bring him back to Paris, and that he left there the mass and his wife—the first he could dispense with, the last he meant to have; and he was now on his way to Parthenay to meet his sister, whom he had sent Rosny to demand. By the time Berenger had heard this, he had succeeded in finding honest Rotrou, who was in a state of great triumph, and readily undertook to give Osbert shelter, and as soon as he should have recovered to send him to head-quarters with some young men who he knew would take the field as soon as they learnt that the King of Navarre had set up his standard. Even the inroads made into the good farmer's stores did not abate his satisfaction in entertaining the prime hope of the Huguenot cause; but Berenger advanced as large a sum as he durst out of his purse, under pretext of the maintenance of Osbert during his stay at the Grange. He examined Rotrou upon his subsequent knowledge of Isaac Gardon and Eustacie, but nothing had been heard of them since their departure, now nearly three years back, except a dim rumour that they had been seen at the Synod of Montauban.

"Well, my friend," said Philip, when about to remount, "this will do rather better than a headlong gallop to Rochelle with Nid-de-Merle at our heels."

"If M. le Baron is safe, it is well," said Aimé shortly.

"Is Selinville there?" said Berenger, coming up. "Here, let me take you to the King of Navarre: he knew your family in Languedoc."

"No, no," petulantly returned the boy. "What am I that he should notice me? It is M. de Ribaumont whom I follow, not him or his cause."

"Boy," said Berenger, dismayed, "remember, I have answered for you."

"I am no traitor," proudly answered the strange boy, and Berenger was forced to be thus satisfied, though intending to watch him closely.

CHAPTER XL.

THE SANDS OF OLONNE.

" Is it the dew of night
  That on her glowing cheek
Shines in the moonbeam ?—Oh, she weeps, she weeps,
 And the good angel that abandoned her
 At her hell baptism, by her tears drawn down
 Resumes his charge . . . and the hope
  Of pardon and salvation rose
  As now she understood
  Thy lying prophecy of truth."
SOUTHEY.

"M. DE RIBAUMONT," said Henry of Navarre, as he stood before the fire after supper at Parthenay, "I have been thinking what commission I could give you proportioned to your rank and influence."

"Thanks to your Grace, that inquiry is soon answered. I am a beggar here. Even my paternal estate in Normandy is in the hands of my cousin."

"You have wrongs," said Henry, "and wrongs are sometimes better than possessions in a party like ours."

Berenger seized the opening to explain his position, and mention that his only present desire was for permission, in the first place, to send a letter to England by the messenger whom the King was despatching to Elizabeth, in tolerable security of her secret countenance; and, secondly, to ride to Nissard to examine into the story he had previously heeded so little, of the old man and his daughter rescued from the waves the day before La Sablerie was taken.

"If Pluto relented, my dear Orpheus, surely Navarre may," said Henry good-humouredly; "only may the priest not be more adamantine than Minos. Where lies Nissard? On the Sables d'Olonne? Then you may go thither with safety while we lie here, and I shall wait for my sister, or for news of her."

So Berenger arranged for an early start on the morrow; and young Selinville listened with a frown, and strange look in his dark eyes. "You go not to England?" he said.

"Not yet?" said Berenger.

"This was not what my lady expected," he muttered; but though Berenger silenced him by a stern look, he took the first opportunity of asking Philip if it would not be far wiser for his brother to place himself in safety in England.

"Wiser, but less honest," said Philip.

"He who has lost all here, who has incurred his grandfather's anger," pursued Aimé, "were he not wiser to make his peace with his friends in England?"

"His friends in England would not like him the better for deserting his poor wife's cause," said Philip. "I advise you to hold your tongue, and not meddle or make."

Aimé subsided, and Philip detected something like tears. He had still much of rude English boyhood about him, and he laughed roughly. "A fine fellow, to weep at a word! Hie thee back to feed my lady's lap-dog, 'tis all thou art fit for."

"There spoke English gratitude," said Aimé, with a toss of the head and flash of the eye.

Philip despised him the more for casting up his obligations, but had no retort to make. He had an idea of making a man of young Selinville, and his notion of the process had something of the bullying tendency of English youth towards the poor-spirited or cowardly. He ordered the boy roughly, teased him for his ignorance of manly exercises, tried to cure his helplessness by increasing his difficulties, and viewed his fatigue as affectation or effeminacy. Berenger interfered now and then to guard the poor boy from a horse-jest or practical joke, but he too felt that Aimé was a great incumbrance, hopelessly cowardly, fanciful, and petulant; and he was sometimes driven to speak to him with severity, verging on contempt, in hopes of rousing a sense of shame.

The timidity, so unusual and inexplicable in a youth of eighteen or twenty, showed itself irrepressibly at the Sands of Olonne. These were not misty, as on Berenger's former journey. Nissard steeple was soon in sight, and the guide who joined them on a rough pony had no doubt that there would be ample time to cross before high water. There was, however, some delay, for the winter rains had brought down a good many streams of fresh water, and the sands were heavy and wet, so that their horses proceeded slowly, and the rush and dash of the waves proclaimed that the flow of the tide had begun. To the two brothers the break and sweep was a home-sound, speaking of freshness and freedom, and the salt breeze and spray carried with them life and ecstasy. Philip kept as near the incoming waves as his inland-bred horse would endure, and sang, shouted, and hallooed to them as welcome as English waves; but Aimé de Selinville had never even beheld the sea before: and even when the tide was still in the distance, was filled with nervous terror as each rushing fall sounded nearer; and, when the line of white foamy crests became more plainly visible, he was impelled to hurry on towards the steeple so fast that the guide shouted to him that he would only bury himself in a quicksand.

"But," said he, white with alarm, and his teeth chattering, "how can we creep with those dreadful waves advancing upon us to drown us?"

Berenger silenced Philip's rude laugh, and was beginning to explain that the speed of the waves could always be calculated by an experienced inhabitant; and his voice had seemed to pacify Aimé a little, when the spreading water in front of a broken wave flowing up to his horse's feet, again rendered him nearly frantic. "Let us go back!" he wildly entreated, turning his horse; but Berenger caught his bridle, saying, "That would be truly death. Boy, unless you would be scorned, restrain your folly. Nothing else imperils us."

Here, however, the guide interposed, saying that it had become too late to pursue their course along the curve of the shore, but they must at once cut straight across, which he had intended to avoid, because of the greater depth of a small river that they would have to cross, which divided further out into small channels, more easily forded. They thus went along the chord of the arc formed by the shore, and Aimé was somewhat reassured, as the sea was at first farther off; but before long they reached the stream, which lost itself in many little channels in the sands, so that when the tide was out there was a perfect network of little streams dividing low shingly or grassy isles, but at nearly high tide, as at present, many of these islets were submerged, and the strife between river and sea caused sudden deepenings of the water in the channels.

The guide eagerly explained that the safest place for crossing was not by the large sandbank furthest inland and looking firm and promising—it was a recent shifting performance of the water's heaping up, and would certainly sink away and bury horse and man. They must ride further out, to the shingly isle; it and the channels on either side had shingly bottoms, and were safe.

"This way," called Berenger, himself setting the example, and finding no difficulty; the water did not rise above his boots, and the current was not strong. He had reached the shingly isle when he looked round for his companions; Humfrey and Philip were close behind him; but, in spite of the loud "*gare!*" of the guide, Aimé, or his horse,—for each was equally senseless with alarm,—were making inwards; the horse was trying to tread on the sandbank, which gave way like the water itself, under its frantic struggles—there was a loud cry—a shrill, unmistakeable woman's shriek—the horse was sinking—a white face and helpless form were being carried out on the waves, but not before Berenger had flung himself from his horse, thrown off his cloak and sword, and dashed into the water; and in the lapse of a few moments he struggled back to the island, where were Philip and Humfrey, leg-deep in water: the one received his burthen, the other helped him to land.

"On, gentlemen, not a moment to lose," cried the guide; and Berenger, still panting, flung himself on his horse, held out his arms, gathered the small, almost inanimate figure upon the horse's neck before him, and in a few minutes more they had crossed the perilous passage, and were on a higher bank where they could safely halt; and Philip, as he came to help his brother, exclaimed, "What a fool the boy is!"

"Hush!" said Berenger, gravely, as they laid the figure on the ground.

"What! He can't have been drowned in that moment. We'll bring him to."

"Hands off!" said Berenger, kneeling over the gasping

form, and adding in a lower voice, "Don't you see?" He wound his hand in the long drenched hair, and held it up, with cheeks burning like fire, and his scar purple.

"A woman!—what?—who?" Then suddenly divining, he exclaimed, "The jade!" and started with wide eyes.

"Stand back," said Berenger; "she is coming to herself."

Perhaps she had been more herself than he knew, for, as he supported her head, her hand stole over his and held it fast. Full of consternation, perplexity, and anger as he was, he could not but feel a softening pity towards a creature so devoted, so entirely at his mercy. At the moment when she lay helpless against him, gasps heaving her breast under her manly doublet, her damp hair spread on his knees, her dark eyes in their languor raised imploringly to his face, her cold hand grasping his, he felt as if this great love were a reality, and as if he were hunting a shadow; and, as if fate would have it so, he must save and gratify one whose affection must conquer his, who was so tender, so beautiful—even native generosity seemed on her side. But in the midst, as in his perplexity, he looked up over the grey sea; he seemed to see the picture so often present to his mind of the pale, resolute girl, clasping her babe to her breast, fearless of the advancing sea, because true and faithful. And at that thought faith and prayer rallied once again round his heart, shame at the instant's wavering again dyed his cheek; he recalled himself, and speaking the more coldly and gravely because his heart was beating over hotly, he said, "Cousin, you are better. It is but a little way to Nissard."

"Why have you saved me, if you will not pity me? she murmured.

"I will not pity, because I respect my kinswoman who has saved our lives," he said, steadying his voice with difficulty. "The priest of Nissard will aid me in sparing your name and fame."

"Ah!" she cried, sitting up with a start of joy, "but he would make too many inquiries! Take me to England first."

Berenger started as he saw how he had been misunderstood.

"Neither here nor in England could my marriage be set aside, cousin. No; the priest shall take charge of you, and place you in safety and honour."

"He shall not!" she cried hotly. "Why—why will you drive me from you—me who ask only to follow you as a menial servant?"

"That has become impossible," he answered, "to say nothing of my brother, my servant, and the guide have seen;" and, as she remembered her streaming hair, and tried, in dawning confusion, to gather it together, he continued: "You shrank from the eye of the King of Navarre. You cannot continue as you have done; you have not even strength."

"Ah! had you sailed for England," she murmured.

"It had only been greater shame," he said. "Cousin, I am head of your family, husband of your kinswoman, and bound to respect the reputation you have risked for me. I shall, therefore, place you in charge of the priest till you can either return to your aunt or to some other convent. You can ride now. We will not wait longer in these wet garments."

He raised her from the ground, threw his own dry cloak round her shoulders and unmanageable hair, and lifted her on his horse; but, as she would have leant against him, he drew himself away, beckoned to Philip, and put the bridle into his hands, saying, "Take care of her. I shall ride on and warn the priest."

"The rock of diamond," she murmured, not aware that the diamond had been almost melting. That youthful gravity and resolution, with the mixture of respect and protection, imposed as usual upon her passionate nature, and daunted her into meekly riding beside Philip without a word—only now and then he heard a low moan, and knew that she was weeping bitterly.

At first the lad had been shocked beyond measure, and would have held aloof as from a kind of monster, but Madame de Selinville had been the first woman to touch his fancy, and when he heard how piteously she was weeping, and recollected where he should have been but for her, as well as all his own harshness to her as a cowardly boy, he felt himself brutally ungrateful, and spoke: "Don't weep so, Madame; I am sorry I was rude to you, but you see, how should I take you for a woman?"

Perhaps she heard, but she heeded not.

"My brother will take good care to shield you," Philip added. "He will take care you are safe in one of your nunneries;" and as she only wept the more, he added, with a sudden thought, "You would not go there; you would embrace the Protestant faith?"

"I would embrace whatever was his."

Philip muttered something about seeing what could be done. They were already at the entrance of the village, and Berenger had come out to meet them, and, springing towards him, Philip exclaimed, in a low voice, "Berry, she would abjure her Popish errors! You can't give her up to a priest."

"Foolery, Philip," answered Berenger, sternly.

"If she would be a convert!"

"Let her be a modest woman first;" and Berenger, taking her bridle, led her to the priest's house.

He found that Père Colombeau was preaching a Lent sermon, and that nobody was at home but the housekeeper, to whom he had explained briefly that the lady with him had been forced to escape in disguise, had been nearly drowned, and was in need of refreshment and female clothing. Jacinthe did not like the sound, but drenched clothes were such a passport to her master's house, that she durst not refuse. Berenger carried off his other companions to the cabaret, and when he had dried himself, went to wait for the priest at the church-door, sitting in the porch, where more than one echo of the exhortation to repentance and purity rang in his ears, and enforced his conviction that here he must be cruel if he would be merciful.

It was long before Père Colombeau came out, and then, if the scar had not blushed for all the rest of his face, the sickly, lanky lad of three years since would hardly have been recognised in the noble, powerful-looking young man who unbonneted to the good curé. But the priest's aspect was less benignant when Berenger tried to set before him his predicament; he coldly asked where the unhappy lady was; and when Berenger expressed his intention of coming the next morning to ask his counsel, he only bowed. He did not ask the brothers to supper, nor show any civility; and Berenger, as he walked back to the cabaret, perceived that his story was but half-believed, and that, if Diane's passion were still stronger than her truth or generosity, she would be able to make out a terrible case against him, and to willing ears, naturally disposed against a young cavalier and a heretic.

He sat much dispirited by the fire of the little wine shop, thinking that his forbearance had been well-nigh thrown away, and that his character would never be cleared in Eustacie's eyes, attaching, indeed, more importance to the blot than would have been done by a youth less carefully reared.

It was quite dark when a knock came to the door: the curé's white head appeared in the lamplight; he nodded kindly to all the guests, and entreated that M. de Ribaumont would do him the favour to come and speak with him.

No sooner were they outside the house, than the curé held out his hand, saying, "Sir, forgive me for a grievous injustice towards you;" then pressing his hand, he added with a voice tremulous with emotion, "Sir, it is no slight thing to have saved a wandering sheep by your uprightness and loyalty."

"Have you then opened her eyes, father?" said Berenger, relieved from a heavy load.

"You have, my son," said the old man. "You have taught her what truth and virtue are. For the rest, you shall hear for yourself."

Before Berenger knew where he was, a door was opened, and he found himself in the church. The building was almost entirely dark; there were two tall lights at the altar in the distance, and a few little slender tapers burning before certain niches and shrines, but without power to conquer with the gloom more than enough to spread a pale circle of yellow light beneath them, and to show mysteriously a bit of vaulting above. A single lamp hung from an arch near the door, and beneath it, near a pillar, knelt, or rather crouched, on the floor, a female figure with a dark peasant cloak drawn over her head.

"The first token of penitence is reparation to the injured," said the priest.

Berenger looked at him anxiously.

"I will not leave you," he added. "See, I shall pray for you yonder, by the altar," and he slowly moved up the aisle.

"Rise, cousin, I entreat you," said Berenger, much embarrassed, as he disappeared in the darkness.

"I must speak thus," she answered, in a hoarse, exhausted voice. "Ah! pardon, pardon!" she added, rising, however, so far as to raise clasped hands and an imploring face. "Ah! can you pardon? It was through me that you bear those wounds; that she—Eustacie—was forced into the masque, to detain you for *that* night. Ah! pardon."

"That is long past," said Berenger. "I have been too near death not to have pardoned that long ago. Rise, cousin, I cannot see you thus."

"That is not all," continued Diane. "It was I—I who moved my father to imprison you." Then, as he bent his head, and would have again entreated her to rise, she held out her hand as if to silence him, and spoke faster, more wildly. "Then—then I thought it would save your life. I thought——" she looked at him strangely with her great dark eyes, all hollow and cavernous in her white face.

"I know," said Berenger, kindly, "you often urged it on me."

There was a sort of movement on the part of the kneeling figure of the priest at the altar, and she interrupted, saying precipitately, "Then—then, I did think you free."

"Ah!" he gasped. "Now——!"

"Now I know that she lives!" and Diane once more sank at his feet a trembling, shrinking, annihilated heap of shame and misery.

Berenger absolutely gave a cry that, though instantly repressed, had the ring of ecstasy in it. "Cousin—cousin!" he cried, "all is forgiven—all forgotten, if you will only tell me where!"

"That I cannot," said Diane, rousing herself again, but

speaking in a dull, indifferent tone, as of one to whom the prime bitterness was past, "save that she is under the care of the Duchess de Quinet;" and she then proceeded, as though repeating a lesson: "You remember the Italian conjurer whom you would not consult? Would that I had not!" she added, clasping her hands. "His prediction lured me! Well, he saw my father privately, told him he had seen her, and had bought her jewels, even her hair. My father sent him in quest of her again, but told not me till the man returned with tidings that she was at Quinet, in favour with the Duchess. You remember that he went from home. It was to demand her; and, ah! you know how long I had loved you, and they told me that your marriage was void, and that all would be well upon the dispensation coming. And now the good father there tells me that I was deceived—cruelly deceived—that such a dispensation would not be granted save through gross misrepresentation." Then, as Berenger began to show tokens of eagerness to come at tidings of Eustacie, she continued, "Ah! it is vain to seek to excuse one you care not for. My father could learn nothing from the Duchess; she avowed that she had been there, but would say no more. However, he and my brother were sure she was under their protection; they took measures, and—and the morning my poor father was stricken, there had been a letter from my brother to say he was on her track, and matters must be ended with you, for he should have her in a week;" and then, as Berenger started forward with an inarticulate outburst, half of horror, half of interrogation, she added, "Where, he said not, nor did I learn from him. All our one interview was spent in sneers that answered to my wild entreaties; but this I know—that you would never have reached Tours a living man."

"And now, now he is on the way to her!" cried Berenger, "and you kept it from me!"

"There lay my hope," said Diane, raising her head; and now, with glittering eyes and altered voice, "How could I not but hate her who had bereaved me of you; her for whose sake I could not earn your love?"

The change of her tone had, perhaps, warned the priest to draw nearer, and as she perceived him, she said, "Yes, father, this is not the way to absolution, but my heart will burst if I say not all."

"Thou shalt not prevail, foul spirit," said the priest, looking earnestly into the darkness, as though he beheld the fiend hovering over her, "neither shall these holy walls be defiled with accents of unhallowed love. You have made your reparation, daughter; it is enough."

"And can you tell me no more?" said Berenger, sadly. "Can you give me no clue that I may save her from the wolf that may be already on her track? Cousin, if you would do this, I would bless you for ever."

"Alas! I would if I could! It is true, cousin, I have no heart to deceive you any longer. But it is to Madame de Quinet that you must apply, and if my brother has thought me worth pursuit, you may be in time! One moment,"—as he would have sprung away as if in the impulse to fly to the rescue,—"cousin; had you gone to England as I hoped, I would have striven to deserve to win that love of yours, but you have conquered by your constancy. Now, father, I have spoken my last save as penitent."

She covered her head and sank down again.

Berenger, bewildered and impelled to be doing something, let the priest lead him out before he exclaimed, "I said nothing to her of pardon!"

"You do pardon?" said the priest.

He paused a moment. "Freely, if I find my wife. I can only remember now that she set me on the way. I would ease her soul, poor thing, and thinking would make me hard again."

"Do the English bring up their sons with such feelings?" asked the curé, pausing for a moment.

"Of course," said Berenger. "May I say that one word, sir?"

"Not now," said the priest; "she had better be left to think of her sin towards Heaven, rather than towards man."

"But do you leave her there, sir?"

"I shall return. I shall pray for her true penitence," said the priest, and Berenger perceived from his tone that one without the pale might inquire no further. He only asked how safe and honourable shelter could be found for her; and the curé replied that he had already spoken to her of the convent of Luçon, and should take her there so soon as it could safely be done, and that Abbess Monique, he trusted, would assist her crushed spirit in finding the path of penitence. He thought her cousin had better not endeavour to see her again; and Berenger himself was ready to forget her very existence in his burning anxiety to outstrip Narcisse in the quest of Eustacie.

CHAPTER XLI.

OUR LADY OF HOPE.

"Welcome to danger's hour,
Brief greeting serves the time of strife."
SCOTT.

As soon as it was possible to leave Nissard, Berenger was on his way back to head-quarters, where he hoped to meet the Duke de Quinet among the many Huguenot gentlemen who were flocking to the Bourbon standard; nor was he disappointed in the hope, for he was presented to a handsome middle-aged gentleman, who told him, with much politeness, that he was aware that his mother had had the honour to receive and entertain Mme. de Ribaumont, and that some months ago he had himself arranged for the conveyance of her letters to England, but, he said, with a smile, he made a point of knowing nothing of his mother's guests, lest his duties as a governor might clash with those of hospitality. He offered to expedite M. de Ribaumont's journey to Quinet, observing that, if Nid-de-Merle were, indeed, on the point of seizing the lady, it must be by treachery; indeed he had, not ten days back, had the satisfaction of hanging an Italian mountebank who had last year stolen a whole packet of despatches, among them letters from Mme. de Ribaumont, and the fellow was probably acting as a spy upon her, so that no time was to be lost in learning from his mother where she was. On the next morning he was about to send forward twenty men to reinforce a little frontier garrison on the river Dronne, and as M. le Baron must pass through the place, it would be conferring a favour on him to take the command. The men were all well mounted, and would not delay; and when once across the frontier of Guyenne, no escort would be needed.

Berenger gladly accepted the proposal. It did not occur to him that he was thus involved in the civil war, and bearing arms against the sovereign. In spite of Queen Elizabeth's alliance with the French court, she connived at her youthful subjects seeking the bubble reputation in the mouths of Valois cannon; and so little did Henry III. seem to Berenger to be his king, that he never thought of the question of allegiance,—nay, if the royal officers were truly concerned in his arrest, he was already an outlaw. This was no moment for decision between Catholic and Calvinist; all he wanted was to recover his wife and forestall her enemies.

Henry of Navarre gave his full consent to the detachment being placed under charge of M. de Ribaumont. He asked somewhat significantly what had become of the young gentleman who had attended M. de Ribaumont, and Philip blushed crimson to the ears, while Berenger replied, with greater coolness than he had given himself credit for, that the youth had been nearly drowned on the Sables d'Olonne, and had been left at Dom Colombeau's to recover. The sharp-witted King looked for a moment rather as Sir Hugh the Heron did when Marmion accounted for his page's absence, but was far too courteous and too *insouciant* to press the matter further, though Berenger saw quite enough of his expression to feel that he had been delivered from his companion only just in time.

Berenger set forth as soon as his impatience could prevail to get the men into their saddles. He would fain have ridden day and night, and grudged every halt for refreshment, so as almost to run the risk of making the men mutinous. Evening was coming on, and his troop had dismounted at a cabaret, in front of which he paced up and down with Philip, trying to devise some pretext for hastening them on another stage before night, when a weary, travel-stained trooper rode up to the door and was at once hailed as a comrade by the other men, and asked, "What cheer at Pont de Dronne?"

"Bad enough," he answered, "unless you can make the more speed there!" Then making obeisance to Berenger he continued his report, saying that Captain Falconnet was sending him to M. le Duc with information that the Guisards were astir, and that five hundred *gens d'armes*, under the black Nid-de-Merle, as it was said, were on their way intending to surprise Pont de Dronne, and thus cut the King of Navarre off from Guyenne and his kingdom beyond it. After this Berenger had no more difficulty with his men, who were most of them Quinet vassals, with homes south of the Dronne, and the messenger only halted for a hasty meal, hastening on to the Duke, that a more considerable succour might at once be despatched.

"Is she there whom they call the Lady of Hope?" asked one of the soldiers, a mercenary, less interested than most of his comrades, as he had only a fortnight since transferred his services from Guise to Quinet.

"Our Lady of Sadness just now," replied the messenger; "her old father is at the point of death. However, she is there, and at our last siege twenty wine-skins would not so well have kept up men's hearts."

"And the little one, the white fairy, is she there too?

They say 'tis a spirit, a changeling that could not brook the inside of a church, but flew out of the Moustier at Montauban like a white swan, in the middle of a sermon."

"I only know I've seen her sleep like a dormouse through prayers, sermon, and all at Pont de Dronne. *Follette* if she be, she belongs to the white elves of the moonlight."

"Well, they say bullets won't touch her, and no place can be taken where she is," replied the trooper. "Nay, that Italian pedlar rogue, the same that the Duke has since hung, has sold to long Gilles and snub-nosed Pierre silver bullets, wherewith they have sworn to shoot the one or the other next time they had a chance."

These words were spoken at no great distance from Berenger, but passed by him as mere men-at-arms' gossip, in his eagerness to expedite the start of his party; and in less than an hour they were *en route* for Pont de Dronne: but hasten as he would, it was not till near noon the next day that he came in sight of a valley, through which wound a river, crossed by a high backed bridge, with a tall pointed arch in the middle, and a very small one on either side. An old building of red stone, looking like what it was—a monastery converted into a fortress—stood on the nearer, or northern bank, and on the belfry tower waved a flag with the arms of Quinet. Higher up the valley, there was an ominous hum, and clouds of smoke and dust; and the *gens d'armes* who knew the country, rejoiced that they were come just in time, and exchanged anxious questions whether the enemy were not fording the river above them, so as to attack not only the fortress on this northern side, but the bridge tower on the southern bank of the river.

Spurring down the hill, the party were admitted, at the well-guarded gateway, into a large thickly-walled yard, where the soldiers and horses remained, and Beranger and Philip, passing through a small arched doorway into the body of the old monastery, were conducted to a great wainscoted hall, where a pulpit projecting from the wall, and some defaced emblematic ornaments, showed that this had once been the refectory, though guard-room appliances now occupied it. The man who had shown them in left them, saying he would acquaint Captain Falconnet with their arrival, and just then a sound of singing drew both brothers to the window. It looked out on what had once been the quadrangle, bounded on three sides by the church, the refectory, and the monks' lodgings, the cloistered arcade running round all these. The fourth side was skirted by the river, which was, however, concealed by an embankment, raised, no doubt, to supply the place of the wall, which had been unnecessary to the peaceful original inhabitants. What attracted Berenger's eyes was, however, a group in the cloister, consisting of a few drooping figures, some of men in steel caps, others of veiled, shrouded women, and strange, mingled feelings swept over him as he caught the notes of the psalm sung over the open grave—

"Si qu'en paix et seurté bonne
Coucherai et reposerai—
Car, Seigneur, ta bonté tout ordonne
Et elle seule espoir donne
Que seur et sain régnant serai."

"Listen, Philip," he said, with moistening eyes; then as they ended, "It is the 4th Psalm: 'I lay me down in peace and take my rest.' Eustacie and I used to sing it to my father. It was well done in these mourners to sing it over him whom they are laying down to take his rest while the enemy are at the gates. See, the poor wife still kneels while the rest disperse; how dejected and utterly desolate she looks."

He was so intently watching her as not to perceive the entrance of a tall, grizzled old man in a steel cap, evidently the commander of the garrison. There was the brief welcome of danger's hour—the briefer, because Captain Falconne was extremely deaf, and, taking it for granted that the new comers were gentlemen of the Duke's, proceeded to appoint them their posts without further question. Berenger had intended to pursue his journey to Quinet without delay, but the intelligence that the enemy were on the southern as well as the northern side of the river rendered this impossible; and besides, in defending this key of Guyenne against Narcisse, he was also defending Eustacie.

The state of affairs was soon made known to him. The old monastery, covering with its walls an extensive space, formed a fortress quite strong enough to resist desultory attacks, and protect the long bridge, which was itself strongly walled on either side, and with a barbican at the further end. In former assaults the attacks had always been on the north, the Catholic side, as it might be called; but now the enemy had crossed the river above the fort, and were investing the place on both sides. Long foreseeing this, the old commandant had guarded the bank of the river with an earthwork, a long mound sloped irregularly on either hand, over which numerous little paths had since been worn by the women within, when on their way to the river with their washing; but he had been setting every one to work to destroy and fill up these, so that the rampart was smooth and sloping, perfectly easy indeed to cross, but high and broad enough to serve as an effectual protection against such artillery as the detached troops of the Guise party were likely to possess; and the river was far too wide, deep, and strong in its main current to be forded in the face of a hostile garrison. The captain had about fifty *gens d'armes* in his garrison, besides the twenty new-comers whom he persisted in regarding as Berenger's charge; and there were, besides, some seventy peasants and silk-spinners, who had come into the place as a refuge from the enemy—and with these he hoped to hold out till succour should come from the Duke. He himself took the command of the north gate, where the former assaults had been made, and he entrusted to his new ally the tower protecting the bridge, advising him to put on armour; but Berenger, trying on a steel cap, found that his head could not bear the weight and heat, and was forced to return to his broad-brimmed Spanish hat, while Philip in high glee armed himself as best he could with what Captain Falconnet could lend him. He was too much excited to eat of the scanty meal that was set before them: a real fight seemed like a fair-day to him, and he was greatly exalted by his brother's post of command —a post that Berenger felt a heavy responsibility only thrust upon him by the commandant's incapacity of hearing how utterly inexperienced he was.

The formal summons to surrender to the King, and the refusal, had duly passed, and it became evident that the first attack was to be on the bridge-gate. Captain Falconnet hurried to the place, and the fighting was hot and desperate. Every assailant who tried to throw his fagot into the moat became a mark for arquebus or pistol, and the weapons that had so lately hung over the hearth at Nid-de-Merle were now aimed again and again at the heads and corslets of Guisards, with something of the same exulting excitement as, only higher, more engrossing, and fiercer than, that with which the lads had taken aim at a wolf, or ridden after a fox. Scaling-ladders were planted and hurled down again; stones were cast from the battlements, crushing the enemy; and throughout Berenger's quick eye, alert movements, and great height and strength, made him a most valuable champion, often applauded by a low murmur of commendation from old Falconnet, or a loud shout of "Ha, well done, the Duke's Englishman," from the *gens d'armes*—for English they would have him to be—on the presumptions afforded by his companions, his complexion, and his slow speech. Nor did Philip and Humfrey fail to render good service. But just as the enemy had been foiled in a sharp assault and were dragging away their wounded, Philip touched his brother, and saying, "I can hold out no longer," showed blood trickling down his right side.

Berenger threw an arm round him, and Captain Falconnet seeing his case, said, "You are hit, *petit Anglais;* you have done gallantly. There will be time for you to take him to his quarters, sir; these fellows have had enough for the present, and you can tarry with him till you hear the bugle. Whither, did you ask? Let me see. You, Renaud, take him to the chapel: the old chancel behind the boarding will be more private; and desire Madame to look to him. Farewell! I hope it may prove slight; you are a brave youth." And he shook hands with Philip, whose intense gratification sustained him for many steps afterwards.

He hardly remembered receiving the hurt, and was at first too busy to heed it, or to call off any one's attention, until a dread of falling, and being trodden on, had seized him and made him speak; and indeed he was so dizzy that Berenger with difficulty kept him on his feet over the bridge, and in the court lifted him in his arms and carried him almost fainting into the cloister, where by the new-made grave still knelt the black-veiled mourner. She started to her feet as the soldier spoke to her, and seemed at first not to gather the sense of his words; but then, as if with an effort, took them in, made one slight sound like a moan of remonstrance at the mention of the place, but again recollecting herself, led the way along a stone passage, into which a flight of stairs descended into the apsidal chancel, roughly boarded off from the rest of the church. It was a ruinous, desolate place, and Berenger looked round in dismay for some place on which to lay down his almost unconscious burthen. The lady bent her head and signed towards the stone sedilia in the wall; then, after two ineffectual essays to make her voice audible, choked as it was with long weeping, she said, low and huskily, "We will make him more comfortable soon;" and added some orders to the soldier, who disappeared up the stairway, and Berenger understood that he was gone to fetch bedding. Then taking from under her heavy mourning cloak a large pair of scissors, she signed to Berenger how to support his brother, while they relieved him of his corslet, sword-belt, and doublet. The soldier had meantime returned with an old woman, both loaded with bedding, which she signed to them to arrange in one of the little bays or niches that served to form a crown of lesser chapels around the chancel. She flung aside her muffling cloak, but her black hood still hung far over her face, and every now and then hand or handkerchief was lifted as if to clear her eyes from the tears that would not cease to gather and blind her; and she merely spoke when some direction to an assistant, some sympathetic word to the patient, was needed. Even Philip in his dizzy trance guessed that he was succeeding to the bed whence one much dearer had gone to his quieter rest in the cloister. Before he was laid there, however, the bugle sounded; there was a loud shout, and Philip exclaimed, "Go, brother!"

"Trust him to me, sir," said the sunken, extinguished voice; "we will do our best for him."

He was forced merely to lift Philip to the bed, and to hurry away, while the soldier followed him saying, consolingly, "Fear not, sir, now our Lady of Hope has him. Nothing goes ill to which she sets her hand."

Another growl of artillery was now heard, and it was time for the warriors to forget the wounded in the exigencies of the present. An attack was made on both gates at once, and the commandant being engaged at his own post, Berenger had to make the utmost of his brief experience, backed by the counsel of a tough old sergeant: and great was his sense of exhilaration, and absolute enjoyment in this full and worthy taxing of every power of mind or body. The cry among the enemy, "Aim at the black plume," attested his prominence; but the black plume was still unscathed when spring twilight fell. The din began to subside; recalls were sounded by the besiegers; and Berenger heard his own exploit bawled in the ear of the deaf commandant, who was advancing over the bridge. The old captain complimented him, told him that he should be well reported of to M. le Duc and Sieur la Noue, and invited him to supper and bed in his own quarters. The supper Berenger accepted, so soon as he should know how it was with his brother; but as to bed, he intended to watch his brother, and visit his post from time to time.

The captain entered by the main door of the chapel, where ten or twelve wounded were now lying, tended by peasant women. Berenger merely passed through, seeing as he went the black hood busy over a freshly-brought-in patient. He found a door which admitted him through the rough screen of boards to the choir where he had been in the earlier part of the day. The moonlight came through the shivered eastern windows, but a canvas curtain had been hung so as to shelter Philip's vaulted recess from the cold draught, and the bed itself, with a chair beside it, looked neat, clean, and comfortable. Philip himself was cheery ; he said the bullet had made a mere flesh-wound, and had passed out on the other side, and the Lady of Hope, as they called her, was just such another as Aunt Cecily, and had made him very comfortable, with clean linen, good cool drinks, and the tenderest hand. But he was very sleepy, so sleepy that he hardly cared to hear of the combat, only he roused himself for a moment to say, "Brother, I have seen Dolly."

"Dolly !"

"Our sister Dolly."

"Ah, Phil ! many a strange visitor has come to me in the Walnut Chamber at home."

"I tell you I was in my perfect senses," returned Philip ; "there she was, just as when we left her. And, what was stranger still, she talked French."

"Sleep and see her again," laughed Berenger.

CHAPTER XLII.

THE SILVER BULLET.

> "I am all wonder, O my son, my soul
> Is stunned within me; powers to speak to him
> Or to interrogate him have I none,
> Or even to look on him."
>
> COWPER'S *Odyssey.*

IN his waking senses Philip adhered to his story that his little sister Dolly had stood at the foot of his bed, called him "*le pauvre,*" and had afterwards disappeared, led away by the nursing lady. It seemed to Berenger a mere delusion of feverish weakness; for Philip had lost a great deal of blood, and the wound, though not dangerous, permitted no attempt at moving, and gave much pain. Of the perfections of the lady as nurse and surgeon Philip could not say enough, and, pale and overwept as he allowed her to be, he declared that he was sure that her beauty must equal Mme. de Selinville's. Berenger laughed, and looking round this strange hospital, now lighted by the full rays of the morning sun, he was much struck by the scene.

It was the chancel of the old abbey church. The door by which they had entered was very small, and perhaps had led merely to the abbot's throne, as an irregularity for his own convenience, and only made manifest by the rending away of the rich wooden stall work, some fragments of which still clung to the walls. The east end, like that of many French churches, formed a semicircle, the high altar having been in the centre, and five tall deep bays forming lesser chapels embracing it, their vaults all gathered up into one lofty crown above, and a slender pillar separating between each chapel, each of which further contained a tall narrow window. Of course, all had been utterly desolated, and Philip was actually lying in one of these chapels, where the sculptured figure of St. John and his Eagle still remained on the wall; and a sufficient remnant of his glowing sanguine robe of love was still in the window to serve as a shield from the *bise*. The high altar of rich marbles was a mere heap of shattered rubbish; but what surprised Berenger more than all the ruined architectural beauty which his *cinque-cento* trained taste could not understand, was, that the tiles of the pavement were perfectly clean, and diligently swept, the rubbish piled up in corners; and here and there the relics of a cross or carved figure lay together, as by a tender, reverential hand. Even the morsels of painted glass had been placed side by side on the floor, so as to form a mosaic of dark red, blue, and green; and a child's toy lay beside this piece of patchwork. In the midst of his observations, however, Captain Falconnet's servant came to summon him to breakfast; and the old woman appearing at the same time, he could not help asking whether the Lady were coming.

"Oh yes, she will come to dress his wound in good time," answered the old woman.

"And when? I should like to hear what she thinks of it," said Berenger.

"How?" said the old woman, with a certain satisfaction in his disappointment; "is our Lady of Hope to be coming down among you gay gallants?"

"But who is this Lady of Hope?" demanded he.

"Who should she be but our good pastor's daughter? Ah! and a brave, good daughter she was too, abiding the siege because his breath was so bad that he could not be moved."

"What was his name?" asked Berenger, attracted strangely by what he heard.

"Ribault, Monsieur—Pasteur Ribault. Ah! a good man, and sound preacher, when preach he could; but when he could not, his very presence kept the monks' *revenants* from vexing us—as a cat keeps mice away; and, ah! the children have been changed creatures since Madame dealt with them. What! Monsieur would know why they call her our Lady of Hope? Espérance is her true name; and, moreover, in the former days this abbey had an image that they called Notre-Dame de l'Espérance, and the poor deceived folk thought it did great miracles. And so, when she came hither, and wrought such cures, and brought blessings wherever she went, it became a saying among us that at length we had our true Lady of Hope."

A more urgent summons here forced Berenger away, and his repetition of the same question received much the same answer from deaf old Captain Falconnet. He was obliged to repair to his post with merely a piece of bread in his hand; but, though vigilance was needful, the day bade fair to be far less actively occupied than its predecessor: the enemy were either disposed to turn the siege into a blockade, or were awaiting reinforcements and heavier artillery; and there were only a few desultory attacks in the early part of the morning. About an hour before noon, however, the besiegers seemed to be drawing out in arms, as if to receive some person of rank, and at the same time sounds were heard on the hills to the eastward, as if troops were on the march. Berenger having just been told by the old sergeant that probably all would be quiet for some time longer, and been almost laughed at by the veteran for consulting him whether it would be permissible for him to be absent a few minutes to visit his brother, was setting out across the bridge for the purpose, his eyes in the direction of the rampart, which followed the curve of the river. The paths which—as has been said—the feet of the washerwomen and drawers of water had worn away in quieter times, had been smoothed and scarped away on the outer side, so as to come to an abrupt termination some feet above the gay marigolds, coltsfoot, and other spring flowers that smiled by the water-side. Suddenly he beheld on the rampart a tiny grey and white figure, fearlessly trotting, or rather dancing, along the summit, and the men around him exclaimed, "The little moonbeam child!" "A fairy—a changeling!"—"They cannot shoot at such a babe!" "Nor could they harm her!" "Hola! little one! *Gare!* go back to your mother!" "Do not disturb yourself, sir; she is safer than you," were the ejaculations almost at the same moment, while he sprang forward, horrified at the peril of such an infant. He had reached the angle between the bridge and rampart, when he perceived that neither humanity nor superstition were protecting the poor child; for, as she turned down the remnant of one of the treacherous little paths, a man in bright steel and deep black had spurred his horse to the river's brink, and was deliberately taking aim at her. Furious at such brutality, Berenger fired the pistol he held in his hand, and the wretch dropped from his horse; but at the same moment his pistol exploded, and the child rolled down the bank, whence a piteous wail came up, impelling Berenger to leap down to her assistance, in the full face of the enemy. Perhaps he was protected for the moment by the confusion ensuing on the fall of the officer; and when he reached the bottom of the bank, he saw the little creature on her feet, her round cap and grey woollen dress stripped half off in the fall, and her flaxen hair falling round her plump, white, exposed shoulder, but evidently unhurt, and gathering yellow marigolds as composedly as though she had been making May garlands. He snatched her up, and she said, with the same infantine dignity, "Yes, take me up; the naughty people spoilt the path. But I must take my beads first." And she tried to struggle out of his arms, pointing therewith to a broken string among the marshy herbage on which gleamed—the pearls of Ribaumont!

In the few seconds in which he grasped them, and then bore the child up the embankment in desperate bounds, a hail of bullets poured round him, ringing on his breastplate, shearing the plume from his hat, but scarcely even heard; and in another moment he had sprung down, on the inner side, grasping the child with all his might, but not daring even to look at her, in the wondrous flash of that first conviction. She spoke first. "Put me down, and let me have my beads," she said in a grave, clear tone; and then first he beheld a pair of dark blue eyes, a sweet wild-rose face—Dolly's all over. He pressed her so fast and so close, in so speechless and overpowering an ecstasy, that again she repeated, and in alarm, "Put me down, I want my mother!"

"Yes, yes! your mother! your mother! your mother!" he cried, unable to let her out of his embrace; and then restraining himself as he saw her frightened eyes, in absolute fear of her spurning him, or struggling from him, "My sweet! my child! Ah! do you not know me?" Then, remembering how wild this was, he struggled to speak calmly: "What are you called, my treasure?"

"I am *la petite Rayonette*," she said, with puzzled dignity and gravity; "and my mother says I have a beautiful long name of my own besides."

"Bérangère—my Bérangère——"

"That is what she says over me, as I go to sleep in her bosom at night," said the child, in a wondering voice, soon exchanged for entreaty, "Oh, hug me not so hard! Oh, let me go—let me go to her! Mother! mother!"

"My child, mine own, I am taking thee!—Oh, do not struggle with me!" he cried, himself imploring now. "Child, one kiss for thy father;" and meantime, putting absolute force on his vehement affection, he was hurrying to the chancel.

There Philip hailed them with a shout as of desperate anxiety relieved; but before a word could be uttered, down the stairs flew the Lady of Hope, crying wildly, "Not there—she is not—" but perceiving the little one in the stranger's arms, she held out her own, crying, "Ah! is she hurt, my angel?"

"Unhurt, Eustacie! Our child is unhurt!" Berenger said, with an agonized endeavour to be calm; but for the moment her instinct was so entirely absorbed in examining into the soundness of her child's limbs, that she neither saw nor heard anything else.

"Eustacie," he said, laying his hand on her arm. She started back, with bewildered eyes. "Eustacie—wife! do you not know me? Ah! I forgot that I am changed."

"You—you—" she gasped, utterly confounded, and gazing as if turned to stone, and though at that moment the vibration of a mighty discharge of cannon rocked the walls, and strewed Philip's bed with the crimson shivers of St. John's robe, yet neither of them would have been sensible of it had not Humfrey rushed in at the same moment, crying, "They are coming on like fiends, sir!"

Berenger passed his hand over his face. "You will know me *when—if* I return, my dearest," he said. "If not, then still, thank God! Philip, to you I trust them!"

And with one kiss on that still, cold, almost petrified brow, he had dashed away. There was a space of absolutely motionless silence, save that Eustacie let herself drop on the chancel step, and the child, presently breaking the spell, pulled her to attract her notice to the flowers. "Mother, here are the *soucis* for the poor gentleman's broth. See, the naughty people had spoilt all the paths, and I rolled down and tore my frock, and down fell the beads, but be not angry, mother dear, for the good gentleman picked them up, and carried me up the bank."

"The bank!" cried Eustacie, with a scream, as the sense of the words reached her ears. "Ah! no wonder! Well might thy danger bring thy father's spirit;" and she grasped the little one fervently in her arms, murmuring, "Thank, thank God, indeed! Oh! my precious one; and did He send that blessed spirit to rescue thee?"

"And will you tie up my frock, and may I put the flowers into the broth?" chattered Rayonette. "And why did he kiss me and hug me so tight; and how did he know what you say over me as we fall asleep?"

Eustacie clasped her tighter, with a convulsive shudder of thankfulness; and Philip, but half hearing, and barely gathering the meaning of her mood, ventured to speak, "Madame——"

As if touched by an electric shock, Eustacie started up, as recalled to instant needs, and coming towards him said, "Do you want anything, sir? Pardon one who has but newly seen a spirit from the other world—brought by his child's danger." And the dazed, trance-like look was returning.

"Spirit!" cried Philip. "Nay, madame, it was himself. Ah! and you are she whom we have sought so long; and this dear child—no wonder she has Dolly's face."

"Who—what?" said Eustacie, pressing her temples with her hands, as if to retain her senses. "Speak; was yonder a living or dead man—and who?"

"Living, thank God! and your own husband; that is, if you are really Eustacie. Are you indeed?" he added, becoming doubtful.

"Eustacie, that am I," she murmured. "But he is dead—they killed him; I saw the blood where he had waited for me. His child's danger brought him from the grave."

"No, no. Look at me, sister Eustacie. Listen to me. Osbert brought him home, more dead than alive—but alive still."

"No!" she cried, half passionately. "Never could he have lived and left me to mourn him so bitterly."

"If you knew—" cried Philip, growing indignant. "For weeks he lay in deadly lethargy, and when, with his left hand, he wrote and sent Osbert to you, your kinsfolk threw the poor fellow into a dungeon, and put us off with lies that you were married to your cousin. All believed, only he—sick, helpless, speechless, as he was—he trusted you still; and so soon as Méricour came, though he could scarcely brook the saddle, nothing would hold him from seeking you. We saw only ruin at La Sablérie, and well-nigh ever since have we been clapped up in prison by your uncle. We were on the way to Quinet to seek you. He has kept his faith whole through wounds and pain and prison and threats,—ay, and sore temptation," cried Philip, waxing eloquent; "and, oh, it cannot be that you do not care for him!"

"Doubt not my faith, sir," said Eustacie, proudly; "I have been as true to him as if I had known he lived. Nor do I know who you are to question me."

At this moment the child pressed forward, holding between her two careful plump hands a red earthenware bowl, with the tisane steaming in it, and the yellow petals strewn over the surface. She and Philip had taken a great fancy to each other, and while her mother was busy with the other patients, she had been left to her quiet play with her fragments of glass, which she carried one by one to display, held up to the light, to her new friend; who, in his weak state, and after his long captivity, found her the more charming playmate because she so strangely reminded him of his own little sisters. She thought herself his little nurse, and missing from his broth the yellow petals that she had been wont to think the charm of tisane, the housewifely little being had trotted off, unseen and unmissed, across the quadrangle, over the embankment, where she had often gathered them, or attended on the "*lessive*" on the river's brink; and now she broke forth exultingly, "Here, here is the tisane, with all the *soucis*. Let me feed you with them, sir."

"Ah! thou sweet one," gasped Philip, "I could as soon eat them as David could drink the water! For these—for these——!" and the tears rushed into his eyes. "Oh! let me but kiss her, madame; I loved her from the first moment. She has the very face of my little sister—my little sister and Berenger's. What, thou little sweeting, (what French word is good enough for her?) didst run into peril for me, not knowing how near I was to thee? What, must I eat it? Love me then."

But the boarded door was thrown back, and "Madame, more wounded," resounded. The thrill of terror, the elastic reaction, at the ensuing words, "from the north gate," was what made Eustacie in an instant know herself to be not widow but wife. She turned round at once, holding out her hand, and saying with a shaken, agitated voice, "*Mon frère*, pardon me, I know not what I say; and, after all, he will find me *bien méchante* still." Then as Philip devoured her hand with kisses, and held it fast, "I must go; these poor men need me. When I can, I will return."

"Only let me have the little one," entreated Philip; "it is almost home already to look at her."

And when Eustacie next looked in on them, they were both fast asleep.

She, poor thing, the only woman with brains among the many scared females in the garrison, might not rest or look the wonder in the face. Fresh sufferers needed her care, and related gallant things of "the Duke's Englishman," things of desperate daring and prowess that sent the blood throbbing to her heart with exultation, but only to be followed by a pang of anguish at having let him go back to peril—nay, perhaps, to death—without a word of tenderness or even recognition. She imaged him as the sunny-faced youth who had claimed her in the royal castle, and her longing to be at his side and cling to him as his own became every moment more fervent and irresistible, until she gladly recollected the necessity of carrying food to the defenders; and snatching an interval from her hospital cares, she sped to the old circular kitchen of the monastery, where she found the lame baker vainly trying to organize a party of frightened women to carry provisions to the garrison of the bridge-tower.

"Give some to me," she said. "My husband is there! I am come to fetch his dinner."

The peasant women looked and whispered as if they thought that, to add to their misfortunes, their Lady of Hope had become distracted by grief; and one or two, who held the old faith, and were like the crane among the sparrows, even observed that it was a judgment for the profane name that had been given her, against which she had herself uniformly protested.

"My husband is come," said Eustacie, looking round with shining eyes. "Let us be brave wives, and not let our men famish."

She lifted up a loaf and a pitcher of broth, and with the latter poised on her erect and graceful head, and elastic though steady step, she led the way; the others following her with a sort of awe, as of one they fancied in a superhuman state. In fact, there was no great danger in traversing the bridge with its lofty parapet on either side; and her mind was too much exalted and moved to be sensible of anything but a certain exulting awe of the battle sounds. There was, however, a kind of lull in the assault which had raged so fiercely ever since the fall of the officer, and the arrival of the reinforcements. Either the enemy had paused to take food, or were devising some fresh mode of attack; and as the line of women advanced, there started forth from under the arch a broad-shouldered, white-faced, golden-bearded personage, who cried joyously, "My dearest, my bravest! this for me!" and lifted the pitcher from her head as he grasped her hand with a flesh and blood clasp indeed, but the bright-cheeked, wavy-haired lad of her dream withered away with a shock of disappointment, and she only looked up with wistful puzzled earnestness instead of uttering the dear name that she had so long been whispering to herself. "Dearest," he said, "this is precious indeed to me, that you should let me feast my eyes once more on you. But you may not tarry. The rogues may renew their attack at any moment."

She had thought of herself as insisting on standing beside him and sharing his peril. Had he been himself she must have done so, but this was a stranger, whose claiming her made her shrink apart till she could feel the identity which, though she believed, she could not realize. Her hand lay cold and tremulous within his warm pressure, but he was too much wrought up and too full of joy and haste to be sensible of anything but of the brave affection that had dared all to come to him; and he was perfectly happy, even as a trumpet-call among the foe warned him to press her fingers to his lips and say, as his bright blue eye kindled, "God grant that we may meet and thank Him to-night! Farewell, my lost and found! I fight as one who has something to fight for."

He might not leave his post, but he watched her with eyes that could not be satiated, as she recrossed the bridge; and, verily, his superabundant ecstasy, and the energy that was born of it, were all needed to sustain the spirits of his garrison through that terrible afternoon. The enemy seemed to be determined to carry the place before it could be relieved, and renewed the storm again and again with increasing violence; while the defenders, disheartened by their pertinacity, dismayed at the effects of the heavy artillery, now brought to bear on the tower, and direfully afraid of having the bridge destroyed, would have abandoned their barbican and shut themselves up within the body of the place had not Berenger been here, there, and everywhere, directing, commanding, exhorting, cheering, encouraging, exciting enthusiasm by word and example, winning proud admiration by feats of valour and dexterity sprung of the ecstatic inspiration of new-found bliss, and watching, as the conscious defender of his own most beloved, without a moment's respite, till twilight stillness sank on the enemy, and old Falconnet came to relieve him, thanking him for his gallant defence, and auguring that, by noonday to-morrow at latest, M. le Duc would succour them, unless he were hampered by any folly of this young Navarre.

Too blissful for the sense of fatigue, Berenger began to impart to the Commandant his delight, but the only answer he got was "Hope, yes, every hope;" and he again recognised what he had already perceived, that the indistinctness of his utterance made him entirely unintelligible to the deaf Commandant, and that shouting did but proclaim to the whole garrison, perhaps even to the enemy's camp, what was still too new a joy not to be a secret treasure of delight. So he only wrung the old Captain's hand, and strode away as soon as he was released.

It was nearly dark, in spite of a rising moon, but beneath the cloister arch was torch-light, glancing on a steel head-piece, and on a white cap, both bending down over a prostrate figure; and he heard the voice he loved so well say, "It is over! I can do no more. It were best to dig his grave at once here in silence—it will discourage the people less. Renaud and Armand, here!"

He paused for a few minutes unseen in the shadow while she closed the eyes and composed the limbs of the dead soldier; then, kneeling, said the Lord's Prayer in French over him. Was this the being he had left as the petted plaything of the palace? When she rose, she came to the arch and gazed wistfully across the moonlit quadrangle, beyond the dark shade cast by the buildings, saying to the soldier, "You are sure he was safe?"

"My Eustacie," said Berenger, coming forward, "we meet in grave times!"

The relief of knowing him safe after the sickening yearnings and suspense of the day, and moreover the old ring of tenderness in his tone, made her spring to him with real warmth of gladness, and cry, "It is you! All is well."

"Blessedly well, *ma mie*, my sweetheart," he said, throwing his arm round her, and she rested against him murmuring, "Now I feel it! Thou art thyself!" They were in the dark cloister passage, and when he would have moved forward she clung closer to him, and murmured, "Oh wait, wait, yet an instant—Thus I can feel that I have thee—the same—my own!"

"My poor darling," said Berenger, after a second, "you must learn to bear with both my looks and speech, though I be but a sorry shattered fellow for you."

"No, no," she cried, hanging on him with double fervour. "No, I am loving you the more already,—doubly—trebly—a thousand times. Only those moments were so precious, they made all these long years as nothing. But come to the little one, and to your brother."

The little one had already heard them, and was starting forward to meet them, though daunted for a moment by the sight of the strange father: she stood on the pavement, in the full flood of the moonlight from the east window, which whitened her fair face, flaxen hair, and grey dress, so that she did truly look like some spirit woven of the moonbeams. Eustacie gave a cry of satisfaction: "Ah! good, good; it was by moonlight that I saw her first!"

Berenger took her in his arms, and held her to his breast with a sense of insatiable love, while Philip exclaimed, "Ay, well may you make much of her, brother. Well might you seek them far and wide. Such treasures are not to be found in the wide world."

Berenger, without answering, carried the little one to the step of the ruined high altar, and there knelt, holding Eustacie by the hand, the child in one arm, and, with the moon glancing on his high white brow and earnest face, he spoke a few words of solemn thanks and prayer for a blessing on their reunion, and the babe so wonderfully preserved to them.

Not till then did he carry her into the lamplight by Philip's bed, and scan therein every feature, to satisfy his eyes with the fulfilled hope that had borne him through those darkest days, when, despairing of the mother, the thought of the child had still sustained him to throw his will into the balance of the scale between life and death. Little Bérangère gazed up into his face silently, with wondering, grave, and somewhat sleepy eyes, and then he saw them fix themselves on his powder-grimed and blood-stained hands. "Ah! little heart," he said, "I am truly in no state to handle so pure a piece of sugar as thou; I should have rid myself of the battle-stains ere touching thee, but how recollect anything at such a moment?"

Eustacie was glad he had broken the spell of silence; for having recovered her husband, her first instinct was to wait upon him. She took the child from him, explaining that she was going to put her to bed in her own rooms up the stone stair, which for the present were filled with the fugitive women and children who had come in from the country, so that the chancel must continue the lodging of Berenger and his brother; and for the time of her absence she brought him water to wash away the stains, and set before him the soup she had kept warm over her little charcoal brazier. It was only when thus left that he could own, in answer to Philip's inquiries, that he could feel either hunger or weariness; nay, he would only acknowledge enough of the latter to give a perfect charm to rest under such auspices. Eustacie had despatched her motherly cares promptly enough to be with him again just as in taking off his corslet he had found that it had been pierced by a bullet, and pursuing the trace, through his doublet, he found it lodged in that purse which he had so long worn next his heart, where it had spent its force against the single pearl of Ribaumont. And holding it up to the light, he saw that it was of silver. Then there returned on him and Philip the words they had heard two days before, of silver bullets forged for the destruction of the white moonlight fairy, and he further remembered the moment's shock and blow that in the midst of his wild amaze on the river's bank had made him gather his breath and strength to bound desperately upwards, lest the next moment he should find himself wounded and powerless.

For the innocent, then, had the shot been intended; and she running into danger out of her sweet, tender instincts of helpfulness, had been barely saved at the extreme peril of her unconscious father's life. Philip, whose vehement affection for the little one had been growing all day, was in the act of telling Berenger to string the bullet in the place of the injured pearl, as the most precious heirloom of Ribaumont bravery, when Eustacie returned, and learning all, grew pale and shuddered as danger had never made her do before: but this strange day had almost made a coward of her.

"And this it has spared," said Berenger, taking out the string of little yellow shells. "Dost know them, sweet heart? They have been my chaplet all this time."

"Ah!" cried Eustacie, "poor, good Mademoiselle Noémi! she threaded them for my child, when she was very little. Ah! could she have given them to you—could it then not have been true—that horror?"

"Alas! it was too true. I found these shells in the empty cradle, in the burnt house, and deemed them all I should ever have of my babe."

"Poor Noémi! poor Noémi! She always longed to be a martyr; but we fled from her, and the fate we had brought on her. That was the thought that preyed on my dear father. He grieved so to have left his sheep—and it was only for my sake. Ah! I have brought evil on all who have been good to me, beginning with you. You had better cast me off, or I shall bring yet worse!"

"Let it be so, if we are only together."

He drew her to him and she laid her head on his shoulder, murmuring, "Ah! father, father, were you but here to see it. So desolate yesterday, so ineffably blest to-day. Oh! I cannot even grieve for him now, save that he could not just have seen us; yet I think he knew it would be so."

"Nay, it may be that he does see us," said Berenger. "Would that I had known who it was whom you were laying down '*en paix et seurté bonne!*' As it was, the psalm brought precious thoughts of Château Leurre, and the little wife who was wont to sing it with me."

"Ah!" said Eustacie, "it was when he sang those words as he was about to sleep in the ruin of the Temple that first I—cowering there in terror—knew him for no Templar's ghost, but for a friend. That story ended my worst desolation. That night he became my father; the next my child came to me!"

"My precious treasure! Ah! what you must have undergone, and I all unknowing, capable of nothing wiser than going out of my senses, and raging in a fever because I could convince no one that those were all lies about your being aught but my true and loving wife. But tell me, what brought thee hither to be the tutelary patron, where, but for the siege, I had overpassed thee on the way to Quinet?"

Then Eustacie told him how the Italian pedlar had stolen her letters, and attempted to poison her child—the pedlar whom he soon identified with that wizard who had talked to him of "Espérance," until the cue had evidently been given by the Chevalier. Soon after the Duke had despatched a messenger to say that the Chevalier de Ribaumont was on the way to demand his niece; and as it was a period of peace, and the law was decidedly on his side, Madame de Quinet would be unable to offer any resistance. She therefore had resolved to send Eustacie away—not to any of the seaports whither the uncle would be likely to trace her, but absolutely to a place which he would have passed through on his journey into Guyenne. The monastery of Notre-Dame de l'Espérance at Pont de Dronne had been cruelly devastated by the Huguenots in order to form a fortress to command the passage of the river, and a garrison had been placed there, as well as a colony of silk-spinners, attracted by the mulberry-trees of the old abbey garden. These, however, having conceived some terror of the ghosts of the murdered monks, had entreated for a pastor to protect them; and Madame la Duchesse thought that in this capacity Isaac Gardon, known by one of the many aliases to which the Calvinist ministers constantly resorted, might avoid suspicion for the present. She took the persecuted fugitives for some stages in an opposite direction, in her own coach, then returned to face and baffle the Chevalier, while her trusty steward, by a long *détour*, conducted them to Pont de Dronne, which they reached the very night after the Chevalier had returned through it to Nid-de-Merle.

The pastor and his daughter were placed under the special protection of Captain Falconnet, and the steward had taken care that they should be well lodged in three rooms that had once been the abbot's apartments. Their stay had been at first intended to be short, but the long journey had been so full of suffering to Isaac, and left such serious effects, that Eustacie could not bear to undertake it again, and Madame de Quinet soon perceived that she was safer there than at the chateau, since strangers were seldom admitted to the fortress, and her presence there attracted no attention. But for Isaac Gardon's declining health, Eustacie would have been much happier here than at the chateau; the homely housewifely life, where all depended on her, suited her; and, using her lessons in domestic arts of nursing and medicine for the benefit of her father's flock, she had found, to her dismay, that the simple people, in their veneration, had made her into a sort of successor to the patroness of the convent. Isaac had revived enough for a time to be able to conduct the worship in the church, and to instruct some of his flock; but the teaching of the young had been more and more transferred to her, and, as she ingenuously said, had taught her more than she ever knew before. He gradually became weaker through more suffering, and was absolutely incapable of removal, when an attack by the Guisards was threatened. Eustacie might have been sent back to Quinet; but she would not hear of leaving him; and this first had been a mere slight attack, as if a mere experiment on the strength of the place. She had, however, then had to take the lead in controlling the women, and teaching them to act as nurses, and to carry out provisions; and she must then have been seen by some one, who reported her presence there to Narcisse—perhaps by the Italian pedlar. Indeed Humfrey, who came in for a moment to receive his master's orders, report his watch, and greet his lady, narrated, on the authority of the lately enlisted men-at-arms, that M. de Nid-de-Merle had promised twenty crowns to any one who might shoot down the heretics' little white *diablesse*.

About six weeks had elapsed since the first attack on Pont de Dronne, and in that time Gardon had sunk rapidly. He died as he lived, a gentle, patient man, not a characteristic Calvinist, though his lot had been thrown with that party in his perplexed life of truth-seeking and disappointment in the aspirations and hopes of early youth. He had been, however, full of peace and trust that he should open his eyes where the light was clear, and no cloud on either side would mar his perception; and his thankfulness had been great for the blessing that his almost heaven-sent daughter had been to him in his loneliness, bereavement, and decay. Much as he loved her, he did not show himself grieved or distressed on her account; but, as he told her, he took the summons to leave her as a sign that his task was done, and the term of her trials ended. "I trust as fully," he said, "that thou wilt soon be in safe and loving hands, as though I could commit thee to them."

And so he died in her arms, leaving her a far fuller measure of blessing and of love than ever she had derived from her own father; and as the enemy's trumpets were already sounding on the hills, she had feared insult to his remains, and had procured his almost immediate burial in the cloister, bidding the assistants sing, as his farewell, that evening psalm which had first brought soothing to her hunted spirit.

There, while unable, after hours of weeping, to tear herself from the grave of her father and protector, had she in her utter desolation been startled by the summons, not only to attend to the wounded stranger, but to lodge him in the chancel. "Only this was wanting," was the first thought in her desolation, for this had been her own most cherished resort. Either the *bise*, or fear of a haunted spot, or both, had led to the nailing up of boards over the dividing screen, so that the chancel was entirely concealed from the church; and no one ever thought of setting foot there till Eustacie, whose Catholic reverence was indestructible, even when she was only half sure that it was not worse than a foible, had stolen down thither, grieved at its utter desolation, and with fond and careful hands had cleansed it, and amended the ruin so far as she might. She had no other place where she was sure of being uninterrupted; and here had been her oratory, where she daily prayed, and often came to hide her tears and rally her spirits through that long attendance on her fatherly friend. It had been a stolen pleasure. Her reverent work there, if once observed, would have been treated as rank idolatry; and it was with consternation as well as grief that she found, by the Captain's command, that this her sanctuary and refuge was to be invaded by strange soldiers! Little did she think——!

And thus they sat, telling each other all, on the step of the ruined chancel, among the lights and shadows of the apse. How unlike the stately Louvre's halls of statuary and cabinets of porcelain, or the Arcadian groves of Montpipeau! and yet how little they recked that they were in a beleaguered fortress, in the midst of ruins; wounded sufferers all around, themselves in hourly jeopardy. It was enough that they had one another. They were so supremely happy that their minds unconsciously gathered up those pale lights and dark fantastic shades as adjuncts of their bliss.

CHAPTER XLIII.

LE BAISER D'EUSTACIE.

> "No pitying voice, no eye, affords
> One tear to grace his obsequies."
>
> GRAY.

GOLDEN sunshine made rubies and sapphires of the fragments of glass in the windows of Notre-Dame de l'Espérance, and lighted up the brown face and earnest eyes of the little dark figure, who, with hands clasped round her knees, sat gazing as if she could never gaze her fill, upon the sleeping warrior beside whom she sat, his clear straight profile like a cameo, both in chiselling and in colour, as it lay on the brown cloak where he slept the profound sleep of content and of fatigue.

Neither she nor Philip would have spoken or stirred to break that well-earned rest; but sounds from without were not long in opening his eyes, and as they met her intent gaze, he smiled and said, "Good morrow, sweet heart! What, learning how ugly a fellow is come back to thee?"

"No, indeed! I was trying to trace thine old likeness, and then wondering how I ever liked thy boyish face better than the noble look thou bearest now!"

"Ah! when I set out to come to thee, I was a walking rainbow; yet I was coxcomb enough to think thou wouldst overlook it."

"Show me those cruel strokes," she said; "I see one"—and her finger traced the seam as poor King Charles had done—"but where is the one my wicked cousin called by that frightful name?"

"Nay, verily, that sweet name spared my life! A little less spite at my peach cheek, and I had been sped, and had not lisped and stammered all my days in honour of *le baiser d'Eustacie!*" and as he pushed aside his long golden silk moustache to show the ineffaceable red and purple scar, he added, smiling, "It has waited long for its right remedy."

At that moment the door in the rood-screen opened. Captain Falconnet's one eye stared in amazement, and from beneath his grey moustache thundered forth the word "*comment!*" in accents fit to wake the dead.

Was this Espérance, the most irreproachable of pastor's daughters and widows? "What, Madame, so soon as your good father is under ground? At least I thought *one* woman could be trusted; but it seems we must see to the wounded ourselves."

She blushed, but stood her ground; and Berenger shouted, "She is my wife, sir!—my wife whom I have sought so long!"

"That must be as Madame la Duchesse chooses," said the Captain. "She is under her charge, and must be sent to her as soon as this *canaille* is cleared off. To your rooms, madame!"

"I am her husband!" again cried Berenger. "We have been married sixteen years."

"You need not talk to me of dowry; Madame la Duchesse will settle that, if you are fool enough to mean anything by it. No, no, mademoiselle, I've no time for folly. Come with me, sir, and see if that be true which they say of the rogues outside."

And putting his arm into Berenger's, he fairly carried him off, discoursing by the way on *feu* M. l'Amiral's saying that "over-strictness in camp was perilous, since a young saint, an old devil," but warning him that this was prohibited gear, as he was responsible for the young woman to Madame la Duchesse. Berenger, who had never made the Captain hear anything that he did not know before, looked about for some interpreter whose voice might be more effectual, but found himself being conducted to the spiral stair of the church steeple; and suddenly gathering that some new feature in the case had arisen, followed the old man eagerly up the winding steps to the little square of leaden roof where the Quinet banner was planted. It commanded a wide and splendid view, to the Bay of Biscay on the one hand, and the inland mountains on the other; but the warder who already stood there pointed silently to the north, where, on the road by which Berenger had come, was to be seen a cloud of dust, gilded by the rays of the rising sun.

Who raised it was a matter of no doubt; and Berenger's morning orisons were paid with folded hands, in silent thanksgiving, as he watched the sparkling of pikes and gleaming of helmets—and the white flag of Bourbon at length became visible.

Already the enemy below were sending out scouts—they rode to the top of the hill—then a messenger swam his horse across the river. In the camp before the bridge-tower men buzzed out of their tents, like ants whose hill is disturbed; horses were fastened to the cannon, tents were struck, and it was plain that the siege was to be raised.

Captain Falconnet did his ally the honour to consult him on the expedience of molesting the Guisards by a sally, and trying to take some of their guns; but Berenger merely bowed to whatever he said, while he debated aloud the *pros* and *cons*, and at last decided that the garrison had been too much reduced for this, and that M. le Duc would prefer finding them drawn up in good order to receive him, to their going chasing and plundering disreputably among the enemy —the Duke being here evidently a much greater personage than the King of Navarre, hereditary Governor of Guyenne though he were. Indeed, nothing was wanting to the confusion of Berenger's late assailants. In the camp on the north side of the river, things were done with some order; but that on the other side was absolutely abandoned, and crowds were making in disorder for the ford, leaving everything behind them, that they might not have their retreat cut off. Would there be a battle? Falconnet, taking in with his eye the numbers of the succouring party, thought the Duke would allow the besiegers to depart unmolested, but remembered with a sigh that a young king had come to meddle in their affairs!

However, it was needful to go down and marshal the men for the reception of the new comers, or to join in the fight, as the case might be.

And it was a peaceful entrance that took place some hours later, and was watched from the windows of the prior's rooms by Eustacie, her child, and Philip, whom she had been able to install in her own apartments, which had been vacated by the refugee women in haste to return home, and where he now sat in Maître Gardon's great straw chair, wrapped in his loose gown, and looking out at the northern gates, thrown open to receive the King and Duke, old Falconnet presenting the keys to the Duke, the Duke bowing low as he offered them to the King, and the King waving them back to the Duke and the Captain. Then they saw Falconnet presenting the tall auxiliary who had been so valuable to him, the joyous greeting of an old friend bestowed on him, his gesture as he pointed up to the window, and the King's upward look, as he doffed his hat and bowed low, while Eustacie responded with the most graceful of reverences, such as reminded Philip that his little sister-in-law and tender nurse was in truth a great court lady.

Presently Berenger came upstairs, bringing with him his faithful foster-brother Osbert, who, though looking gaunt and lean, had nearly recovered his strength, and had accompanied the army in hopes of finding his master. The good fellow was full of delight at the welcome of his lady, and at once bestirred himself in assisting her in rectifying the confusion in which her guests had left her apartment.

Matters had not long been set straight when steps were heard on the stone stair, and, the door opening wide, Captain Falconnet's gruff voice was heard, "This way, Monseigneur; this way, Sire."

This was Madame la Baronne de Ribaumont's first reception. She was standing at the dark walnut table, fresh starching and crimping Berenger's solitary ruff, while under her merry superintendence those constant playfellows, Philip and Rayonette, were washing, or pretending to wash, radishes in a large wooden bowl, and Berenger was endeavouring to write his letter of good tidings, to be sent by special messenger to his grandfather. Philip was in something very like a Geneva gown; Eustacie wore her prim white cap and frill, and coarse black serge kirtle; and there was but one chair besides that one which Philip was desired to retain, only two three-legged stools and a bench.

Nevertheless, Madame de Ribaumont was equal to the occasion; nothing could have been more courtly, graceful, or unembarrassed than her manner of receiving the King's gallant compliments, and of performing all the courtesies suited to the hostess and queen of the place: it was the air that would have befitted the stateliest castle hall, yet that in its simplicity and brightness still more embellished the old ruinous convent-cell. The King was delighted, he sat down upon one of the three-legged stools, took Rayonette upon his knee, undertook to finish washing the radishes, but ate nearly all he washed, declaring that they put him in mind of his old hardy days on the mountains of Béarn. He insisted on hearing all Rayonette's adventure in detail; and on seeing the pearls and the silver bullet, "You could scarcely have needed the token, sir," said he with a smile to Berenger; "Mademoiselle had already shown herself of the true blood of the bravest of knights."

The tidings of the attack on Pont de Dronne had caused the Duke to make a forced march to its relief, in which the King had insisted on joining him; and they now intended to wait at Pont de Dronne till the rest of the troops came up, and to continue their march through Guyenne to Nérac, the capital of Henry's county of Foix. The Duke suggested that if Philip were well enough to move when the army proceeded, the family might then take him to Quinet, where the Duchess would be very desirous to see Madame; and therewith they took leave with some good-humoured mirth as to whether M. de Ribaumont would join them at supper, or remain in the bosom of his family, and whether he were to be regarded as a gay bridegroom or a husband of sixteen years' standing.

"Nay," said the King, "did his good Orpheus know how nearly his Eurydice had slipped through his fingers again? how M. de Quinet had caught the respectable Pluto yonder in the grey moustache actually arranging an escort to send the lady safe back to Quinet *bon gré malgré*—and truly a deaf Pluto was worse than even Orpheus had encountered!"

So laughing, he bowed again his compliments; but Eustacie

demanded, so soon as he was gone, what he meant by calling her by such names. If he thought it was her Christian name, it was over-familiar—if not, she liked it less.

"It is only that he last saw you in the Infernal Regions, *ma mie*," said Berenger; "and I have sought you ever since, as Orpheus sought Eurydice."

But her learning did not extend so far; and when the explanation was made, she pouted, and owned that she could not bear to be reminded of the most foolish and uncomfortable scene in her life—the cause of all her troubles; and as Berenger was telling her of Diane's confession that her being involved in the pageant was part of the plot for their detention at Paris, Osbert knocked at the door, and entered with a bundle in his arms, and the air of having done the right thing.

"There, sir," he said with proud satisfaction, "I have been to the camp across the river. I heard there were good stuffs to be had there for nothing, and thought I would see if I could find a coat for Monsieur Philippe, for his own is a mere ruin."

This was true, for Eustacie had been deciding that between blood and rents it had become a hopeless case for renovation; and Osbert joyfully displayed a beautifully-embroidered coat of soft leather, which he had purchased for a very small sum of a plunderer who had been there before him. The camp had been so hastily abandoned that all the luggage had been left, and, like a true valet, Osbert had not neglected the opportunity of replenishing his master's wardrobe. "And," said he, "I saw there one whom M. le Baron knows,—M. de Nid-de-Merle."

"Here!" cried Eustacie, startled for a moment, but her eyes resting reassured on her husband.

"Madame need not be alarmed," said Osbert; "M. le

Baron has well repaid him. Ah! ah! there he lies, a spectacle for all good Christians to delight in."

"It was then he, *le scélérat?*" exclaimed Berenger; "I had already thought it possible."

"And he fell by your hands!" cried Eustacie. "That is as it should be."

"Yes, Madame," said Osbert; "it did my very heart good to see him writhing there like a crushed viper. M. le Baron's bullet was mortal, and his own people thought him not worth the moving, so there he lies on the ground howling and cursing. I would have given him the *coup de grâce* myself, but that I thought M. le Baron might have some family matters to settle with him; so I only asked what he thought now of clapping guiltless folk into dungeons, and shooting innocent children like sparrows; but he grinned and cursed like a demon, and I left him."

"In any one's charge?" asked Berenger.

"In the fiend's, who is coming for him," said the descendant of the Norseman. "I only told Humfrey that if he saw any one likely to meddle he should tell them he was reserved for you. Eh! M. le Baron is not going now. Supper is about to be served, and if M. le Baron would let me array him with this ruff of Spanish point, and wax the ends of his belle moustache——"

"It is late," added Eustacie, laying her hand on his arm; "there may be wild men about—he may be desperate! Oh, take care!"

"*Ma mie*, do you not think me capable of guarding myself from a wild cat leap of a dying man? He must not be left thus. Remember he is a Ribaumont."

Vindictiveness and revenge had their part in the fire of Eustacie's nature. Many a time had she longed to strangle Narcisse; and she was on the point of saying, "Think of his attempts on that little one's life—think of your wounds and captivity;" but she had not spent three years with Isaac Gardon without learning that there was sin in giving way to her keen hatred; and she forced herself to silence, while Berenger said, reading her face, "Keep it back, sweet heart! Make it not harder for me. I would as soon go near a dying serpent, but it were barbarity to leave him as Osbert describes."

Berenger was too supremely and triumphantly happy not to be full of mercy; and as Osbert guided him to the hut where the miserable man lay, he felt little but compassion. The scene was worse than he had expected; for not only had the attendants fled, but plunderers had come in their room, rent away the coverings from the bed, and torn the dying man from it. Livid, nearly naked, covered with blood, his fingers hacked, and ears torn for the sake of the jewels on them, lay the dainty and effeminate tiger-fop of former days, moaning and scarcely sensible. But when the mattress had been replaced, and Berenger had lifted him back to it, laid a cloak over him, and moistened his lips, he opened his eyes, but only to exclaim, "You there! as if I had not enough to mock me! Away!" and closed them sullenly.

"I would try to relieve you, cousin," said Berenger.

The answer was a savage malediction on hypocrisy, and the words, "And my sister?"

"Your sister is in all honour and purity at the nunnery of Luçon."

He laughed a horrible, incredulous laugh. "Safely disposed of ere you cajoled *la petite* with the fable of your faithfulness! Nothing like a Huguenot for lying to both sides;" and then ensued another burst of imprecations on the delay that had prevented him from seizing the fugitives—till Berenger felt as if the breath of hell were upon him, and could not help vindicating himself, vain though he knew it to be: "Narcisse de Ribaumont," he said gravely, "my word has never been broken, and you know the keeping of it has not been without cost. On that word believe that Madame de Selinville is as spotless a matron as when she perilled herself to save my life. I never even knew her sex till I had drawn her half drowned from the sea, and after that I only saw her in the presence of Dom Colombeau of Nissard, in whose care I left her."

Narcisse's features contorted themselves into a frightful sneer as he muttered, "The intolerable fool! and that he should have got the better of me, that is if it be true—and I believe not a word of it."

"At least" said Berenger, "waste not these last hours on hating and reviling me, but let this fellow of mine, who is a very fair surgeon, bind your wound again."

"Eh!" said Narcisse, spitefully, turning his head, "your own rogue? Let me see what work he made of *le baiser d'Eustacie*. Pray, how does it please her?"

"She thanks Heaven that your chief care was to spoil my face."

"I hear she is a prime doctress; but of course you brought her not hither lest she should hear *how* you got out of our keeping."

"She knows it."

"Ah! she has been long enough at court to know one must overlook, that one's own little matters may be overlooked."

Berenger burst out at last, "Her I will not hear blasphemed: the next word against her I leave you to yourself."

"That is all I want," said Narcisse. "These cares of yours are only *douceurs* to your conceited heretical conscience, and a lengthening out of this miserable affair. You would scoff at the only real service you could render me."

"And that is——"

"To fetch a priest. Ha! ha! one of your sort would sooner hang me. You had rather see me perish body and soul in this Huguenot doghole! What! do you stammer? Bring a psalm-singing heretic here, and I'll teach him and you what you *may* call blasphemy."

"A priest you shall have, cousin," said Berenger gravely; "I will do my utmost to bring you one. Meanwhile, strive to bring yourself into a state in which he may benefit you."

Berenger was resolved that the promise should be kept. He saw that despair was hardening the wretched man's heart, and that the possibility of fulfilling his Church's rites might lead him to address himself to repentance; but the difficulties were great. Osbert, the only Catholic at hand, was disposed to continue his vengeance beyond the grave, and only at his master's express command would even exercise his skill to endeavour to preserve life till the confessor could be brought. Ordinary Huguenots would regard the desire of Narcisse as a wicked superstition, and Berenger could only hurry back to consult some of the gentlemen who might be supposed more unprejudiced.

As he was crossing the quadrangle at full speed, he almost ran against the King of Navarre, who was pacing up and down reading letters, and who replied to his hasty apologies by saying he looked as if the fair Eurydice had slipped through his hands again into the Inferno.

"Not so, Sire, but there is one too near those gates. Nid-de-Merle is lying at the point of death, calling for a priest."

"*Ventre Saint-Gris!*" exclaimed the King, "he is the very demon of the piece, who carved your face, stole your wife, and had nearly shot your daughter."

"The more need of his repentance, Sire, and without a priest he will not try to repent. I have promised him one."

"A bold promise!" said Henry. "Have you thought how our good friends here are likely to receive a priest of Baal into the camp?"

"No, Sire, but my best must be done. I pray you counsel me."

Henry laughed at the simple confidence of the request, but replied, "The readiest way to obtain a priest will be to ride with a flag of truce to the enemy's camp—they are at St. Esmé—and say that M. de Nid-de-Merle is a prisoner and dying, and that I offer safe-conduct to any priest that will come to him—though whether a red-hot Calvinist will respect my safe-conduct or your escort is another matter."

"At least, Sire, you sanction my making this request?"

"Have you men enough to take with you to guard you from marauders?"

"I have but two servants, Sire, and I have left them with the wounded man."

"Then I will send with you half a dozen Gascons, who have been long enough at Paris with me to have no scruples."

By the time Berenger had explained matters to his wife and brother, and snatched a hasty meal, a party of gay, soldierly-looking fellows were in the saddle, commanded by a bronzed sergeant who was perfectly at home in conducting messages between contending parties. After a dark ride of about five miles, the camp at the village of St. Esmé was reached, and this person recommended that he himself should go forward with a trumpet, since M. de Ribaumont was liable to be claimed as an escaped prisoner. There was then a tedious delay, but at length the soldier returned, and another horseman with him. A priest who had come to the camp in search of M. de Nid-de-Merle was willing to trust himself to the King of Navarre's safe-conduct.

"Thanks, sir," cried Berenger; "this is a work of true charity."

"I think I know that voice," said the priest.

"The priest of Nissard!"

"Even so, sir. I was seeking M. de Nid-de-Merle, and had but just learnt that he had been left behind wounded."

"You came to tell him of his sister?"

And as they rode together the priest related to Berenger that Madame de Selinville had remained in the same crushed, humiliated mood, not exactly penitent, but too much disappointed and overpowered with shame to heed what became of her provided she were not taken back to her brother or her aunt. She knew that repentance alone was left for her, and permitted herself to be taken to Luçon, where Mère Monique was the only person whom she had ever respected. There had no doubt been germs of good within her, but the crime and intrigue of the syren court of Catherine de Medici had choked them; and the first sense of better things had been awakened by the frank simplicity of the young cousin, while, nevertheless, jealousy and family tactics had led her to aid in his destruction, only to learn through her remorse how much she loved him. And when in his captivity she thought him in her power, but found him beyond her reach, unhallowed as was her passion, yet still the contemplation of the virtues of one beloved could not fail to raise her standard. It was for his truth and purity that she had loved him, even while striving to degrade these qualities; and when he came forth from her ordeal unscathed, her worship of him might for a time be more intense, but when the idol was removed, the excellence she had first learnt to adore in him might yet lead that adoration up to the source of all excellence. All she sought *now* was shelter wherein to weep and cower unseen; but the priest believed that her tears would soon spring from profound depths of penitence such as often concluded the lives of the gay ladies of France. Mère Monique had received her tenderly, and the good priest had gone from Luçon to announce her fate to her aunt and brother.

At Bellaise he had found the Abbess much scandalized. She had connived at her niece's releasing the prisoner, for she had acquired too much regard for him to let him perish under Narcisse's hands, and she had allowed Véronique to personate Diane at the funeral mass, and also purposely detained Narcisse to prevent the detection of the escape; but the discovery that her niece had accompanied his flight had filled her with shame and fury.

Pursuit had been made towards La Rochelle, but when the neighbourhood of the King of Navarre became known, no doubt was entertained that the fugitives had joined him, and Narcisse, reserving his vengeance for the family honour till he should encounter Berenger, had hotly resumed the intention of pouncing on Eustacie at Pont de Dronne, which had been decided on upon the report of the Italian spy, and only deferred by his father's death. This once done, Berenger's own supposed infidelity would have forced him to acquiesce in the annulment of the original marriage.

It had been a horrible gulf, and Berenger shuddered as one who had barely struggled to the shore, and found his dear ones safe, and his enemies shattered and helpless on the strand. They hurried on so as to be in time. The priest, a brave and cautious man, who had often before carried the rites of the Church to dying men in the midst of the enemy, was in a secular dress, and when Berenger had given the password, and obtained admittance, they separated, and only met again to cross the bridge. They found Osbert and Humfrey on guard, saying that the sufferer still lingered, occasionally in a terrible paroxysm of bodily anguish, but usually silent, except when he upbraided Osbert with his master's breach of promise or incapacity to bring a priest through his Huguenot friends.

Such a taunt was on his tongue when Père Colombeau entered, and checked the scoff by saying, "See, my son, you have met with more pardon and mercy even on earth than you had imagined possible."

There was a strange spasm on Narcisse's ghastly face, as though he almost regretted the obligation forced on him, but Berenger scarcely saw him again. It was needful for the security of the priest and the tranquillity of the religious rites that he should keep watch outside, lest any of the more fanatical of the Huguenots should deem it their duty to break in on what they had worked themselves into believing offensive idolatry.

His watch did not prove uncalled for. At different times he had to plead the King's safe-conduct, and his own honour, and even to defend his own Protestantism by appealing to his wounds and services. Hearts were not soft enough then for the cruelty of disturbing a dying man to be any argument at all in that fierce camp; but even there the name of Père Colombeau met with respect. The saintly priest had protected too many enemies for any one who had heard of him to wish him ill.

Nearly all night was Berenger thus forced to remain on guard, that the sole hope of Narcisse's repentance and salvation might not be swept away by violence from without, renewing bitterness within. Not till towards morning was he called back. The hard, lingering death struggle had spent itself, and slow convulsive gasps showed that life was nearly gone; but the satanic sneer had passed away, and a hand held out, a breathing like the word "pardon" seemed to be half uttered, and was answered from the bottom of Berenger's kind and pitying heart. Another quarter of an hour, and Narcisse de Ribaumont Nid-de-Merle was dead. The priest looked pale, exhausted, shocked, but would reveal nothing of the frame of mind he had shown, only that if he had been touched by any saving penitence, it was owing to his kinsman.

Berenger wished to send the corpse to rest in the family vault at Bellaise, where the Chevalier had so lately been laid; and the priest undertook to send persons with a flag of truce to provide for the transport, as well as to announce the death to the sister and the aunt. Wearied as he was, he would not accept Berenger's earnest invitation to come and take rest and refreshment in the prior's rooms, but took leave of him at the further side of the fortress, with almost reverent blessings, as to one not far from the kingdom of heaven; and Berenger, with infinite peacefulness in his heart, went home in the silence of the Sunday morning, and lay sleeping away his long fatigue through the chief part of the day, while Pastor Merlin was preaching an eloquent sermon upon his good brother Isaac Gardon, and Eustacie shed filial tears, more of tenderness than sorrow.

CHAPTER XLIV.

THE GALLIMAFRÉ.

"Speats and raxes, speats and raxes, speats and raxes."
Lord Somerville's billet.

Never wont to let the grass grow under his feet, Henry of Navarre was impatient of awaiting his troops at Pont de Dronne, and proposed to hasten on to Quinet, as a convenient centre for collecting the neighbouring gentry for conference. Thus, early on Monday, a party of about thirty set forth on horseback, including the Ribaumonts, Rayonette being perched by turns in front of her father or mother, and the Duke de Quinet declaring that he should do his best to divide the journey into stages not too long for Philip, since he was anxious to give his mother plenty of time to make preparations for her royal guest.

He had, however, little reckoned on the young King's promptitude. The first courier he had despatched was overtaken at a *cabaret* only five leagues from Pont de Dronne, baiting his horse, as he said; the second was found on the road with a lame horse; and the halt for the night was made so far on the way that only half a day's journey remained beyond it. The last stage had been ridden, much to the Duke's discontent, for it brought them to a mere village inn, with scarcely any accommodation. The only tolerable bed was resigned by the King to the use of Philip, whose looks spoke the exhaustion of which his tongue scorned to complain. So painful and feverish a night ensued that Eustacie was anxious that he should not move until the Duke should, as he promised, send a mule litter back for him ; but this proposal he resented ; and in the height of his constitutional obstinacy, appeared booted and spurred at the first signal to mount.

Nor could Eustacie, as she soon perceived, annoy him more than by showing her solicitude for him, or attracting to him the notice of the other cavaliers. As the only lady of the party, she received a great deal of attention, with some of which she would gladly have dispensed. Whether it were the King's habit of calling her "*la Belle Eurydice*," or because, as she said, he was "*si laid*" and reminded her of old unhappy days of constraint, she did not like him, and had almost displeased her husband and his brother by saying so. She would gladly have avoided the gallantries of this day's ride by remaining with Philip at the inn ; but not only was this impossible, but the peculiar ill-temper of concealed suffering made Philip drive her off whenever she approached him with inquiries ; so that she was forced to leave him to his brother and Osbert, and ride forward between the King and the Duke, the last of whom she really liked.

Welcome was the sight of the grand old château, its mighty wings of chesnut forest stretching up the hills on either side, and the stately avenue extending before it ; but just then the last courier was discovered, reeling in his saddle under the effects of repeated toasts in honour of Navarre and Quinet.

"We are fairly sped," said the Duke to Eustacie, shrugging his shoulders between amusement and dismay.

"Madame la Duchesse is equal to any gallimafré," said Eustacie, demurely ; at which the Duke laughed heartily, saying, "It is not for the family credit I fear, but for my own!"

"Nay, triumph makes everything be forgiven."

"But not forgotten," laughed the Duke. "But, *allons*. Now for the onset. We are already seen. The forces muster at the gateway."

By the time the cavalcade were at the great paved archway into the court, the Duchess stood at the great door, a grandson on either side, and a great burly fresh-coloured gentleman behind her.

M. de Quinet was off his horse in a second, his head bare, his hand on the royal rein, and signing to his eldest son to hold the stirrup; but, before the boy had comprehended, Henry had sprung down, and was kissing the old lady's hand, saying, "Pardon, Madame! I trust to your goodness for excusing this surprise from an old friend's son."

Neither seeing nor caring for king or prince, the stranger gentleman at the same moment pounced upon Eustacie and her little girl, crying aloud in English, "Here she is! My dear, I am glad to see you. Give her to me, poor Berenger's little darling. Ah! she does not understand. Where's Merrycourt?"

Just then there was another English exclamation, "My father! Father! dear father!" and Philip, flinging himself from the saddle, fell almost prone on that broad breast, sobbing convulsively, while the eyes that, as he truly boasted, had never wasted a tear on his enemies, were streaming so fast that his father's welcome savoured of reproof: "What's all this? Before these French too."

"Take care, father," cried Berenger, leaping from his horse; "he has an ugly wound just where you are holding him."

"Wounded! my poor boy. Look up."

"Where is your room, sir?" said Berenger, seeing his hosts entirely occupied with the King; and at once lifting the almost helpless Philip like a little child in his strong arms, he followed Sir Marmaduke, who, as if walking in his sleep, led the way up the great stone staircase that led outside the house to the upper chambers.

After a short interval, the Duchess, in the plenitude of her glory at entertaining her dear Queen's son, came up *en grande tenue*, leading the King by the hand, the Duke walking backwards in front, and his two sons each holding a big wax candle on either side.

"Here, Sire, is the chamber where the excellent Queen did me the honour to repose herself."

The Duke swung open the door of the state bedchamber. There, on the velvet-hung bed sat *le gros Chevalier Anglais*, whom she had herself installed there on Saturday. Both his hands were held fast in those of a youth who lay beside him, deadly pale, and half undressed, with the little Ribaumont attending to a wound in his side, while her child was held in the arms of a very tall, bald-headed young man, who stood at the foot of the bed. The whole group of interlopers looked perfectly glorified with happiness and delight. Even the wounded youth, ghastly and suffering as he was, lay stroking the big Englishman's hand with a languid, caressing air of content, almost like that of a dog who has found his master. None of them were the least embarrassed, they evidently thought this a visit of inquiry after the patient; and while the Duchess stood confounded, and the Duke much inclined to laugh, Eustacie turned eagerly, exclaiming, "Ah! Madame, I am glad you are come. May I beg Mademoiselle Perrot for some of your cooling mallow salve. Riding has sadly inflamed the wound."

"Riding—with such a wound! Are we all crazed?" said

Madame la Duchesse, absolutely bewildered out of her dignified equanimity: and her son, seeing her for once at a loss, came to her rescue. "His grace will condescend to the Andromeda Chamber, Madame. He kindly gave up his bed to our young friend last night, when there was less choice than you can give him."

They all moved off again; and, before Eustacie was ready for the mallows, Madame de Quinet, for whom the very name of a wound had an attraction, returned with two handmaidens bearing bandages and medicaments, having by this time come to the perception that the wounded youth was the son of the big Englishman who had arrived with young Méricour in search of her little *protegée*, and that the tall man was the husband so long supposed to be dead. She was curious to see her pupil's surgery, of which she highly approved, though she had no words to express her indignation at the folly of travelling so soon. Indeed, nothing but the passiveness of fatigue could have made her despotism endurable to Philip; but he cared for nothing so long as he could see his father's face, and hear his voice—the full tones that his ear had yearned for among the sharp expression of the French accent—and Sir Marmaduke seemed to find the same perfect satisfaction in the sight of him; indeed, all were so rejoiced to be together, that they scarcely exerted themselves to ask questions. When Berenger would have made some explanation, Sir Marmaduke only said, "Tell me not yet, my dear boy. I see it is all right, and my head will hold no more yet but that I have you and the lad again! Thank God for it! Never mind how."

When, however, with some difficulty they got him away from Philip's bedside down to supper, the King came and made him high compliments upon the distinguished bravery of his sons, and Méricour interpreted, till Sir Marmaduke—

though answering that of course the lads must do their duty, and he was only glad to hear they had done it—became more and more radiant and proud, as he began to gather what their trials, and what their steadfastness and courage had been. His goodly face, beaming with honest gladness, was, as Henry told the Duchess, an absolute ornament to her table.

Unable, however, to converse with any one but Berenger and Méricour, and pining all the time to get back to his son, the lengthy and ceremonious meal was a weary penance to him; and so soon as his release was possible, he made his way upstairs again, where he found Philip much refreshed by a long sleep, and only afraid that he should find the sight of his father merely a dream; then, when satisfied on that head, eager to hear of all at home—"the sisters, the dogs, my mother, and my little brother?" as he arranged his inquiry.

"Ha! you heard of that, did you?"

"Yes," said Philip, "the villains gave us letters once—only once—and those what they thought would sting us most. O father, how could you all think such foul shame of Berry?"

"Don't speak of it, Phil; I never did, nor Aunt Cecily, not for a moment; but my Lord is not the man he was, and those foes of yours must have set abroad vile reports for the very purpose of deceiving us. And then this child must needs be born, poor little rogue. I shall be able to take to him now all is right again; but by St. George, they have tormented me so about him, and wanted me to take him as a providence to join the estates together, instead of you and Berry, that I never thought to care so little for a child of my own."

"We drank his health at Nid-de-Merle, and were not a little comforted that you would have him in our place."

"I'd rather—— Well, it skills not talking of it, but it just shows the way of women. After all the outcry Dame Annora had made about her poor son, and no one loving him or heeding his interest save herself, no sooner was this little fellow born than she had no thought for any but he, and would fain have had her father settle all his lands on him, protesting that if Berry lived, his French lands were enough for him. Out of sight, out of mind, is the way with women."

Womanhood was always made accountable for all Lady Thistlewood's follies, and Philip acquiesced, asking further, "Nay, but how came you hither, father? Was it to seek us or Eustacie?"

"Both, both, my lad. One morning just after Christmas, I rid over to Combe with my dame behind me, and found the house in commotion with a letter that young Sidney, Berry's friend, had just sent down by special messenger. It had been writ more than a year, but, bless you, these poor foreigners have such crooked ears and tongues that they don't know what to make of a plain man's name, and the only wonder was that it ever came at all. It seems the Duke here had to get it sent over by some of the secret agents the French Protestants have in England, and what do they do but send it to one of the Vivians in Cornwall; and it was handed about among them for how long I cannot say, till there was a chance of sending it up to my Lord of Warwick; and he, being able to make nothing of it, shows it to his nephew, Philip Sidney, who, perceiving at once whom it concerned, sends it straight to my Lord, with a handsome letter hoping that it brought good tidings. There then it was, and so we first knew that the poor lady had not been lost in the sack of the town, as Master Hobbs told us. She told us how this Duchess had taken her under her protection, but that her enemies were seeking her, and had even attempted her child's life."

"The ruffians! even so."

"And she said her old pastor was failing in health, and prayed that some trusty person might be sent to bring home at least the child to safety with her kindred. There was a letter to the same effect, praising her highly too, from the Duchess, saying that she would do her best to guard her, but the kinsmen had the law on their side, and she would be safer in England. Well, this was fair good news, save that we marvelled the more how you and Berry should have missed her; but the matter now was who was the trusty person who should go. Claude Merrycourt was ready——"

"How came he there?" demanded Philip. "I thought he had gone, or been sent off with Lady Burnett's sons."

"Why, so he had; but there's more to say on that score. He was so much in favour at Combe, that my Lord would not be denied his spending the holiday times there; and, besides, last summer we had a mighty coil. The Horners of Mells made me a rare good offer for Lucy for their eldest son, chiefly because they wanted a wife for him of my Lady Walwyn's and Mistress Cecily's breeding; and my wife was all for accepting it, having by that time given up all hope of poor Berry. But I would have no commands laid on my girl, seeing that I had pledged my word not to cross her in the matter, and she hung about my neck and prayed me so meekly to leave her unwedded, that I must have been made of stone not to yield to her. So I told Mr. Horner that his son Jack must wait for little Nancy if he wanted a daughter of mine—and the stripling is young enough. I believe he will. But women's tongues are not easy to stop, and Lucy was worn so thin, and had tears in her eyes—that she thought I never marked—whenever she was fretted or flouted, and at last I took her back to stay at Combe for Aunt Cecily to cheer up a bit; and—well, well, to get rid of the matter and silence Dame Nan, I consented to a betrothal between her and Merrycourt—since she vowed she would rather wait single for him than wed any one else. He is a good youth, and is working himself to a shadow between studying and teaching; but as to sending him alone to bring Berry's wife back, he was over-young for that. No one could do that fitly save myself, and I only wish I had gone three years ago, to keep you two foolish lads out of harm's way. But they set up an unheard-of hubbub, and made sure I should lose myself. What are you laughing at, you Jacksauce?"

"To think of you starting, father, with not a word of French, and never from home further than once to London."

"Ah! you thought to come the travelled gentleman over me, but I've been even with you. I made Dame Nan teach me a few words, but I never could remember anything but that 'mercy' is 'thank ye.' However, Merrycourt offered to come with me, and my Lord wished it. Moreover, I thought he might aid in tracing you out. So I saw my Lord alone, and he passed his word to me that, come what would, no one should persuade him to alter his will to do wrong to Berenger's daughter; and so soon as Master Hobbs could get the *Throstle* unladen, and fitted out again, we sailed for Bordeaux, and there he is waiting for us, while Claude and I bought horses and hired a guide, and made our way here on Saturday, where we were very welcome; and the Duchess said she would but wait till she could learn there were no bands of the enemy at hand, to go down with me herself to the place where she had sent the lady. A right worthy dame is this same Duchess, and a stately; and that young King, as they call him, seems hard to please, for he told Berry that his wife's courtliness and ease in his reception were far above aught that he found here. What he means is past a plain man, for as to Berry's wife she is handy, and notable enough, and 'tis well he loves her so well; but what a little brown thing it is, for a man to have gone through such risks for. Nothing to look at beside his mother!"

"If you could only see Madame de Selinville!" sighed Philip—then. "Ah! sir, you would know the worth of Eustacie had you seen her in yonder town."

"Very like!" said Sir Marmaduke; "but after all our fears at home of a fine court madam, it takes one aback to see a little homely brown thing, clad like a serving wench. Well, Dame Nan will not be displeased, she always said the girl would grow up no beauty, and 'tis the way of women to brook none fairer than themselves! Better so. She is a good Protestant, and has done rarely by you, Phil."

"Truly, I might be glad 'twas no court madam that stood by me when Berry was called back to the fight: and for the little one, 'tis the loveliest and bravest little maid I ever saw. Have they told you of the marigolds, father?"

"Why, the King told the whole to the Duchess, so Berry said, and then drank the health of the daughter of the bravest of knights; and Berry held her up in his arms to bow again, and drink to them from his glass. Berry looked a proud man, I can tell you, and a comely, spite of his baldness; and 'tis worth having come here to see how much you lads are thought of—though to be sure 'tis not often the poor creatures here see so much of an Englishman as we have made of Berry."

Philip could not but laugh. "'Tis scarce for that that they value him, sir."

"Say you so? Nay, methinks his English heart and yours did them good service. Indeed, the King himself told me as much by the mouth of Merrycourt. May that youngster's head only not be turned! Why, they set him at table above Berenger, and above half the King's gentlemen. Even the Duchess makes as if he were one of her highest guests—he a poor Oxford scholar, doubting if he can get his bread by the law, and flouted as though he were not good enough for my daughter. 'Tis the world topsy turvy, sure enough! And that this true love that Berenger has run through fire and water after, like a knight in a pedlar's ballad, should turn out a mere little, brown, common-looking woman after all, not one whit equal to Lucy!"

Sir Marmaduke modified his disappointment a little that night, when he had talked Philip into a state of feverishness and suffering that became worse under Madame de Quinet's reproofs and remedies, and only yielded to Eustacie's long and patient soothing. He then could almost have owned that it was well she was not like his own cherished type of womanhood, and the next day he changed his opinion still more, even as to her appearance.

There was a great gathering of favourers of the Huguenot cause on that day; gentlemen came from all parts to consult with Henry of Navarre, and Madame de Quinet had too much sense of the fitness of things to allow Madame de Ribaumont to appear at the ensuing banquet in her shabby, rusty black serge, and tight white borderless cap. The whole wardrobe of the poor young Duchess de Quinet was placed at her service, and, though with the thought of her adopted father on her heart, she refused gay colours, yet when, her toilette complete, she sailed into Philip's room, he almost sprang up in delight, and Sir Marmaduke rose and ceremoniously bowed as to a stranger, and was only undeceived when little Rayonette ran joyously to Philip, asking if *Maman* was not *si belle, si belle.*

The effects of her unrestful nights had now passed away, and left her magnificent eyes in their full brilliancy and arch fire; the blooming glow was restored to her cheek; and though neck, brow, and hands were browner than in the shelter of convent or palace, she was far more near absolute beauty than in former days, both from countenance and from age. Her little proud head was clustered with glossy locks of jet, still short, but curling round her brow and neck whose warm brunette tints contrasted well with the delicate, stiffened cobweb of her exquisite standing ruff, which was gathered into a white satin bodice, with a skirt of the same material, over which swept a rich black brocade train open in front, with an open body and half-sleeves with falling lace, and the hands, delicate and shapely as ever, if indeed a little tanned, held fan and handkerchief with as much courtly grace as though they had never stirred broth nor wrung out linen. Sir Marmaduke really feared he had the court madam on his hands after all, but he forgot all about his fears, as she stood laughing and talking, and by her pretty airs and gestures, smiles and signs, making him enter into her mirth with Philip, almost as well as if she had not spoken French.

Even Berenger started, when he came up after the counsel to fetch her to the banqueting-hall. She was more entirely the Eustacie of the Louvre than he had ever realized seeing her, and yet so much more; and when the Duchess beheld the sensation she produced among the *noblesse*, it was with self-congratulation in having kept her in retirement while it was still not known that she was not a widow. The King of Navarre had already found her the only lady present possessed of the peculiar aroma of high-breeding which belonged to the society in which both he and she had been most at home, and his attentions were more than she liked from one whose epithet of Eurydice she had never quite forgiven; at least, that was the only reason she could assign for her distaste, but the Duchess understood her better than did Berenger, nay, better than she did herself, and kept her under the maternal wings of double form and ceremony.

Berenger, meanwhile, was in great favour. A command had been offered him by the King of Navarre, who had promised that if he would cast in his lot with the Huguenots, his claims on all the lands of Ribaumont should be enforced on the King of France when terms were wrung from him, and Narcisse's death removed all valid obstacle to their recognition; but Berenger felt himself bound by all home duties to return to England, nor had he clear convictions as to the absolute right of the war in which he had almost unconsciously drawn his sword. Under the Tudors the divine right of kings was strongly believed in, and it was with many genuine misgivings that the cause of Protestant revolt was favoured by Elizabeth and her ministers; and Berenger, bred up in a strong sense of loyalty, as well as in doctrines that, as he had received them, savoured as little of Calvinism as of Romanism, was not ready to espouse the Huguenot cause with all his heart; and as he could by no means have fought on the side of King Henry III. or of the Guises, felt thankful that the knot could be cut by renouncing France altogether, according to the arrangement which had been defeated by the Chevalier's own super-subtle machinations.

At the conference of gentlemen held at Quinet, he had been startled by hearing the name of the Sieur de Bellaise, and had identified him with a grave, thin, noble-looking man, with an air of high-bred and patient poverty. He was a Catholic but no Guisard, and supported the middle policy of the Montmorency party, so far as he possessed any influence; but his was only the weight of personal character, for he had merely a small property that had descended to him through his grandmother, the wife of the unfortunate Bellaise who had pined to death in the dungeon at Loches, under Louis XI. Here, then, Berenger saw the right means of ridding himself and his family of the burthen that his father had mourned over, and it only remained to convince Eustacie. Her first feeling when she heard of the King's offer, was that at last her ardent wish would be gratified, she should see her husband at the head of her vassals, and hear the war-cry motto, "*A moi Ribaumont.*" Then came the old representation that the Vendéen peasants were faithful Catholics who could hardly be asked to fight on the Calvinist side. The old spirit rose in a flush, a pout, a half-uttered query why those creatures should be allowed their opinions. Madame la Baronne was resuming her haughty temperament in the *noblesse* atmosphere; but in the midst came the remembrance of having made that very speech in her Temple ruin—of the grave sad look of rebuke and shake of the head with which the good old minister had received it—and how she had sulked at him till forced to throw herself on him to hinder her separation from her child. She burst into tears, and as Berenger, in some distress, began to assure her that he would and could do nothing without her consent, she struggled to recover voice to say, "No! no! I only grieve that I am still as wicked as ever, after these three years with that saint, my dear father. Do as you will, only pardon me, the little fierce one!"

And then, when she was made to perceive that her husband would have to fight alone, and could not take her with him to share his triumphs or bind his wounds, at least not except by bringing her in contact with Henry of Navarre and that atmosphere of the old court, she acquiesced the more readily. She was a woman who could feel but not reason;

and, though she loved Nid-de-Merle, and had been proud of it, Berenger's description of the ill-used Sieur de Bellaise had the more effect on her, because she well remembered the traditions whispered among the peasants with whom her childhood had been passed, that the village crones declared nothing had gone well with the place since the Bellaises had been expelled, with a piteous tale of the broken-hearted lady, that she had never till now understood.

For the flagrant injustice perpetrated on her uncle and cousin in the settlement on Berenger and herself she cared little, thinking they had pretty well repaid themselves, and not entering into Berenger's deeper view, that this injustice was the more to be deplored as the occasion of their guilt; but she had no doubt or question as to the grand stroke of yielding up her claims on the estate to the Sieur de Bellaise. The generosity of the deed struck her imagination, and if Berenger would not lead her vassals to battle, she did not want them. There was no difficulty with Sir Marmaduke; he only vowed that he liked Berenger's wife all the better for being free of so many yards of French dirt tacked to her petticoat, and Philip hated the remembrance of those red sugar-loaf pinnacles far too much not to wish his brother to be rid of them.

M. de Bellaise, when once he understood that restitution was intended, astonished Sir Marmaduke by launching himself on Berenger's neck with tears of joy; and Henry of Navarre, though sorry to lose such a partisan as the young Baron, allowed that the Bellaise claims, being those of a Catholic, might serve to keep out some far more dangerous person whom the Court partly might select in opposition to an outlaw and a Protestant like M. de Ribaumont.

"So you leavé us," he said in private to Berenger, to whom he had taken a great liking. "I cannot blame you for not casting your lot into such a witch's cauldron as this poor country. My friends think I dallied at court like Rinaldo in Armida's garden. They do not understand that when one hears the name of Bourbon one does not willingly make war with the Crown, still less that the good Calvin left a doctrine bitter to the taste, and tough of digestion. May be, since I have been forced to add my spoon to stir the cauldron, it may clear itself; if so, you will remember that you have rights in Normandy and Picardy."

This was the royal farewell. Henry and his suite departed the next morning, but the Duchess insisted on retaining her other guests till Philip's cure should be complete. Meantime, Claude de Méricour had written to his brother and arranged a meeting with him. He was now no boy who could be coerced, but a staid, self-reliant, scholarly person, with a sword by his side and an English passport to secure him, and his brother did not regard him as quite the disgrace to his family he had at first deemed him. He was at least no rebel; and though the law seemed to French eyes infinitely beneath the dignity of a scion of nobility, still it was something not to have him a heretic preacher, and to be able at least to speak of him as betrothed to the sister of the Baron de Ribaumont. Moreover, that Huguenot kinsman, whose extreme Calvinist opinions had so nearly revolted Méricour, had died and left him all his means, as the only Protestant in the family; and the amount, when Claude arranged matters with his brother, proved to be sufficient to bear him through his expenses handsomely as a student, with the hope of marriage so soon as he should have kept his terms at the Temple.

And thus the good ship *Throstle* bore home the whole happy party to Weymouth, and good Sir Marmaduke had an unceasing cause for exultation in the brilliant success of his mission to France.

After all, the first to revisit that country was no other than the once homesick Philip. He wearied of inaction, and thought his county neighbours ineffably dull and lubberly, while they blamed him for being a fine, Frenchified gentleman, even while finding no fault with their old friend Berenger, or that notable little, lively, housewifely lady his wife, whose broken English and bright simplicity charmed everyone. Sorely Philip needed something to do; he might have been a gentleman pensioner, but he had no notion, he said, of loitering after a lady to boat and hunt, when such a king as Henry of Navarre was in the field; and he agreed with Eustacie in her estimate of the Court, that it was horribly dull, and wanting in all the sparkle and brilliancy that even he had perceived at Paris.

Eustacie gladly retreated to housewifery at Combe Walwyn, but a strenuous endeavour on Lady Thistlewood's part to marry her stepson to a Dorset knight's daughter, together with the tidings of the renewed war in France, spurred Philip into wringing permission from his father to join the King of Navarre as a volunteer.

Years went by, and Philip was only heard of in occasional letters, accompanied by presents to his sisters and to little Rayonette, and telling of marches, exploits, and battles,—how he had taken a standard of the League at Coutras, and how he had led a charge of pikemen at Ivry, for which he received the thanks of Henry IV. But, though so near home, he did not set foot on English ground till the throne of France was secured to the hero of Navarre, and he had marched into Paris in guise very unlike the manner he had left it.

Then home he came, a bronzed gallant-looking warrior,

the pride of the county, ready for repose and for aid to his father in his hearty old age, and bearing with him a pressing invitation from the King to Monsieur and Madame de Ribaumont to resume their rank at Court. Berenger, who had for many years only known himself as Lord Walwyn, shook his head. "I thank the King," he said, "but I am better content to breed up my children as wholly English. He bade me to return when he should have stirred the witch's cauldron into clearness. Alas! all he has done is to make brilliant colours shine on the vapour thereof Nay, Phil; I know your ardent love for him, and marvel not at it. Before he joined the Catholic Church I trusted that he might have given truth to the one party, and unity to the other; but when the clergy accepted him with all his private vices, and he surrendered unconditionally, I lost hope. I fear there is worse in store. Queen Catherine did her most fatal work of evil when she corrupted Henry of Navarre."

"If you say more, Berry, I shall be ready to challenge you!" said Philip. "When you saw him, you little knew the true king of souls that he is, his greatness, or his love for his country."

"Nay, I believe it; but tell me, Philip, did you not hint that you had been among former friends—at Luçon, you said, I think?"

Philip's face changed. "Yes; it was for that I wished to see you alone. My troop had to occupy the place. I had to visit the convent to arrange for quartering my men so as least to scandalize the sisters. The Abbess came to speak to me. I knew her only by her eyes! She is changed—aged, wan, thin with their discipline and fasts—but she once or twice smiled as she alone in old times could smile. The place rings with her devotion, her charity, her penances, and truly her face is "—he could hardly speak—" like that of a saint. She knew me at once, asked for you all, and bade me tell you that *now* she prays for you and yours continually, and blesses you for having opened to her the way of peace. Ah! Berry, I always told you she had not her equal."

"Think you so even now?"

"How should I not, when I have seen what repentance has made of her?"

"So!" said Berenger, rather sorrowfully; "our great Protestant champion has still left his heart behind him in a French convent."

"Stay, Berenger! do you remember yonder villain conjurer's prediction that I should wed none but a lady whose cognizance was the leopard?"

"And you seem bent on accomplishing it," said Berenger.

"Nay! but in another manner—that which you devised on the spur of the moment. Berenger, I knew the sorcerer spake sooth when that little moonbeam child of yours brought me the flowers from the rampart. I had speech with her last night. She has all the fair loveliness that belongs of right to your mother's grandchild, but her eye, blue as it is, has the Ribaumont spirit; the turn of the head and the smile are what I loved long ago in yonder lady, and, above all, she is her own sweet self. Berenger, give me your daughter Bérengère, and I ask no portion with her but the silver bullet. Keep the pearls for your son's heirloom; all I ask with Rayonette is the silver bullet."

THE END.

LONDON: R. CLAY, SONS, AND TAYLOR, PRINTERS.

www.ingramcontent.com/pod-product-compliance
Lightning Source LLC
Chambersburg PA
CBHW020509270326
41926CB00008B/804

* 9 7 8 3 7 4 4 6 4 6 8 1 9 *